WHAT WOULD MA SAY?

KATHLEEN DOYLE

POOLBEG

Published 2010
by Poolbeg Books Ltd
123 Grange Hill, Baldoyle
Dublin 13, Ireland
E-mail: poolbeg@poolbeg.com

13 5 7 9 10 8 6 4 2

A catalogue record for this book is available from the British Library.

ISBN 978-1-84223 435-8

Typeset by TYPE DESIGN in Sabon 10.5/14
Printed by CPI Mackays, UK

www.poolbeg.com

About the author

Kathleen McGrath was born Kathleen Doyle in 1948. She is married to Alan, and they have three children – Martina, Alan Junior and Amanda – three granddaughters – Danielle, Jessica and Robin – and one great-grandson, Conor. Kathleen set up her own hairdressing business, running three salons. She has now retired and lives in Tallaght. This is her first book.

Acknowledgements

I would like to thank Poolbeg Press, especially Kieran and Paula, for giving me the opportunity to tell my story. With special thanks to Brian for all your support and help with the editing. To José (my Spanish Angel), Brenda and Bernie who helped along the way – many thanks. To my youngest sister, Patricia: I can never thank you enough for taking on the challenge to transcribe my scribbles into a typed manuscript. To all my brothers and sisters: without you, there would never have been a book. I thank each and every one of you. To my three children and grandchildren, thanks for bearing with me on this adventure.

Last but not least, to my best friend and soulmate Alan: you have encouraged me so much since the first day we met in everything I set out to do – love you.

While everything in this book is true, a few names have been changed.

To Ma,
I hope I did yeh proud . . .

1

From Jam Jars to China

The phone rang. It was my sister Clare. The call I was expecting but didn't want to hear.

'Kathleen, Ma is gone,' she cried. 'Ma's dead.'

I had only been down with Ma the day before. As soon as I'd walked into the house I could see how weak she looked. She was eighty-four and had been sick a lot over the past two years and her mind was starting to wander. There were days when I would go in to see her and she wouldn't know who I was. I'd get so upset when that happened.

I thought to myself, *This is it. Her time has come.* I could see in her eyes that she was ready to go. The life was gone completely out of her. She was like a little child sitting in her chair, helpless, unable to do anything for herself.

My sister Carmel, who lives in the family home and looked after Ma so well, tapped me on the shoulder.

'You're miles away there, Kathleen. Have you heard anythin' I've said?'

'Sorry, Carmel, I was thinkin'. Wha' did yeh say?'

'You'll have to try and get some food and water into Ma. She's eaten nothin' for me since yesterday.' Her eyes filled up as she spoke.

'Yeh look tired, Carmel. You go and have a break for a few hours and don't be worryin'. I'll take care of everythin'.'

It wasn't long before the house was empty and I was alone with Ma. I knew in my heart that there wasn't much time left and was grateful for the next few hours we were to spend together. Just the two of us. I sat there holding her hand, trying to get her to sip some water for me. But she wasn't having any of it. As weak as she was, she still put her hand up to stop me, shaking her head from side to side, saying, 'No'. She gestured for me to bend down.

'What is it?' I asked. 'Wha' are yeh tryin' to say, Ma?' It took her a minute or two of struggling in such a low voice to get the words out. But I was so happy when I heard what she had to say. 'Kathleen, make's a cup of tea.' I couldn't believe it. She knew who I was.

They were the last words that Ma spoke to me. I sat there for the next couple of hours, Ma sipping on her tea and me pouring my heart out at last, telling her all the things I had bottled up inside me all these years.

'D'yeh know, Ma, sometimes I used to think as a child growin' up, tha' yeh didn't love me. Yeh never said the words, ever.'

She looked at me the whole time I spoke, listening and giving me the nod every now and then.

'Ah, don't take any notice of me, Ma. I'm just rammagin' on here. They're just thoughts from a child, Ma, tha's all. Thoughts from a child, from long ago.'

She then gave my hand a little squeeze, and with the other hand pointed towards her eye and then to her heart, holding it there for a few seconds longer and then, last but not least, straight at me. Eye for 'I', heart for 'love', and 'you'.

I cried and cried as I spoke the words back. 'And I love yeh too, Ma.' I hugged and kissed her. The words had never been spoken, but they were there all this time, inside her head and mine. That was all that mattered to me.

* * *

The next day, when Clare told me Ma had died, I was sad but didn't cry at first. I knew she couldn't hold on any longer. She had done her time on this earth and what a great job she had done. She was at peace now. All her worrying was over.

In the days leading up to Ma's funeral, the whole family gathered in the house to support one another. There was myself, Carmel, Noel, Clare, Marion, Thomas, Jacinta, Patricia, Mano and Paul, remembering all the funny stories, laughing and crying at the same time. The only one missing was Phil, the oldest of all of us. He had been so young when he died, barely forty; such a character, always full of life. If he'd been here now, God only knows what antics he'd be getting up to. How I wished he could have been there. He'd have helped us get through a very hard time with his funny ways, just like he always did when we were growing up. We all missed him so much.

I could hear Noel and Thomas reminiscing about the day they robbed a dead pig with Phil and how they hid it in the wardrobe so Da wouldn't see it. Then Clare turned around and brought up the day that we all made a swimming pool in the kitchen. The other sisters got their spoke in straight away: 'Wha' are yeh talkin' about, Clare? At least the whole gang of us did tha' together. Remember when yeh went and painted the table and chairs, and every plate and jam jar in the house gold and silver – and yeh did tha' all on yer own!'

'Tha's because I was tryin' to keep meself awake,' said Clare. 'I was afraid to go asleep because of the ghost.'

On went the storytelling while all the grandchildren sat there in amazement listening to all the things that we had got up to! How Ma put up with us I will never know. We went on for hours, all of us going over events from so long ago.

Ma was laid out in the very sitting-room that she had spent

most of her life in, where all the bedlam and mayhem went on. Be it good, sad or funny, that's where it all happened. We all felt it was only fitting that she would leave from the home that she and Da had built around us so many years ago.

Down through the years, Ma had always spoken about having a big send-off when she passed away. I would tell her not to be talking about such things, as you never want to think of your parents dying. But no, Ma would never let it go. She made each and every one of us promise to keep her wishes.

'Remember tha' film *Madame X*?' she would say. 'There was these big black stallions and a glass carriage bringin' the woman to her restin' place. Well, tha's wha' I want and if I don't get it I'll come back and haunt every one of yiz. Oh, and another thing, yeh're to make sure the horses trot nice and slow, so as everybody on the road can see me. When me day comes, I want to go out in style. I might not have had much in me life, but by God, when I'm ready to leave this earth, I want everybody to remember the day tha' Lil Doyle died.'

And what a send-off she got. For the outspoken woman that she was, and for all her toughness, she was so well liked that people came from far and near to pay their respects. You couldn't put a price on all the flowers in the house. All Ma's favourites. She loved flowers so much she used to spend half of her pension every week doing the flowers for the church, telling us, 'Now tha' I'm able to, I want to thank the Holy Mother herself for all the years tha' she helped me through all me hard times.'

The day of Ma's funeral was such a lovely November day, the sun splitting the trees. We were all down in the house from early to say our last goodbye. I remember standing back and looking at all the family, from the youngest to the oldest, dressed in black as a mark of respect. I thought Ma would be well pleased with them all.

When the horses and carriage arrived at the house, we were all speechless. I had never seen the likes of it before at any funeral. It was everything Ma had wished for and more. The two black horses were groomed to perfection. They stood tall with their black plumes on the tops of their heads, waiting patiently. The coachmen looked so impressive dressed in traditional uniform – double-breasted coats with big silver buttons, expensive cravats, top hats, snow-white gloves and black leather polished boots. They stood silently on either side of the glass carriage, which was gleaming so beautifully. It was perfect.

It was now my turn to go in to Ma to say my last few words. As I stood there holding Ma's hand, I finally broke down and cried. Such a loss and emptiness came over me as I said goodbye. 'Yeh were a great Ma and will never be forgotten. Yeh'll live on forever in all our hearts. It's time to go now Ma, your carriage awaits yeh.'

My brothers placed the coffin into the glass carriage as Ma left the house for the last time. The horses trotted slowly up the road, while all the neighbours, young and old, stood still, the older men taking off their caps out of respect for Lil Doyle. When we got to the church I couldn't believe the number of people there. It was packed to capacity. We played Ma's favourite songs as the priest said Mass. I sat there listening to all the family as everyone broke down crying. They too were feeling the loss I felt inside.

Her cremation in Mount Jerome was so peaceful. There were no more words spoken. While the song 'In the Arms of an Angel' played, we all sat there in silence. As the curtains slowly closed, I felt Ma was at peace at last. I sat there on my own for a few moments, thinking, 'Well, wha' de yeh say, Ma? Is it everythin' yeh wished for? Did we do yeh proud? I think so, Ma; it was a funeral fit for a queen.'

* * *

The day slowly came to an end. I felt so tired and drained, I thought I would never get home to put my head down. Later, unable to sleep, I made my way downstairs. As I sat there drinking a cup of tea, I thought about the first time Ma sat in this very kitchen with me.

Over the years, Ma had been visiting myself and Alan every Sunday and sometimes used to stay for the weekend. We had bought a new house at the bottom of the mountains in Tallaght. I thought I'd never get her up to see it. We were only in the door and as usual the cup of tea and a smoke had to come first.

'Are yeh right, Ma? Come on and I'll show yeh around while the kettle is boilin'.'

As we went around the house, you could see she was surprised and well pleased, but didn't say it. She had mellowed a lot over the years and only now you could have a bit of crack with her. I laughed as we walked in and out of the rooms.

'Ma, which toilet would yeh like to use today? There's the blue one, the green one and there's the yellow one downstairs. Your choice.'

'Would yeh get away with yerself, Kathleen Doyle, I wouldn't be able for yeh with yer showin' off. There was a time yeh hadn't got a pair of knickers to yer name, and don't yeh ever forget tha', de yeh hear me now?'

In a way I suppose I was showing off. I wanted Ma to be so proud of me for what I had achieved throughout the years. As a child, I craved the slightest bit of attention. Even the tiniest bit of praise meant so much to me. But I rarely got it.

'All the same, Kathleen, did yeh ever think tha' yeh'd see the likes of it? Three toilets and all in yer own house, for only yiz to use and nobody else. Isn't it a far cry from the tenements and the shite bucket, and you know tha' more than the rest of the kids – helpin' me carry it down all them stairs to tha' filthy toilet in the yard. We've come a long way since then, so we have.'

'Yeh should be very proud, Ma. Yeh built a lovely home around yerself and Da over the years and look at the way all the kids turned out. Yeh did well.'

'I have to say – and I'll say it straight to yer face, Kathleen – it was a long, hard road, but yiz didn't turn out too bad for a shower of ticks.'

And by that she meant we had done well for ourselves, which we all did. Believe it or not, that was a big compliment coming from Ma.

'Kathleen, me mouth's waterin' here. Are yeh makin' me tha' cup of tea or wha'?'

I took out my special set of china cups and saucers as Ma sat there puffing away. 'Wha' de yeh say, Ma? Will we go all posh for the day to celebrate the new house or would yeh prefer a jam jar?'

The look on her face was priceless. I was still showing off and I didn't care.

'God be with the days, Kathleen, when we had nothin' else only jam jars to drink our cup of tea out of. Such poverty, how did we ever get through it all?'

I sat there listening to Ma while she reminisced about the past. I let my own mind slowly fade back to a time gone by so long ago.

2

The Tenement

My name is Kathleen Doyle. I'm one of twelve children, five brothers and six sisters. I was born in a tenement house – number 7, Cook Street – off the back of Christ Church Cathedral in Dublin City, in 1948.

Ma was small in height, about five foot, but she was heavily built. She had very dark skin and the most beautiful head of long black hair that you ever saw. An ordinary woman with very little education behind her, but maybe not so ordinary in the way she learned how to survive and handle life. She was so strong and tough, cunning, smart and very streetwise and that's how she was able to get through so much turmoil in her life.

She could be very witty in her own way. I laugh now when I think of the things she used to say with her friend Maisie. They were gas when they got together; that would be the only time Ma would let herself go and probably be the Ma that I didn't know but should have known.

Maisie was the complete opposite to Ma. She was very tall and thin, her blonde hair always tied back in a bun. When I think back to those times, she was some character and the only one who ever made Ma laugh. One day as they sat in the kitchen having a cup of tea and smoking their Woodbines, I heard Maisie speak to Ma.

'Lil Doyle.'

'Wha's tha', Maisie?'

'How come yeh nearly go like one of them Comanche Indians out of them cowboy pictures the minute the sun comes out? Would yeh have a look at the colour of yeh?'

Ma replied, trying to keep her face as serious as anything, 'Well now, Maisie, if the truth be told I think one of me grannies must have went off with a foreigner of some kind. Yeh know, when them big ships came here with them Vikings and Spaniards on board? Yeh know, years and years ago, when they invaded and pillaged the life outta everyone.'

'Jaysus, Lil, yeh were listenin' in school all the same. Yeh know yer bit of history and stuff. Good for you, cause I know fuck-all.'

'No, Maisie, I swear there's foreign blood flowin' through me veins, so there is. I'm tellin' yeh, there is.'

'Yeh mean one of yer grannies was, like, a bit iffy, Lil? Yeh know, yeh know?' she said, giving Ma the nod and a wink.

Ma couldn't keep her face straight any longer. She was bursting her sides with the laughing.

'Go away, yer a mad thing, Lil, pullin' me leg like tha'. If yer Ma heard yeh sayin' tha', she'd kick the fuckin' daylights out of yeh, so she would, talkin' about yer ancestral people like tha'.'

The two of them sat there laughing and joking, telling yarns to one another.

'Sure, wha' else have we got, Maisie, only a bit of a laugh to keep us goin'.'

'Yeh never said a truer word, Lil. An oul' laugh keeps the heart sweet, so it does.'

I loved when Maisie would visit. She brought out the best in Ma.

* * *

Da was eight years older than Ma, a slim man, about five foot ten in height, with fair hair going a bit bald on top. He was a very good man, quiet in his own way. He always helped around the house with the cleaning and cooking and never minded helping out with us kids while Ma was out and about.

Phil was his name. He loved the church, sang in choir, and would help the priest to serve Mass and do the collections. Anything that needed doing around the church, Da was there. Some say that he might have gone to the priesthood only he met Ma. You couldn't blame him for getting sidetracked – she was beautiful.

But he had his downfalls, as we were to learn through the years. Very early in our lives, Da turned to drink and gambling. He became weak and didn't face up to his responsibilities very well, which was the root of all the poverty and heartache in Ma's life and ours. Life would have been a lot easier, and so much better, if he didn't drink, but that wasn't to be.

My brother Phil was born first. He had the same name as my father – the first son always carried the name. I came along eleven months later.

Back then, most working-class people in the city lived in tenement houses, which were three or four storeys high with only one toilet to serve the whole house. We lived in one very small room at the top of the tenement house. There was a small table with two chairs, one wardrobe, a double bed for Ma and Da, a single bed which myself and Phil shared and an old chest that Ma used to keep a few sheets and clothes in. The gas cooker was by the window and candles were used for lighting. There was no electricity, or at least if there was, we didn't have it – probably because it had been cut off.

The fireplace was very big. At the side of the fire there would be a stack of turf or logs and if there were an extra few bob to spare, the black bucket would be filled with coal.

We had a big milk churn. Da filled it up with water from the tap in the yard every day. In the evenings when the fire would get going and the room warmed up, Ma would do her best, but the water was never very warm and we'd be shivering as we stood there, waiting our turn to be washed from head to toe. I dreamed of sinking into a hot bath filled with bubbles.

The room had two windows. Some of the glass was missing in one of them and when the wind would blow through the lace curtains, Ma would say, 'It's grand in the summer, yeh get plenty of fresh air, good for the lungs; but in the winter the arse is blown off yeh.' She was forever at Da to fix the window.

I didn't like living in the tenement; it was such a dark and dreary house. It wasn't too bad during the day when the sunlight shone through, but at night, as soon as you went in through the front door, there was complete darkness. Ma always carried a candle in her bag, to make sure that none of us would slip and hurt ourselves.

There was nowhere for us to play except the street around the tenements or sometimes the small park at Christ Church. It was the only place in the area with a few trees and a bit of grass. I used to love when we would go up there – we would play around for hours and have the best fun ever.

Da's family lived up the hill from us. There was Granny Mariah; she was very good to us. A big woman, tall and with snow-white hair, I never remember her smiling, but then again she hadn't got much to smile about living with Granda Phil. He was a pig and a mean old shitebag. He was a lot smaller than my granny, a frail little man who looked more dead than alive and was never out of the bed. Every time we saw him, he was giving out about one thing or another. He used to frighten the shite out of me.

Then there were Da's sisters, Maggie, Mary and Emmie. They loved Da to bits and, in their eyes and Mariah's eyes, he could do no wrong. He was the only boy. They were very funny. Maggie was very posh and spoke really well. She always had her make-up on and used to tell the other two they were so common. She'd say to me, 'Listen to yer Auntie Maggie, Kathleen, and you'll go far.'

Mary and Emmie would chime in, 'Who de yeh think yeh are, Maggie Doyle, callin' us common? Yeh'd think yeh had a bag of marbles in yer mouth! And as for yer face, yeh'd get yerself a job in a circus, so yeh would; it's a clown yeh look like, with all tha' muck yeh have on.' They would always be slagging each other, but not in a bad way; they were the best of friends.

On my Ma's side was Granny Kitty. God, she was a big woman; she must have weighed about twenty-five stone. There was talk in the family that she couldn't get a pair of knickers to fit her, that she had to make them herself, and I could well believe it.

My Granda John. He always had a big smile for us but didn't have much to say. He would sit there in his rocking chair smoking his clay pipe. He would give myself and Phil a penny or two to buy a few sweets. He was nice. I liked him.

They had this lovely little red-bricked house at the back of the fish and fruit market, off Smithfield. I loved going there; they had plenty of rooms and they had their own toilet, which only they used.

My brother Phil said to Ma one day when we were visiting, 'Hey, Ma, why don't we have nice shiny windows and a toilet like me granny?'

That was the first time I saw Ma give 'the look'. I thought she was going to kill him there and then for saying that in front of everyone. You could see her face change but she was trying to be nice at the same time as she spoke to Phil.

'Yeh know the window is too high and we haven't got a ladder to reach tha' far. As for the toilet, well, yeh'll just have to shit in the bucket for now, won't yeh, luv?' As she bent down pretending to fix his hair, she whispered in his ear, 'I'm goin' to give yeh such a kick up the hole when I get yeh home, yeh'll go flyin' through the fuckin' winda' for makin' a show of me in front of me family.'

We learned that day what the look meant and never, ever to say anything out of place in front of family or strangers again.

The bucket was kept out on the landing and was emptied a few times a day. I used to hate when we had to go down to the toilet, which was out the yard at the back of the house. At night, I had to carry a candle down three flights of stairs while Ma would be carrying the bucket. When we got down to the yard, the toilet was forever blocked. There would be bits of newspaper and shit floating around, right up to the top, while the piss would be overflowing down the sides. The smell was so bad, I'd pull my dress up to my mouth and cover my nose, while Ma would be fucking and blinding out of her, calling whoever had used the toilet last all the bastards under the sun for not cleaning up after themselves.

'Mark my words, Kathleen, some day we won't have to do this.' She would try to unblock the toilet with an old wire coat-hanger.

If he wasn't working, Da did the bucket run on the weekends with Phil. I remember one day Da and Phil were taking the bucket down to the yard to empty it. Phil slipped and knocked Da down the stairs; there was piss and shit all over the two of them. Oh my God, you'd want to have heard the roars of Ma when she had to clean it up. The whole of Christ Church must have heard her that day. The fucking and blinding would start all over again.

'Tha' brother of yers is a gobshite, Kathleen. If he's not trippin' up, he's droppin' things. Accident prone, so he is. Tha's it, you'll have to carry the candle every time.'

Phil was no more accident prone than I was. He was just a cute little fucker, to say the least. 'But tha's not fair, Ma,' I mumbled.

'Wha's tha' yeh said, Kathleen? Are yeh givin' me lip now?'

'No, Ma, I was only sayin' . . .'

'Well, *don't*.' She gave me the staring look that would nearly cut you in two.

I learned a very important lesson that day: keep your mouth shut and your thoughts to yourself. You could think what you liked, but you couldn't say it out loud, not to Ma anyway. That was the way I would have to behave all through my young life, always keeping everything bottled up inside me. Back then I was too nervous to speak out.

I looked up at Phil who was standing at the top of the stairs with a sly grin on his face. I swear the little bastard had tripped on purpose because he didn't want to go down to the smelly yard himself, knowing full well that I would have to do it. I was just sorry that I didn't think of it first; but then again I don't think it would have made much of a difference. If I'd been the one who'd tripped, I wouldn't have got off that easily. There would be no excuses made for me. Phil was always Ma's blue-eyed boy.

From then on, at such an early age, I became Ma's right arm. She depended on me for so much and forgot I was a child like the rest of the kids. As far back as I can remember, that's the way things were for myself, always: minding the kids, cleaning, and helping Ma.

3

Kidnapped

Ma couldn't stand being stuck in the room all day. It was so small and cluttered.

She wasn't one for lying in bed and made sure we didn't either. She would be up from early, getting us ready to take us off for the rest of the day. We would be out and about, rambling around a few of the shops in town, with Ma picking up a few bargains here and there, before going over to Granny Kitty's.

Granny Kitty had a lovely little donkey and cart from which she sold the biggest and tastiest fish on Wednesdays and Fridays and the freshest vegetables and fruit you ever saw the rest of the week, all around Smithfield and the back of the quays. They came from near and far to buy from her. She was one of the best-known traders in the inner city. Kitty always had plenty of money tucked away in her apron and she was very good to us. Some days, if the weather wasn't too bad, she would take us with her. I loved when that would happen. We would have the best fun ever. She'd have me roaring as loud as I could.

'Get yer fresh fish straight from the sea today.'

And my brother Phil would shout, 'Cabbage and spuds straight from the farm.'

Some days we'd head off to Howth with Granny Kitty. It would take us a long time to get there. Granny always tried to be there as early as she could to catch the first trawlers docking. All the fishermen knew her very well and she knew every one of them by their first name.

'There yeh are, Kitty, first as usual.'

'Well, Johnny, doesn't the early bird always catch his worm.'

'Kitty, not a truer word could yeh say.'

She'd be asking them if they'd got a good catch and they would go on about how rough the water was. Granny would pick every piece of fish herself and made sure she got the best for all her customers.

'Kathleen, Phil,' she would say, 'come over here and count the fish with me and make sure I'm not doin' meself out of a penny.'

We would sort the fish out into different boxes, then she'd start the haggling.

'Johnny, I've twenty-five smoked cod here, thirty fresh cod, twenty mackerel, fifty of them whitin' – they went very well last week. The ray looks very big, so I'm takin' only twelve pieces. Wha' will yer price be today? Now, before yeh say a word, don't be gettin' into me with yer high prices. Yeh know I'm yer best customer.'

'Ah now, Kitty, don't I work hard out on them high waters, with the wind batterin' the face off me. You'll get rid of tha' lot in no time, you bein' one of the best fishmongers in the city of Dublin.'

As soon as they agreed on a price, there would be the spit and a shake of the hands. Only then would the deal be sealed.

Granny Kitty was great at selling. On a Friday morning the bells for twelve o'clock mass would only be ringing out, with not a fish left in sight, every box empty. She had the gift of the gab.

We would get a penny each and we would be straight down

WHAT WOULD MA SAY?

to the shop for some clove rock and a few bulls eyes. Kitty always handed Ma a little parcel of food and a half crown when we were leaving, giving Ma the nod and the eye at the same time, saying, 'Put tha' by for a rainy day, Lil, de yeh hear me now? None of us know wha's ahead of us.'

Of course, Ma never did this, as she always needed a few bob for one thing or another; if she didn't owe it to somebody it would be spent straight away.

* * *

On the way home from town with Ma, we would drop into the small park in the grounds of Christ Church. Sally, Mary and Kathleen, Ma's sisters, would be there with their kids. The sisters were very close and would meet up every chance they got. We would play around, climbing the trees and chasing one another. Ma and her sisters always brought their knitting with them; they would be sitting there, backbiting everyone who lived on the Hill while they smoked their Woodbines.

One day I heard Mary say to Ma, 'Are you gone again, Lil Doyle?'

'For fuck's sake, Mary! Will yeh be quiet, the kids will hear yeh.'

I cocked my ears up when I heard that.

'Ma, are yeh goin' somewhere?' I asked.

They all laughed and told me not to be listening. 'Get away with yerself, Kathleen. Go and play with the rest of the kids and don't be always ear-wiggin'.'

A few months later my sister Carmel was born. That was the start of me minding Ma's babies; I was about four years old at that stage.

It was around that time that I was kidnapped.

* * *

I remember the day so well; Ma was in the best of form.

'Wha' a lovely day it is, Kathleen. The sun is splittin' the trees out there. It's a great day to get the washin' dry. Come 'ere and hold these pillowcases for me while I fill them up.'

'Okay, Ma.'

'It's a right load of clothes I have to wash. I wonder would oul' Granny Mariah keep an eye to yiz while I slip up to the wash house?'

Ma had no washing machine in those days; she had to wash everything by hand. The wash house had a dozen or more sinks but you had to bring your own washboard, which was made of wood with a metal-ridged front. It was back-breaking work and wasn't easy for her.

Ma was rammaging on, talking away to me like I was a grown-up. I was standing there listening to all she was saying, shaking my head up and down, not saying a word back to her, while Phil was grinning over at me, knowing he was never made do anything, and all the while all I wanted was to play with him.

'Right, tha's done, Kathleen. Hold this washboard for me while I settle Carmel into the pram.'

One of my aunties helped her carry the pram down the stairs. Phil was a lazy little fucker who was always falling and crying, so she put him sitting on the pram with the washing and off we walked up the Hill to Granny Mariah's, which was just around the corner from us.

As soon as we got there, Ma shouted up the stairs to Gran, 'Mariah, will yeh keep an eye to the kids for me? I'm just goin' up to the wash house in Francis Street.'

'Is tha' you, Lil Doyle?' Mariah looked down at us from the top window. 'Wha' was tha' yeh said?'

Ma mumbled under her breath. 'Deaf oul' fuck.' Then out loud, 'I said, would yeh mind keepin' an eye on the kids for me.'

'I will, but yeh better not be long, Lil, I have to get oul'

Phil's dinner ready and yeh know him – there'll be blue murder if it's not sittin' on the table waitin' for him.'

'I know wha' he's like, Mariah, so I'll be as quick as I can.' As soon as Mariah popped her head back in the window, Ma muttered, 'The oul' shite bag.'

'Come 'ere, Phil, sit with yer sisters. Kathleen, keep an eye to Carmel. If she cries, stick the soother in her mouth and rock the pram. Mariah will make her way down to yiz in a while. I won't be long. And wha'ever yeh do, don't move from the front of the house – de yeh hear me now? Are yiz listenin' to me? Don't move!'

We were playing around the steps, me with my skipping rope and Phil with a few marbles, when this man came along on a pushbike and stopped right beside us. He looked straight over at me and asked, 'De yeh know where the shops are, luv?'

'There's one, mister, right beside yeh.'

'No, I'm not lookin' for a sweet shop; I want one tha' sells hammers and nails.'

'Them ones are over there, around the corner.' I pointed down the road.

'I'm not from around here so I don't really know where yeh mean. Will yeh be a good little girl and show me and I'll give yeh a few sweets all for yerself?'

'Did yeh hear tha', Phil? I can get us a few sweets for nothin'. Will yeh watch Carmel for me while I show him the shop? It won't take long. I'll be back in a few minutes.'

Phil pulled at my dress. 'Kathleen, don't go. Ma will kill yeh. She said we're not to move.'

'Don't be a sissy. I won't tell if you don't.' I was a brazen little bitch and wouldn't take heed of what Phil was saying.

So off I went on the crossbar of this man's bike, not realising the danger that was ahead. As he went cycling down the Hill, we passed by Mrs Maguire, Gran's friend. I could hear her in the distance, calling out, 'Mariah, yer Kathleen's on a fella's bike. He's seems to be headin' for the Forty Steps.'

21

The Forty Steps was an old ruin that was used when the boats used to dock along the canal for people making their way from Cook Street up to High Street. Later on, through the years, part of it was turned into a small school for the children of the area. There were two rooms – one for the boys and one for the girls.

With the shops being only around the corner, I wasn't too long on his bike. He stopped and lifted me off, putting the bike against the wall at the entrance to the Forty Steps, which is across the road from where I lived.

'Hey, mister, the shops is not here.' I pointed across the road. 'It's over there, around the corner. Now, can I have me sweets?' I stuck my hand out.

'They're in my bag up here, luv. Come on with me and I'll get them for yeh, and if yeh're a good little girl there might be a bar of chocolate as well.'

My eyes lit up when I heard that. Chocolate was something we rarely got and I knew Phil would be chuffed when I got back, so off I went, skipping along, holding his hand – too innocent to know or understand the danger I was in. That was, until I heard Ma's voice calling out to me, over and over.

'Kathleen! Kathleen! Where are yeh? Answer me!'

I felt afraid then; I knew there was something wrong. Ma kept calling me.

'Kathleen! Kathleen!'

I shouted down. 'Ma, Ma, I'm here!' I was getting more frightened by the minute.

By this stage the man was dragging me along the steps, telling me to be quiet as he slapped me in the face. My knees were all torn and scratched. I kept telling him as I cried and sobbed, 'Please, mister, I want to go home now. I don't want any of yer sweets. Please!'

He wouldn't listen.

I was nearly up the top of the steps when Ma and a few of the men off the Hill reached me. The man pushed me to the ground and tried to run, but there was only one way out and that was through Ma and, believe me, there was no way he was getting past her. Nobody asked any questions. They went and kicked the living daylights out of him. He had his hands up to his face and kept shouting as he fell to the ground, 'Stop, stop, I didn't touch her!'

Ma was on top of him, screaming and punching.

'Touch my Kathleen, would yeh? Yeh dirty fuckin' bastard of a man. By the time I'm finished with yeh, yeh won't be using yer balls ever again. I'll kick them so far up into yer stomach tha' yeh'll be pissin' out of yer mouth, yeh pig!' She roared as she put the boot in once more.

I kept trying to tell everyone that he was giving me sweets, not balls, but nobody would listen to me.

The men had to drag Ma off the man. 'Stop, Lil, you've done enough damage. Now take Kathleen and off home with yeh. We'll take care of him.' And that they did.

While Ma made her way over to me, I could see the man move as the men from the Hill carried on finishing what Ma had started, kicking the shit out of him again and again.

I kept saying, 'I'm sorry, Ma, I'm sorry.' She picked me up. I waited to get a dig for not doing what I was told. I thought she was going to bash me also, but no, to my surprise she cried, hugged and kissed me so hard I could feel her tears against my face.

'Kathleen, Kathleen,' she kept saying. 'Thank God yeh're safe. Did he touch yeh? Did he do anythin' to yeh? Tell me, tell me!'

'He slapped me face, Ma, and dragged me along the steps. Look at me knees. They're all cut and bleedin'.'

'Don't worry, I'll look after them as soon as we get home,' she said, hugging and kissing me again and again. It felt good.

We made our way down the steps. The bike was lying on the ground. Ma picked it up. 'He won't be usin' this again in a hurry, the pig! I'll sell this on and make meself a few shillin's.'

Ma held on tight to me with one hand as she pushed the bike with the other. As we made our way back up the Hill, Mrs Maguire and a few of the neighbours came running over to us.

'Lil, it was meself tha' told Mariah. I knew tha' fella was up to no good, with him not bein' from around here. Is she all right? Did he harm her?'

'Just a few cuts and scratches when he was pullin' her up the steps.'

'God luv her, the poor little mite.' One of them rubbed the top of my head.

'Thanks to the Holy Mother I got to her on time. God only knows wha' would have happened,' said Ma as she blessed herself, launching into telling them the ins and outs of what had gone on at the top of the steps.

'I hope yeh kicked him good and hard,' all the women chimed in.

'Well, let's just say he'll be findin' it very hard to walk for a good while.'

'Good for you, Lil, and no better woman to do it.'

'I'll be on me way now, and thanks for askin' about me child. Oh, another thing; if anyone asks yeh tha' doesn't live on the Hill, yeh know nothin'. Keep yer mouth zipped.'

'Yeh don't have to worry there, Lil. Mum's the word.'

When we got to the top of the Hill, I could see that Carmel and Phil were crying. Gran was sitting on the steps with them. Ma got into one of her mad rages again and didn't half lash Gran out of it for not looking after us kids.

'Holy Jaysus, Mariah, why didn't yeh try and stop him?'

'I was still upstairs, Lil, how could I?'

'Yeh stupid fuckin' oul' wan! You were supposed to be keeping an eye on the kids for me. I trusted yeh with them. Only I got meself there when I did, God only knows wha' could have happened. Kathleen could have been destroyed for life.'

'Don't talk to me like tha', Lil Doyle! The cheek of yeh. Yeh'll mind yer own kids in future. Anyway, didn't I get a few of the men to help yeh? An' I thank each and every one of them for tha'.'

'But I didn't need anyone to sort tha' bastard out for me, I can well take care of meself and me family, yeh can be sure of tha'. And I won't be askin' yeh for any more help, I can tell yeh tha' for nothin'.'

She bundled Phil into the pram on top of Carmel, took me by the hand and we made our way back down the Hill. When we were walking away, I looked back. I could see Gran was real upset, but Ma didn't care. That day she had herself so worked up and she soon let Da know that too when he came home from work.

Well, you'd want to have seen the shock on Da's face when Ma told him the goings-on of the day. He picked me up and put me sitting on his lap and held on to me so tight as he listened to the story unfold. I didn't realise the seriousness of all this. I was just enjoying all the attention I was getting for a change.

'We'll have to go to the police, Lil, and let them know wha' happened.'

'There will be no police brought into this, Phil. Tha' bastard got wha' was due to him today and won't be botherin' any little children for a long time, and I mean a long time! So we'll leave it at tha'. Right Phil? And say no more.'

Da knew not to argue with Ma. Once she had her mind made up about something, there would be no going back.

'Anyway, Phil, I have something else on me mind I want to talk to yeh about. I have been thinkin' about this for a while. Me mind's made up now after wha' happened to Kathleen today. We're movin'. I'm puttin' in to the Corporation for a house. The kids are not safe around the Hill any more. I'll put our name down first thing in the mornin', then I'll go on over to see me father. He might be able to put in a good word for us, with him workin' there. Maybe he'll get our name moved up the list. Tha' way we might not be waitin' too long for a house.'

* * *

Ma stuck to her guns as always and had her name on the list the following day, with Granda doing his bit on the side.

Things were never the same for us or Ma after that day. She wouldn't let us out of her sight. Before that, we used to play around the Hill with all our cousins, getting up to all sorts, having the best of fun ever, but that all stopped after that day.

I didn't understand what all the fuss was over. I was just happy that Ma kicked the shit of that man and not me. From that day on, I always listened to what she had to say.

4

Da Sacked

Da had a very good job, working in a factory that made chocolate, among other things. He was so religious and honest that he wouldn't take a sweet for love nor money. We were often watering from the mouth for the want of a bit of chocolate. I heard Ma say so many times, 'Go on, Phil, get us a few bits of the broken chocolate; sure nobody will miss a few squares.' His answer was always 'No!'

But, after the shock of me going off with the stranger on his bike for a few sweets, he was so afraid that Phil or I would do the same thing again. So what did he only go and do? He took a few bars of chocolate. He got himself caught and they gave him the sack. It nearly killed him, everybody knowing that he was after robbing from the factory, him always helping the priest and all.

Da was out of work for months, so Ma got herself a job patching the old potato sacks from the Daisy Market. Herself and her friend Maisie would sit at home for hours sewing by hand, while they tore the back off everyone on and off the Hill, drinking tea and smoking their few Woodbines.

I loved my Da being at home with us. He was so good, always helping Ma with cleaning and tidying around. He would be up from early looking after us kids, keeping us busy and out of harm's way. While Ma and Maisie would be working away on the sacks, Da would tell us the best stories ever.

The one we all loved the best was 'The Jelly Mountain'. He told us that story over and over and over again. Da would sit there with Carmel on his lap while Phil and I would sit on the bed.

'I have a new story to tell yiz today, and if yeh're good and do wha' yeh're told, I might even bring yeh to the Jelly Mountain. I was there many times when I was a little boy – the nicest place you ever saw in the whole world. Very deep in the forest it is, where only good children can go.'

That's when Phil and I started jumping up and down, one shouting over the other, 'I want to go, take me, Da! I'll be good, I'll be good!'

'Right, then. It's settled. Yiz can come with me the next time I'm goin'. But in the meantime, I'll tell yiz all about it. Be quiet now and listen. The first thing yeh see as soon as yeh get there is this big red jelly mountain, wobbling all over the place. Now, yeh have to make yer way up to the top first. An' when yeh're doin' tha', yeh can eat as much jelly as yeh like. And that's only the start. Now, when yeh're ready to slide down, guess where yeh splash and land.'

'Tell us, Da, tell us!' we kept shouting.

'Only into a pool of custard. And when yeh're finished there, isn't there only a river of chocolate across from the mountain, and yeh can swim away there to yer heart's content, drinkin' as much chocolate as yeh can for as long as yeh want.'

We would sit there with our mouths wide open, wishing we were in Jellyland.

'Now, after tha' yeh head over to the lemonade waterfall. Yeh have to make sure and drink plenty of it while yeh're washin' all the chocolate off yerself, before yeh go over to Lollypop Land where all the trees have every kind of sweets tha' yeh ever wanted growin' out of them. Oh, I nearly forgot. It never rains there; the sun shines there all day long. So yeh will be able to play in the golden cornfields until we're ready to come home. Now, who's goin' to be good?'

We would jump up, screaming, '*We are, Da, we are!*'

* * *

Ma didn't seem to mind Da being around in the beginning but, after a while, you could see that it was starting to get on her nerves.

She was in a right mood one day and didn't half let rip at Da.

'Phil Doyle!' she roared at him. When Ma said the second name, I knew: *here we go, trouble again.* I would take my brother Phil and sister Carmel and sit out on the landing, and then all hell would break loose. 'Phil Doyle, yeh can't keep hiding yerself up here in the room. Fuck everybody out there, who cares what they think.'

'I do, Lil, I care. How can I hold me head up knowin' everybody knows I did a bit of robbin'.'

'Ah, for Jaysus' sake, Phil, will yeh give it over. A few bars of chocolate, tha's all it was. Now yeh'd better get up off yer arse and get yerself a job. The blood's drippin' from the tops of me fingers from sewing these bloody sacks. And on top of all tha' I'm fallin' behind with me bills.'

Da just kept reading his paper, not taking any heed of what Ma was saying.

'Phil, I'm talkin' to yeh. Are yeh listenin'? Jaysus, Maisie, I think he's goin' deaf, or is he ignorin' me?'

'Phil ignore yeh? Are yeh mad, Lil? Not at all, look at him, he's away with the fairies, Lil. In another world, so he is.'

'Well, I won't be long bringin' him back into the real world.' She shouted at the top of her voice, 'Phil Doyle! Did yeh hear wha' I said?'

'Right, right, Lil. I heard yeh the first time. There's no need to be shoutin'. And de yeh have to talk to me like tha' in front of Maisie?'

'Then why didn't yeh *fuckin'* answer me if yeh heard me, lettin' me go on and on?' roared Ma.

'Don't mind me, Phil,' said Maisie. 'This is nothin' to wha' goes on between me and Jojo Murphy. Yeh're only in the ha'penny place here.'

Da would never curse or take the Lord's name in vain, not like Ma. He just took his cap and coat, passing us on the stairs, giving Ma a staring look for a change.

'I want yiz to keep out of yer mother's way for a little while. Kathleen, will yeh mind yer brother and sister out there on the front steps; get yerselves a bit of fresh air at the one time. I'm off to try to get meself a bit o' work. Anythin' to keep yer mother quiet and off me back. Come on while I carry the pram down the stairs. Hold on to Carmel for me. Are yeh right then, Phil – move yerself. Now promise me, Kathleen, tha' yeh won't move or talk to anybody tha' doesn't live around here. Remember wha' happened to yeh only a while ago.'

'I won't, Da. I'll never do tha' again.'

'Tha's a good girl. I'll be on me way, and if it's not too late when I get back, we'll go up to the park. Yerself and Phil can have a bit of a play around before it gets dark.'

* * *

We were playing around outside when Granny Mariah came over to us.

'Kathleen, where's yer father gone? I saw him headin' up towards Thomas Street.'

'He went out lookin' for a job, Gran.'

'Thanks be to God he's after gettin' himself out and about. I have meself sick worryin' about him. I'm prayin' mornin' noon and night to the good Lord, hopin' he'll help yer father get a bit of work for himself.'

'So is me Ma, Gran.'

'Hmm, is she now, Kathleen?' She rolled her eyes in the air. 'Where is yer mother anyway?'

'Sewin' up in the room with Maisie.'

'Go up and tell her I want her.'

I ran straight up the stairs. 'Ma, me Granny Mariah wants yeh.'

'Wha' does tha' oul fuck want now, Maisie? She has a nerve comin' around here. I haven't seen her in months since the big row I had with her about Kathleen and the kids.'

I shouted down, 'Gran, me Ma said wha' de yeh want?'

'Ask her can yeh go down to the butcher's for a bit of tripe for yer Grandad's tea. Me legs is very bad today, I can't walk very far.'

Ma opened her mouth, but Maisie cut across her. 'Before yeh say any more, Lil, and yeh know I'm not one for interferin', but don't be too hard on Mariah, she's not the worst. Tha's probably just an excuse about her legs . . . for her to come around and talk to yeh. After all, Phil's her only son and yeh know she loves to drop in every chance she gets to see him. Blood is blood, Lil, and yeh know he loves his mother.'

'Ah, I suppose yeh're right, Maisie. If the truth be known, I shouldn't really be askin' her to mind the kids. She is gettin' old and a bit forgetful.'

'Now, I'm only sayin', Lil . . . I hope yeh don't mind.'

'No, no. Yeh're a good friend Maisie. It's not everybody tha' I'd let put me in me place. But I have to agree, yeh're right. Kathleen, I see it's startin' to rain out there. Bring Carmel and Phil back up. The pair of yiz push the pram under the stairs. Yer Da can bring it back up later. Tell yer Gran to come up and have a cup of tea. I'll slip down in a little while to the shop and get the few bits for her.'

When I told Gran what Ma said, I knew she was happy by the smile on her face, which you didn't see very often.

I thought I'd never get to tell Phil that Gran and Ma were friends again.

'Tha's great,' says Phil. 'I missed her comin' around with the little bags of sweets.'

I had to agree, so did I.

* * *

Ma was talking away to Gran and Maisie when Da burst in the door. 'Lil, I've got great news. I got meself a job on the docks. It's just day-by-day work.'

'Oh my God, tha's great, Phil. Now, isn't it better than sittin' around here all day. I'll be able to pay me few bills again.'

You could see Ma was well pleased with the news and Da was even happier when he saw Gran sitting there with Carmel in her arms.

From then on, Da left the house at six o'clock in the morning to make sure he was at the top of the queue, hoping each day to get some work – which he always did. Ma only had to sew the sacks a few days a week, which meant we were able to go down to my Granny Kitty's again, my favourite place to go.

Everything was great for a while until one day Da was carrying a heavy sack of flour off the boat. He slipped and fell in the water, and sure he couldn't swim. Only that one of the fellas jumped in after him, he was a goner. He lost his nerve and no way would he go back to work on the boats again and was out of work once more.

Ma was on his back all the time about getting work, telling him he should have stayed in the job until something else came up.

'Lil, don't yeh care what happens to me? De yeh realise tha' I almost drowned? I was nearly out to Dollymount before they got me out of the water.'

'Go 'way, yeh shaggin' eejit, Phil. Yeh would have been dead ten times over with you not bein' able to swim.'

'Did yeh hear tha', Kathleen? Would I lie before the holy mother of God's statue standing there in the corner?'

'No, Da, yeh wouldn't.'

Ma just looked over at us and shook her head.

'Sure, when I was goin' up and down in the water I thought I saw Moby Dick swimming away from me with the big harpoon stuck in his back.'

'Ah, for fuck's sake, Phil, will yeh stop. Kathleen, don't be mindin' yer Da. Some of the water must have got into his brains. Moby Dick, me arse!'

'Da, who's Moby Dick?' says my brother Phil.

'Did I never tell yeh tha' story? Come over here, the pair of yiz, and sit down beside me. Well, wasn't he only the biggest fish tha' yeh ever saw in yer whole life, the length and width of the hill out there, so it was. Isn't tha' right, Lil?'

Ma just looked over and shook her head, once more not saying a word.

'Righ' then, gettin' back to me story. There was this man called Captain Ahab, who owned his own ship called *The Pequod*. He spent most of his life out on the open sea; a whale-catcher he was. He kept hearin' about this big white whale from all the other fishermen and about how nobody could ever catch him. Well, didn't he go an' get it into his head tha' he was goin' to be the one to capture Moby Dick. Which he did. Himself and the whale got into a fierce fight one day, with the whale bitin' one of the captain's legs off.'

'Wha' happened, Da? Did he die, did he die?' I asked.

'De yeh know wha' kept him alive, Kathleen? Hate and revenge. He became obsessed with Moby Dick and spent years roamin' the sea lookin' for him until one day he finally caught him with one of his big harpoons. He lodged it deep into the whale's flesh. He struggled and struggled for God only knows how long. Wha' de yeh think happened then?'

At this stage, Phil was jumping up and down on the bed with excitement. 'Quick, Da, tell us, tell us!'

Even Ma stopped sewing, waiting to see what was going to be said next.

'Ahab, the bloody eejit, went and got the good leg caught in his own harpoon's rope and, unable to free himself, was dragged out to the cold sea by the whale and was lost forever.'

Da told the story of his own encounter with 'Moby Dick' many times over the years, with the waves getting higher and the fish getting even bigger.

* * *

So Ma was back to sewing the sacks every day. Granny Kitty knew a woman who was selling a little sewing machine cheap. She bought it for Ma, so the blood wouldn't be dripping from her fingers from the big needles. That kept Ma happy and off Da's back.

Da got himself a few hours' work up in the Phoenix Park picking the papers up and emptying the small bins. He didn't get paid very much but what he did get he gave to Ma. He was so good back then, never keeping a penny for himself. Everything was always for Ma and us kids.

'Lil, it's not much, but every little helps. It's the best I can do for now.'

'Tha's grand, Phil. Sure won't it keep our heads above water.'

'Don't be mentioning water to me, for God's sake, Lil! I'll be bringing a panic attack on meself.'

They both laughed as Ma went back to her sewing, while Da took Carmel in his arms and we all went up to the Christ Church park to play.

Da went out every day looking for work. He put his name down everywhere. Then, one day, two letters came. Ma and Da looked at one another. We never got letters, never mind two at the same time.

'Jaysus, Phil, wha' could they be for? You open them; yeh know I'm not good at the oul' readin'.'

He sat there for a minute looking at the letters.

'Will yeh open them, for Jaysus' sake, Phil!'

Da sat there reading away to himself, not saying a word to Ma. Then he jumped up off the chair.

'I don't believe it! The Lord answered me prayers, Lil.'

'Will yeh tell me wha' they say? The suspense is killin' me.'

'I'm after gettin' offered two good jobs – one in the Corporation and one in Guinness.'

'Tha's great, Phil. We'll have a steady wage comin' in. Me mind will be at ease at last. I won't have to worry any more.'

'Wha'll I do? I don't know which one to pick. Wha' de yeh think, Lil?'

'I don't know, Phil, I'm not sure. Go over and talk to your Da, see wha' he says.'

Off Da went to Granda Phil and they made their way down to the Irish pub at the bottom of the Hill to make the big decision.

Back then it wasn't very often Da took a drink, but when he did you always knew. You could hear him singing at the top of his voice, from one end of Christ Church to the other. He thought he could sing like an opera singer. He'd make up all of his own words, pretending he knew how to sing in Italian. That night, the whole of Cook Street was awake, including Maisie, who opened her window and roared at the top of her lungs.

'Is tha' you Phil Doyle? Who de yeh think yeh are, Mario Lanza, yeh fuckin' eejit? Wakin' us all up! I won't be able to go back to sleep now, I'll be fallin' out of me standin' tomorrow, yeh bloody gobshite.'

With a struggle Da finally got up the stairs and into the room.

'Jaysus, Phil, yeh have the whole house awake with the roars of yeh.'

'I've made up me mind, Lil. I'm takin' the job in the Corporation.'

35

My brother Phil and myself were under the covers laughing our heads off at Da swaying from one side of the room to the other. We had never seen him that bad before.

'Lil, I've made up me mind. I'm takin' the job in the Corporation.'

'I heard yeh the first time,' whispered Ma. 'Now, shut the fuck up and get into the bed. The whole Hill will be talkin' about us tomorrow.'

'Let them talk. I'm a happy man tonight.'

And so he was; he never had to go out looking for work again.

* * *

Da was up early the next morning. He was green in the face and as sick as anything.

'I'm dyin', Lil. Me head's burstin'.'

'And so yeh should be, yeh fuckin' eejit. Makin' a show of me!'

'It's not every day a man gets offered two jobs. Yeh should be pleased and proud, not givin' out to me.'

'Ah, I suppose yeh're right, Phil. To hell with everybody! Now drink tha' sup of tea and get yer arse down to the Corporation before they give the job to somebody else.'

He was up and on his way out before Ma could say another word.

Maisie was standing at the door as Da was walking out.

'Tha's a lovely voice yeh have there, Phil. Yeh had the whole house awake last night with the roars of yeh.'

'Sorry about tha', Maisie.' Da gave her a nod of the head, tipped the peak of his cap and kept going.

'Jaysus, Lil, he looks a bit rough around the edges. He must have had a right sup on him last night.'

'He's not used to drinkin', Maisie, I can tell yeh. He's in a right state. Anyway never mind all tha', come in, come in. I've great news. Sit down there and we'll have a cup of tea. Phil's after gettin' offered two jobs – Dublin Corporation and Guinness – but he's takin' the one in the Corporation.'

'Tha's great news, Lil. Is tha' wha' all tha' singin' was about last night? I never knew your Phil could sing. He hasn't got a bad voice there at all.'

'It's only when he takes a few pints, Maisie, which doesn't be very often, I can tell yeh tha' for nothin', thank God. He starts with all tha' opera stuff. I don't have a clue wha' he does be sayin' and neither does he. Anyway, I was thinkin' to meself last night, why don't yeh tell your Jojo there's a job goin' in Guinness?'

'Ah, for fuck sake, Lil. Are yeh serious or wha'? Yeh couldn't give him a job there. Sure, yeh'd find him dead after a week, he'd be after drinkin' tha' much of the stuff. And if tha' didn't happen they'd go bankrupt in no time.'

'I wasn't thinkin' there, Maisie, I forgot about his drink problem.'

'Would yeh mind, Lil, if I told me brother Jimmy about the job?'

'Not at all, Maisie, tell him I think the job in Guinness is only temporary, tha's why Phil went for the Corporation. Sure wouldn't it do him for a while, Maisie and yeh never know, he might get himself a full-time job out of it after a while.'

'Thanks, Lil. Yeh're real good thinkin' of me and all. I'll run down to me Ma's and tell Jimmy to go up straight away. Put the teapot on there, I'll be back in a few minutes with a packet of Woodbines for yeh and a few jam doughnuts to celebrate.'

Da was never out of work from that day on.

5

The Fever

Da was working away in his new job and delighted with life and Ma was as happy as Larry, with not a worry in the world. Until one morning my brother Phil woke up with spots all over him.

'Wha's wrong with yeh, Phil? Yer face is full of freckles.'

His hair was wringing wet and he didn't answer me. I kept nudging him. 'Are yeh after pissin' on yerself, Phil?' I whispered in his ear. 'If yeh did, Ma will kill yeh.'

'Wha's tha' yeh said, Kathleen?' Ma shouted over. 'Did he piss in tha' bed again? Phil, didn't I tell yeh to go in the bucket last night before yeh went asleep? Kathleen, I'm still feedin' Carmel. Will yeh get him up for me and while yeh're at it, strip the sheets off the bed.'

'Okay, Ma.'

I tried to push him out of the bed but he just lay there lifeless, with not a sound coming from him.

'Ma, he won't move for me. Look at him. He's messin'.'

She took one look at Phil and screamed.

'Holy Mother of God! Quick, Kathleen, take Carmel,' she said. She wrapped Phil in a blanket. 'Go down to Maisie. Tell her I think young Phil has the fever. I have to go to the doctor quick. Ask Maisie if she will keep an eye to yiz 'til yer father comes home.'

'Wha's the fever, Ma?'

'For God's sake, Kathleen, just do wha' I tell yeh. This is no time to be askin' me twenty questions. Move now. Go on, go on.'

I ran down the stairs as quick as I could, with Carmel in my arms roaring and shouting as I banged on the door. 'Maisie, Maisie, open up quick!'

'For Jaysus' sake. Wha' the hell is goin' on with yeh, Kathleen, with all yer screamin' and shoutin'?'

'Phil has marks all over him and he's after pissin' on himself. Ma said he has the fever.'

'Holy Mother of God,' she said, blessing herself. 'Come in, come in, Kathleen.'

'Maisie, wha' does the fever mean?'

She kept blessing herself. I was afraid to tell her I was after wetting my knickers with the fright of Ma turning green in the face and running to the doctor's place.

'Here, give me Carmel. Sit down there, Kathleen. Did yeh have anythin' to eat?'

'No, Ma just ran with Phil.'

'I have a drop of porridge over, yiz can have tha'.'

'Wha's wrong with Phil, Maisie?'

'Yer brother is a very sick boy if he has the fever,' she said, as she blessed herself another dozen times. 'All we can do now is pray and hope the Holy Mother herself is listenin' to us.'

* * *

When Da came home from work, Maisie told him about Phil. He too turned green in the face.

'Quick, Maisie. Give me the kids and thanks for lookin' after them. I'll leave them with me mother. I'll have to get over to Lil as quick as I can. She'll be frantic on her own.'

'Da, Da, I want to go with yeh, please, I want to see me brother.'

'Shush, Kathleen,' says Da.

'She's cryin' all day, Phil. Let her go with yeh. I'll come and look after her while yeh're in with Lil.'

Da dropped Carmel off at Granny Mariah's. As soon as she heard the word 'fever', the rosary beads were taken out and she too blessed herself a dozen times. Maisie took me by the hand as Da took us over to the doctor, who told us Ma had gone on to the fever hospital.

There we found Ma sitting outside the door, crying her eyes out.

'Lil, wha' did they say?' asked Da.

'He's bad, Phil, the water's drippin' outta him. His temperature's sky-high. Me child's rantin' and ravin' all over the place.'

'Try and calm down, will yeh, Lil. It might not be tha' bad.'

'Don't tell me to be calm, me child's fightin' for his life in there.'

'Shush, Lil, here's the doctor.'

The doctor looked serious. 'I'm afraid your son has scarlet fever. We have to try and keep his temperature down and hope the fever breaks. I have to be honest with you, your son is a very sick child.'

'Holy Mother of God, Phil. There's children dyin' from tha'.' The tears rolled down her face.

Maisie stepped in straight away, trying to calm down both of them. 'Now, now, Lil, the Holy Mother herself is lookin' down on him. Don't be thinkin' like tha'. Gettin' yerself into a state. We'll drop into the church on the way home and light a few candles,' said Maisie, giving Da the eye to try and get Ma to leave the hospital, which she did, after a lot of persuasion.

'Is Phil okay, Ma?'

'He's real sick, Kathleen. They have to keep him in hospital,' she said, bursting out crying again.

We picked Carmel up from Gran's and headed home. As soon as she got through the door, Ma lit up a Woodbine, her hands shaking. 'I'll have to get a bit of heat into this room. God love yiz, yeh must be freezin'. Phil, get tha' fire goin' as quick as yeh can and I'll make a bite to eat.'

Carmel and I were fed, stripped and in the bed in no time. Carmel was asleep as soon as her head hit the pillow, as usual, with her thumb in her mouth and a finger up her nose. I cried myself to sleep that night because I missed Phil so much. I always slept at one end of the bed while he slept at the other. We were like two peas in a pod. At night, I used to rub my feet on Phil's to heat them up. Now, I was worried that there would be no one to keep him warm that night.

I woke up and could hear Ma crying and talking to Da.

'Lil, yeh'll have to be strong and try to keep yerself together. Yeh have the other two kids to take care of.'

I lay there thinking to myself, *What does Da mean? My Ma's real strong. She can bash anybody.* I was too young to understand the seriousness of Phil's fever.

* * *

Ma and I went to the hospital every day to see Phil, stopping at the church on the way to light a few candles. Then, on the way home, we would light more candles. At the hospital, we weren't allowed into Phil's room, so we had to stand outside the door and look through a small pane of glass. We stood there for such a long time. Every now and then Ma would pick me up in her arms to let me have a look at him. He lay there looking lifeless.

'Kathleen, look at his little face. He's gone so thin, the flesh is walkin' off him.'

One day we went up to Granny Kitty's from the hospital. Ma cried uncontrollably, telling all the family, 'It's touch and go. They'll know tonight if he'll pull through.'

They all started crying and took out the rosary beads and prayer books. They sat there for hours on end, praying, praying and praying again. I looked around at all the grown-ups, not understanding what all this meant. I asked Ma if it meant that if they all touched Phil and then go, that he would get better. I could hear a few of my aunties in the background giggling and praying at the same time. Ma couldn't answer me. She walked away, not saying a word.

We all went to the church that evening. Everybody was putting money in the candle box. I sat there looking at all the money God was making out of my brother being sick. I told him that night that unless he made Phil better, every chance I'd get I'd be robbing all his candles, and he wouldn't be making money any more.

God must have had a good think about what I said that night because Phil pulled through and everything was great again. I didn't tell Ma what I'd said in the church. It was my secret.

After Phil's fever broke, we were allowed to go in to sit with him. Ma hugged him so tight I thought she was never going to let him go. After a while, the doctor came over and was talking away to Ma, so I jumped up onto the bed.

'When are yeh comin' home? I missed yeh. Did yeh miss me, Phil?'

He just smiled, not saying a word.

'I was here every day with Ma. We were standin' over there behind the door. See tha' one with the bit of glass? Well, I was lookin' in at yeh all the time. The nurse kept washin' yeh cause yeh were sweatin' and she even washed yer bum cause I think yeh pissed on yerself again.'

Phil started laughing and showing off his pearly whites. I knew then he was okay and would be coming home to me soon.

* * *

43

He was skin and bone for a long time. Ma treated him like a God from then on. He was her blue-eyed boy and that was that. In her eyes, he could do no wrong – and he didn't half milk it.

'Kathleen, hand yer brother his dinner . . . Help him with his shoes . . . You carry the bags, yeh know Phil's legs are weak, he's not able.'

When she wasn't looking, the little fucker would be getting me back up and giving me the sly grin, but when Ma wasn't around and when I got the chance, I'd give him a good kick up the hole. That would soon knock the grin off his face, but deep down inside me I was so happy he was better.

* * *

Phil was home from hospital a good few weeks now, getting stronger and stronger by the day and starting to look more like his old self again, which made Ma very happy. But he wasn't talking very much.

One morning we were sitting at the table eating our porridge when Ma let out an unmerciful scream.

'Jaysus, Kathleen. Wha's tha' walkin' down Phil's face?'

'Where, Ma?'

'There! For God's sake, Kathleen, look – it's after movin'.'

Of course, Phil jumped up and started crying as usual.

'Christ, come over to me till I check yer head. It's walkin'.'

'Walkin', walkin' where, Ma?'

'Never mind, Kathleen. Run downstairs and ask Maisie for a lend of her fine comb.'

I was down the stairs in seconds, banging the door and shouting. 'Maisie, Maisie, me Ma wants yeh. Phil's head is movin' and walkin' as well. Have yeh got a fine comb?'

'For Jaysus' sake, Kathleen, will yeh keep yer voice down, the whole house can hear yeh.'

Maisie followed me back up to Ma. 'Wha's wrong with yeh, Lil?'

'Would yeh have a look at the state of his head.'

Maisie had a quick look. 'Jaysus, Lil, how did his head get so bad? They're like a herd of buffaloes runnin' around. They're tha' big. How did he catch them?'

'I bet yeh he got them off tha' scaldy-eyed young wan who lives down the bottom of the Hill. Yeh know who I'm talkin' about. I don't think she gets washed from one end of the week to the other. The hum off her would turn yer stomach. Will yeh check Kathleen's hair for me? I'll go crazy mad if her head is the same. Her lovely long black plaits, she'll have to get them cut off.'

'Don't be panickin', Lil. It's only a few fleas. Here, give me a bit of newspaper. Bend yer head over, Kathleen,' she said, and began combing through my hair. I thought my brains were going to come out, she dug the comb in that hard.

'There, yeh see, Lil. There wasn't tha' many. Only a dozen or so. Now have yeh got a bottle of vinegar, Lil?'

'Vinegar? For wha'?'

'Did yeh never hear about tha'? I can't believe nobody ever told yeh. Just in case we miss any fleas, the vinegar will smother any little bastards tha's left.'

'Maisie, I'm ashamed of me life. I'm sewin' them bloody sacks from mornin' 'til night. I didn't think to check their heads.'

'Will yeh go away, Lil. Everybody gets fleas and hoppers.'

'Ma, where do they come from?' asked Phil.

'Yeh get them from somebody tha's not clean, or it could be the dust from the sacks or the turf,' said Ma as she sat there combing Phil's hair back. 'Would yeh have a look at him, Maisie? De yeh know who young Phil always reminds me of, with his hair combed back off his face and all curly at the back?'

'Who's tha', Lil?'

'Ah, yeh know yer man tha' does be in the films. Wha's this his name is? It's on the tip of me tongue. I have it. Errol Flynn, the movie star, tha's who.'

'I wouldn't be able for yeh, yeh're a scream, Lil. Movie star, me arse.' She stood back from me. 'There. The plaits are done now. Wha' de yeh think?'

'God, Maisie, I'd be lost without yeh.'

'Don't be gettin' all sloppy on me now. Put the teapot on the fire there and give me a Woodbine.'

'I've none, Maisie. Phil will be in from work soon. We'll get one off him. Kathleen, Carmel's asleep, so take Phil with yeh and sit at the front steps so tha' vinegar can dry well into yer hair. And don't move, de yeh hear me?'

'Right, Ma.'

We made our way down the stairs and were sitting on the front steps when Phil turned to me. 'Yeh know wha', Kathleen, I'm goin' to get me Da to make a sword out of this bit of wood I found under the stairs and if anybody starts pickin' on us again I'll give them a bang on the head and then stick it up their arse.'

'Jaysus, yeh're talkin', Phil! Don't let anyone hear yeh, for fuck's sake, or yeh'll be gettin' yer own arse roasted, especially if Ma hears yeh.'

Scaldy-Eyes and her friends came over to us. They started jeering, calling us 'lousy heads'.

'Yeh have fleas, Kathleen Doyle. I know yeh have. Yiz are rotten. Yeh can smell the stuff in yer hair.'

I jumped up.

'Who de yeh think yeh are, with yer scaldy eyes and yer smelly knickers? Me Ma said tha' yeh could do with a good wash.'

All her friends started laughing at her. She ran off crying, with Phil fucking and blinding as he chased her with his plank of wood.

It was starting to get dark so we made our way back up the stairs. Carmel was at the age where she was starting to talk so I had to keep telling Phil to stop saying 'fuck' in front of her. Or in front of Ma, for that matter.

'If Da hears yeh, he'll be lightin' candles for a month. I'm tellin' yeh, Phil, Ma will ram a bar of soap in yer mouth. Yeh'll be sick as anythin'.'

I think I was better off when he was crying all the time and not talking.

* * *

It was starting to get cold so Da fixed the panes of glass that were broken. Granny Kitty bought herself new curtains so she gave us the old ones. Ma said that they were nearly new.

'Come on, the three of yiz, we'll go up to the Iveagh Market in Francis Street and see if I can get a cheap tablecloth to go with the curtains. When we're there we'll have a root through the second-hand stuff and see if I can get some boots for yiz.'

We used to love going to the market. Ma would be yapping for ages while the three of us would be off dressing up in all sorts of clothes, me with a straw hat and flowery dress, while Phil would have a bowler hat and a coat down to his ankles. Carmel was small and still sucking her thumb, so we would stick a wig on her or any oul' hat to keep her happy. We'd have great fun. They were happy days.

* * *

It wasn't long after Phil's sickness that I heard Ma telling my Aunt Emmie, 'I'm gone again.' By this stage, I had learned what these words meant: another baby on the way. This time it was to be my brother Noel.

47

6

Noel's Birth

It was Christmas Eve and it was very cold outside. The snow was thick on the ground. Da lit the fire early that morning and kept an eye to Phil and Carmel while myself and Ma went for the last of the Christmas shopping. We met Maisie up Thomas Street. She was carrying a big Christmas tree.

'Howyeh, Lil. Where are yeh off to?'

'Just gettin' the last few bits in, Maisie.'

'I'm half-dead carryin' this tree. Tha' bastard of a husband of mine, Jojo Murphy, is down in the pub, pissed drunk after spendin' all me wages on drink – didn't give me a penny, Lil. He's only a bollocks, I swear he is, a pig if yeh ever met one.'

Jojo was a very big man, well over six foot and built like a lion. Da always said that he had hands like shovels – 'If yeh got a dig off him, sure yeh'd be dead.'

Ma wasn't saying much. Maisie was still going on and on and on . . .

'I had to go down to me Ma and borrow a few bob to get me over the Christmas. Thank God, I had the kids' things in.'

At this stage Ma was bent over, holding herself. She was nearly on her knees.

'Jaysus, Lil, are yeh all right?'

I could see a big gush of water pouring down Ma's legs.

'Me waters are gone, Maisie, I've started.'

'Christ, Lil, here's me givin' out like fuck and you in the height of labour! Let's get yeh back home.'

'Wha's wrong, Ma?' I asked.

'I'm okay, Kathleen; just a few cramps in me stomach. I'll be all right when I lie down.'

Maisie was dragging the Christmas tree with one hand and trying to help Ma with the other. It took us ages to get back home, with Ma stopping every few yards, bending over with the pain.

'Kathleen, run on down the hill and tell yer Da I'm on me way with yer mother. Tell him she's started.'

I was gasping for breath as I got to the end of the stairs, screaming my lungs out.

'Da, quick, Da, come down! Ma is all bent up and she's after pissin' on herself and Maisie said she's after startin' somethin'.'

Da came running down the stairs. 'Jaysus Christ, Kathleen, will yeh watch yer tongue. If anybody hears yeh. Yeh're startin' to sound more like yer mother every day.'

'I think Ma is sick. Sorry, Da.'

Da only had the words out of his mouth when we heard this unmerciful roar from Maisie: 'Phil Doyle, come down here quick! Lil's started.'

Da went running ahead of me. 'Wha' are yeh sayin' Maisie? Started wha'?'

'For fuck's sake, Phil, yeh know wha' I mean. Do I have to spell it out for yeh? Sure she didn't even get to the top of Thomas Street. Will yeh look at her, the child is on its way.'

'Christ, Lil, I thought yeh said tha' it wouldn't be happenin' 'til after Christmas?'

'Will yeh shut the fuck up, Phil, and just get me up the stairs. I must have got me dates mixed up.'

With Maisie in the front and Da at the back, after a

struggle, they finally got Ma up the stairs and into the bed.

'Phil, yeh better get the doctor here quick,' said Maisie. 'I'll stay and look after Lil and the kids until yeh get back.'

My brother Phil and myself just stood there, while Carmel slept in the pram. Ma was twisting and turning, screaming and shouting, as Maisie wiped her face with a towel.

'Lil, try and keep yerself calm. Phil is on his way with the doctor.'

In the middle of all this mayhem, I could hear Ma tell Maisie, 'Their few bits is under the bed, wrapped in one of the oul' sacks.' Ma was in the height of labour and she was still worrying about us and Santy.

It wasn't too long before Da walked in with the doctor and nurse.

Maisie told Da to take us downstairs to her place.

'I'll be down in a couple of minutes meself, Phil.'

'Wha' about Santy?' he whispered in Maisie's ear.

'It's okay, Phil, Lil told me where everythin' is. I'll take care of all tha', you've more to be worryin' about tonight. Go on over to yer Ma's. It'll be well into the morning before the child's born.'

Da told us the fire had to stay lit because Ma was sick. 'And we have to stay with Maisie for the night as Santy won't be able to come down our chimney.' The look on our faces told Da what we were thinking. 'Don't be worryin', the pair of yiz, I'll let Santy know where yeh are.'

* * *

The three of us slept in Maisie's bed that Christmas Eve. I was awake first. Santy left me a lovely doll, Phil a truck and Carmel a teddy bear.

Maisie had four kids herself. We were all running around like lunatics while she made us something to eat. Jojo was lying across the kitchen table, still drunk from the night before.

Maisie burst open the door and let out her usual scream, 'For fuck's sake, will yiz be quiet! Everybody on the Hill will think I'm murderin' yiz. Kathleen, when yeh're finished tha' bit of bread get the other two and go up to yer Ma. She has somethin' to tell yiz.'

'Is me Ma better, Maisie?'

'There's not a bother on her, Kathleen. Now, run along; she has a nice little surprise for yiz.'

We got our toys and went up to Ma, who was sitting up in the bed, with Da standing beside her. She had this little bundle in her arms, which I thought was a doll, until it started to cry.

I got such a fright, I jumped. 'Ma, is it real?'

'Of course, Kathleen. Isn't he lovely?'

'Where did it come from?' Phil asked.

'Santy left him.'

'I thought he couldn't get down the chimney with the fire, Ma.'

'Tha's right, Kathleen, but wasn't the door half-open? Santy popped his head in to see who was here and, this bein' his last stop, he said tha' he had one more parcel left. Would I like it? Sure, I couldn't say no to Santy, could I?' She pulled the blanket back to show us. 'This is yer new brother. I'm goin' to call him Noel. The three of yiz come over and sit up here beside me.'

Da lifted Carmel up and put her under the blankets with Ma.

Phil was jumping up and down on the bed – 'A brother for me to play with!' He was well pleased with himself.

I just smiled as I looked down at Noel. 'He's nice, Ma.' But, as young as I was, what was really going through my head was, 'Here's another little fucker for me to mind.' I rolled my eyes up to the ceiling.

'Right then, Lil, we better start gettin' the Christmas dinner ready,' said Da. 'Kathleen, get the spuds out of the bag. Phil, bring tha' head of cabbage over here. Where's the chicken, Lil?'

'I think Maisie left the bag out on the landin'.'

'Are yeh sure tha' it'll be all right now? Yeh should have brought it in – yeh wouldn't know wha' would be crawlin' around out there in the depths of the night.'

'Well now, Phil Doyle, I wasn't thinking of chickens last night, was I, with me waters broke, and the child halfway into the world? Yeh fuckin' eejit, yeh're gettin' me all worked up now and me tryin' to get me milk goin' to feed the baby.'

'Holy Mother of God, Lil, could you please, on Christmas Day, of all days, not curse.'

Ma was mumbling to herself and we all knew when she started fucking and blinding, you'd best be quiet.

'Kathleen, get Phil and Carmel, put their coats on and I'll bring yiz to Mass first. We'll let yer mother get a bit of peace and quiet, and maybe then she might calm herself down by the time we get back.'

We dropped in to see Granny Mariah to tell her about the new baby and to wish her a Happy Christmas. While we were there, Da asked if she had a spare bar of soap.

'Wha's tha' for, Da?' I asked.

'To wash yer mother's mouth out – a terrible woman she is, Kathleen, with that tongue of hers.' He gave me a little smile, so I'd know full well that he was making up a yarn.

Little did he know that it should be two bars of soap he should be getting.

One for Ma and one for me.

7

The Move

Ma roared down from the top of the landing.

'Maisie, will yeh come up to me for a minute? I've somethin' to tell yeh.'

'Okay, Lil. I'm after makin' a lovely pot of stew – will I bring yeh up a bowl?'

'Tha's great, Maisie. Are yeh sure yeh don't need it for yerself?'

'No, my lot's fed. Anyway, wouldn't you give me some if yeh had it over?'

'When have I ever got anythin' over?'

Ma was a bit quiet and not her usual self that day.

'Wha's wrong with yeh, Lil? I never saw yeh down in the dumps as bad as this before. Have yeh got tha' thing where all yer bits inside go a bit mad after a baby and have yeh cryin' and all? Jaysus, wha' the fuck is it called?'

'Maisie, wha' are yeh talkin' about?'

'I have it Lil – hormones. Tha's it, hormones. I hear they can make yeh go crazy mad.' She was trying to put a smile back on Ma's face.

'Go away, yeh mad thing. It's nothin' to do with me hormones. I was dreadin' havin' to tell yeh this, bu' . . . I'm goin' to be leavin' the city. I've put in for a house.'

Maisie kept talking, not taking any heed of what Ma had just said. She didn't want to know.

'I'm just windin' yeh up, Lil. I'll heat this bowl of stew; yeh need all yer strength after bringin' tha' Noel fella into the world. He must have been at least twelve pounds the night he was born; sure look at the size of him now for three weeks old! Yeh could nearly put a bag on his back and send him to school, he's tha' big.'

'Maisie, will yeh shut the fuck up and listen to me? Please! Me Da knows someone in Dublin Corporation; he's goin' to see if he can pull a few strings and get me name moved up on the list. Tha' way we won't have to wait years for a house.'

Maisie just sat there with the tears falling down her face; she couldn't stop crying.

'Lil, yeh don't have to move. One of the houses up the Hill has a few rooms goin' cheap. I'll see if I can get them for yeh.'

'No, Maisie, I'm sick to death goin' down to tha' bloody yard, cleanin' tha' filthy toilet. Anyway, me mind's made up after wha' happened to Kathleen. All I want is a house with me own toilet and garden for the kids. At least I know they will be safe. The traffic around here is gettin' worse. Only yesterday mornin' I couldn't keep count of the cars goin' up and down Christ Church Hill; me nerves were gone watchin' and worryin' about them. There's a place called Crumlin . . .'

'Ah, for fuck's sake, Lil! Tha's out in the wilderness. Yeh know tha' young wan, "Scaldy-Eyes", who lives down the Hill? Well, they're after gettin' a house out there. I met her Ma and she was tellin' me they haven't even got proper shops, only a little bit of a one, and they're robbers with their prices. And tha's not all; there's cows lookin' in yer back garden at yeh. Jaysus, Lil, it's in the arsehole of the country. Yeh'll go mad out there on yer own.'

'Maisie, don't be gettin' yerself all upset; yeh'll bring on an asthma attack. I'll make yeh a cup of tea and we'll have a smoke. Come on now, stop cryin'.'

'I can't help it, Lil, yeh're me only friend. Tha' Jojo Murphy doesn't give two fucks about me. Have yeh seen him lately? He's pissed drunk every night, the pig.'

'Sure haven't yeh got yer Ma, Maisie?'

'I know I have me Ma, and she's real good and all, but it won't be the same. If I slip up and say "fuck" or "piss" in front of her, she starts chasin' me with the holy water. And who's goin' to lend me a cup of sugar or a Woodbine when I've none? There's only yerself, Lil. I've nobody else.'

'Why don't yeh come down to me Da's with me and see wha' he says? Maybe he could put yer name down on the list with mine; we might even get a house beside one another. Jaysus, Maisie, I'd love nothin' better than to have yeh with me. Tha' would be all me dreams come together.'

'No fuckin' way, Lil. Yeh wouldn't get me out there for love nor money, not even for yerself.'

'Wha' are yeh goin' to do when they start pullin' down all the tenement houses? It's goin' to happen, Maisie – mark my words, it's on the cards.'

'I don't care, Lil, I'll get meself somethin' – one or two rooms over a shop. I'll never leave. I love the city too much.'

'Come on, Maisie, walk down to me Da's. We'll have a yap on the way. We'll worry about it when the time comes.'

* * *

Noel was nine months old when the letter finally came about the house.

'Phil, you open it. I can't look; if they turn us down I'll go mad. Hurry up and tell me wha' it says.'

'Lil, will yeh stay quiet and let me read it first.'

Da stood up and blessed himself as he read down the page.

'Will yeh tell me wha' it says, Phil!'

The suspense was killing Ma; it seemed to take ages for Da to read the letter and then there was a scream out of him.

'Yes, yes! We got the house in Crumlin!'

'Jaysus! Oh my God, I can't believe it.'

We kids were jumping and screaming. We knew something good was happening. Da picked up myself and Carmel and swung us around. Ma was jumping and dancing with Phil. Everyone was happy that day.

'Lil, yeh'll have to go over to yer Da and thank him for puttin' a word in for us. Tell him I'll buy him a pint when I get paid.'

'Yeh're right, Phil, I will. Kathleen, get the pram ready.'

The pram was more like a small bus. It was huge and the wheels were so big you could put them on one of the horses up the lane and use it as a cart. Carmel was put up the top of the pram, Noel down the other end and Phil, with his weak legs, was put in the middle. As usual, I was left running after Ma.

When we got down to Granny Kitty's, Granda John was there.

'Ah, Lil, come in and sit down. Have yeh heard any word about the house, luv?'

Ma threw her arms around him. 'Here's the letter, Da – it came this mornin'. I can't believe it, a house of me own. How will I ever thank yeh?'

'Shush . . . Now, Lil, don't be lettin' anyone know I put a word in for yeh. There's people years on the housin' list. Yeh'd be gettin' me into trouble, so say no more about it.' He went back to reading his paper.

'Lil, let me know when yeh get yer key and wha' day yeh're movin' and I'll come over with Fanny and the cart to give yeh a hand,' said Granny Kitty. Fanny was her donkey.

'Tha'll be great, Ma. Now, I'll just have a quick cup of tea with yeh and then I'd better be on me way home. It's gettin' late.'

Over the next week there was great excitement around the area. A good few people had got letters saying they'd got houses too. Ma was happy about that.

'At least we'll know a few families from town, Phil. It won't feel so lonely.'

* * *

The day finally came to move. My uncle Billy, who was married to Da's sister Emmie, said he could get a loan of a small wagon for ten shillings. Da gave him the money and they shook hands on it.

'Tha's grand, Billy, we'll be able to do the trip in one go, 'cause we've Kitty's cart as well.'

While all the running up and down the stairs was going on, Maisie made over to Ma.

'So, yeh're really goin', Lil. I still can't believe it.'

'Yeah, I am, Maisie. I'm goin' to miss yeh.'

Maisie was sobbing like I never saw before. Ma put her arms around her.

'Please don't cry, Maisie, you'll start me off. Sure I'll be back in to see me Ma and Da every week and I'll come over to see yeh. I promise. And yeh can even come out for a day with the kids and we can catch up on all the gossip. Won't it be like an outin' for yeh, comin' out to the country. Wha' de yeh say?'

'We'll see, Lil. I'm goin' down to me Ma now; I can't stand here and watch yeh go. It's too hard. Me heart is broke.'

They cried, hugged and kissed one another and said their goodbyes.

Da turned to Ma. 'Lil, there's no room for the pram. It's too big.'

'Okay, Phil, you go ahead with the wagon. Put the oul' chest on the cart with Kathleen and young Phil and I'll walk with the pram and the two younger kids.'

Sitting on top of the cart, Phil and I waved goodbye to all the neighbours as Ma started the long walk to Crumlin.

* * *

I thought we were never going to get to the house. It seemed to be taking forever, between Granny stopping and talking to half of Dublin on the way, Fanny having a shit every few minutes, and Phil crying in my face that he was going to piss on himself.

'Here yiz are now,' said Granny. 'There's yer new house; I can see yer father and Billy. Hold on to young Phil and don't let him move, Kathleen, while I settle Fanny down.' She pulled the reins in. 'Slow down girl, slow, slow.'

We were here at last. Myself and Phil stood there beside Granny, looking at our new house. We couldn't believe our eyes. It was huge; we had our own front gate with a long garden and a path in the centre leading to a red hall door, with '51' in brass number plates and a brass letterbox. It looked ever so posh, just like my Granny Kitty's house.

Phil tipped me. 'Kathleen, look at tha' gate over there at the side of the house. Let's see wha's behind it.'

It was the back garden, which was three times bigger than the front garden.

'Ma will be over the moon when she sees this, Phil. Tha's all she talks about – the garden and the toilet. Come on, let's go and check out the rest.'

When we went inside, we looked at one another in amazement. There were rooms everywhere. Downstairs we had a kitchen and a parlour. After living in one room, this looked like a mansion to us. We ran upstairs, each trying to get in front of the other. To our surprise, there were two bedrooms with small fireplaces and a bathroom off the landing.

'Da, did yeh see this?' I roared. 'We have a bath and it's in the same room as the toilet!'

'Tha's right, Kathleen; yer Mother will be well pleased when she sees tha', like I am with the garden. Wait and see, I'll soon have vegetables growin' the length and breadth of it. Enough of all tha' now; come and help me get these few bits in before yer mother arrives.'

Da was struggling in with the beds, giving us the small stuff, when a man came over to him.

'Can I give yeh a lift with tha'?' He put his hand out. 'I'm Mr O'Brien from next door.'

Phil and myself looked at each other. 'There's goin' to be a fight, Kathleen. I'm off.'

'Where are yeh runnin' to, Phil? Come back here, yeh eejit; just wait and see wha' happens. I keep tellin' yeh, always listen first.'

'Yeh told me to run for cover when yeh hear the second name being mentioned.'

'Tha's only when it's between Ma and Da. Now shut the fuck up and listen.'

Da put his hand out.

'I'm Phil, pleased to meet yeh. We're movin' from town. Lil the wife is on her way with the rest of the family.'

Da was shaking his hand so hard I thought it was going to fall off. He was delighted with himself to meet a friendly face. It looked like a good start.

'I'd better get the furniture in quick. It looks like there's rain on the way.'

Da and Mr O'Brien were talking away as they carried everything in. He told Da they were living there a few years and that it was a grand new house we got.

Phil kept tipping me. 'There's no fight, Kathleen. It must be different out in the country.'

'You're right there, Phil, it must be.'

We ran around pressing all the switches on and off, even though there were no bulbs yet. Granny Kitty let out such a scream that Mr O'Brien nearly dropped the one and only wardrobe we had.

'Stop tha' now, the pair of yiz! You'll break them,' she roared.

'Is it true, Gran?' I asked. 'Da says the lights are magic and there'll be no more candles ever again.'

'Tha's right, Kathleen. Now, come 'ere, young Phil. Help me get the fire goin'. We'll have to get a bit of heat into this house. Yer Mother will be cold and tired by the time she gets here. And when yeh're finished tha', there's a box of food on the back of me cart. Go out and get it while I talk to yer father.'

Gran wasn't long sorting out the food into the kitchen press and getting a fire going. 'Phil, the gas is turned on. I checked it meself. Will yeh make a bit of dinner for Lil and the kids? There's a grand blazin' fire on in there. I can't wait any longer. I'll have to be on me way before it gets dark. I've to get Fanny back to the yard; she has to be fed and bedded down for the night.'

'I'll take it from here, Kitty; and thanks again. I'd have been lost without yeh.'

'Isn't tha' wha' families are for? To be there when it's needed.'

'Yeh never said a truer word, Kitty.'

* * *

We were standing at the front door waving Granny off when I saw Ma coming up the road. 'Ma, Ma! Up here, we're up here, Ma!'

Myself and Phil were jumping up and down, screaming our heads off.

'Ma, Ma, wait 'til yeh see the house! It's huge!'

'Phil, Kathleen, for God's sake will yiz be quiet!' roared Da. 'Wha' will the neighbours think?'

'Sorry, I was afraid Ma couldn't see us.'

'Well, she certainly heard yiz, tha's for sure.'

Ma stood at the front gate, worn out from the long walk to Crumlin. Well, you'd want to have seen the look on her face – it was priceless. Suddenly, she started to cry.

'I can't believe it, Phil; me own house at last.'

She pushed the pram through the side gate and into the kitchen.

The first thing she did was to go straight upstairs and look for the toilet, with myself and Phil running behind her.

'Wha' did I tell yiz? Didn't I say we'd have our own toilet one day?' Ma smiled at us through the tears running down her face.

'Ma, why are yeh cryin'?'

'Because I'm happy, Kathleen. Now, come on, help me make the beds and sort some of the stuff out while yer Da makes a bit of dinner. Young Phil, will yeh go down and keep an eye to Carmel and Noel.'

Ma went on talking about all the things she was going to do with the house as soon as she got a few shillings behind her.

'Ma, we've been up here ages. I'm starvin'; can we go downstairs now?'

'Okay, Kathleen, we'll finish this tomorrow. Anyway, me diddies are full to the top. I'll have to go down and feed Noel before he starts screamin' the house down. I swear, Kathleen, I never saw a baby drink so much on top of his dinner; he'll have me two diddies worn out in no time.'

When we came down, Da had a blanket spread out on the floor in front of the fire.

'Now, sit down there, the three of yiz, and eat yer dinner. I'll ask around tomorrow and see if I can pick up a few chairs, now tha' we have somewhere to put them. Lil, are yeh ready for yer dinner?'

'No, not yet, I have to feed Noel.'

'Okay, I want to talk to yeh anyway.'

'Yeh do? About wha', Phil?'

'Hold on a minute, Lil – Phil, Kathleen, Carmel, come over here and listen to wha' I have to say as soon as yeh're finished.'

Da started telling Ma all about Mr O'Brien helping him and how nice he was.

'Wasn't he very good to do tha', Phil, and him not even knowin' us. I'll go in tomorrow and thank himself.'

'Tha's grand, Lil. Now, when yeh go into him, I'd like yeh

to say tha' you're Mrs Doyle – will yeh do tha' for me?'

'Wha' the hell are yeh goin' on about, Phil? I'll say tha' me name is Lil; everybody calls me Lil.'

'I know, I know, but it seems to be different out here. When I was goin' in and out with the furniture, a few people was goin' by and they were all callin' one another Mr and Mrs. They don't seem to call yeh by yer first name. We don't want to be lettin' ourselves down, do we?'

Everything went real quiet. Ma just sat there with her diddy stuck in Noel's mouth, thinking for a minute and giving the look at the same time.

'Right then, if yeh say it's the proper thing to do. Yeh heard yer Da – from now on, all grown-ups outside the family will be called by Mr or Mrs and I'll do the same – BUT! . . .' Ma looked across at Da. '. . . I'll be gettin' called Lil and tha's the end of tha' and there'll be no more talkin' on the matter.'

'Okay then, Lil. But there's just one more thing – will yeh try and keep yer voice down and stop the cursin'? We don't want people thinkin' we're a shower of bowsies.'

Well, when I heard that, I nearly choked on the bit of sausage that was still in my mouth. I gave Phil and Carmel the eye and we ran out and sat on the stairs. All hell broke loose. Ma was screaming at the top of her voice.

'Would yeh ever go and fuck off! Don't start goin' all high and mighty with me, Mr Phil Doyle. If I want to say "fuck" I'll say "fuck" and I'll raise me voice as high as I want when it suits me. I'll not put any airs or graces on for nobody. Yeh take me as I am, and you should know tha' more than anybody.'

'See wha' I mean, Kathleen, Phil? Are yiz listenin' to yer mother? I'm just tryin' to get yeh to be a bit quieter, Lil, and not be losin' yer temper so quick and easy. Will yeh even try and cut the bad language out? I don't think tha's too much to ask.'

Da was running around the house at the same time, closing

all the windows and doors, while Ma was still shouting at him, making sure she got her point across.

That was our first night in Crumlin.

* * *

The next morning there was a hard banging on the hall door.

'I'll get it, Ma,' I roared with excitement. We had never had our own front door before.

'No,' said Phil, 'I'm doin' it.' He tried to push me out of the way.

'Yeh little bastard.' We nearly killed each other trying to get to the door first, but I won.

'Hello, mister, wha's yer name?'

'I'm Paddy and I'm here to switch the lights on.'

'Who's tha', Kathleen?' Ma roared out to me.

'Ma, it's Mr Paddy. He's goin' to switch the lights on.'

Da came running out of the kitchen, 'Come in, come in! Will you two move out of the man's way. Kathleen, take Carmel and go out and play in the garden.'

You could see that Da felt great saying that. We had a garden at last.

'Sorry about tha'. They're just excited about the new house. Yeh know yerself; kids, they're always under yer feet.'

'I've got a few meself; they drive yeh round the bend half the time.'

Da stood there talking away to Mr Paddy while he got on with the job. He had the work done in no time. Ma made him a cup of tea and chatted with him about what it was like living in the country.

As soon as Mr Paddy left, Da called us in from the garden.

'Okay, in with the three of yiz. I have a surprise for yeh. Now, just stand there and watch.'

We waited with excitement while Da ran around the house, putting bulbs in every room, pressing on all the switches as he went along.

'Now, wha' did I tell yeh – didn't I say the lights were magic?'

We never saw the likes of it before, the whole house lit up like a Christmas tree.

It really was magic.

8

On the Mitch

I didn't start school until I was six years old and I hated the place from the first day I walked into it. As I stood there with Ma waiting in the long cold corridor, all I could see were these huge big statues with vases of flowers at their feet.

Two nuns were walking towards us. It was my first time ever to see a nun, and from day one they frightened the shit out of me. I hid behind Ma's back, peeping out all the while. Their long black habits flowed down to their ankles, the black and white veils clinging tight on their heads. All I could see were these faces glaring at me, with not a smile. They wore giant rosary beats, tied around their waists like belts, with big crucifixes on the end. I could hear the beads swishing from side to side as they made their entrance, letting me know with the full tone and force of their voices who was boss.

Then one of them stepped out in front of the other. 'My name is Sister Joseph.' She went on talking away to Ma, setting down all the rules I was to obey, which I very seldom ever did. I was so afraid that the first day; when the nun tried to pull me from behind Ma's back, I held on so tight to her dress, hoping she wouldn't let the nun take me away.

'I don't want to go, Ma,' I cried. 'Please don't make me stay.'

'Come on now, Kathleen, yeh're not to carry on. Yeh're a big girl now,' said Ma. 'Yeh have to go with the Sister.'

The Sister was starting to look very annoyed at this stage. She gave my hand a nice little squeeze, pulled me away from Ma and walked me firmly down the corridor, putting me into line with all the other kids. They were all standing there with one finger pressed against their lips, not a whisper or a sound coming from any of them. As time went on I would soon learn what that was all about. If any of the nuns caught you speaking to one another, you would get lashed across the legs with the cane that was strapped beside their beads, or a box in the head that would nearly knock you to the floor. I was an awful chatterbox and got the cane more times than not.

I always seemed to be one of the kids picked out of the line and put cleaning the toilets or scrubbing the marble corridors. They would pick two of us out at a time, hand us our scrubbing brushes and tell us they would be back to inspect our work later. We would be down on our knees, scrubbing and cleaning away, along the edges and in and out of all the corners, making sure not a scrap of dirt was left. If there was, you'd know what to expect – another lash of the cane. One or two of the bigger girls would follow us with a bucket and mop.

This was always done during school hours, when you were supposed to be learning. When you would eventually get to your class, you were expected to be able to catch up and know what the teacher had been talking about while you weren't there, and if you didn't know that, you were in trouble again. You couldn't win; their rules were impossible at times, for me anyway.

* * *

I haven't got many good memories of school. But one day in particular sticks out in my mind.

Sister Carmel – that was her name. She was very kind and

so different from the rest of the nuns. One morning, she came over, took me out of the line and told me to stand to one side. I was shitting myself, not knowing what to expect. While she walked me down to her office, to my surprise, she started asking me about Ma and Da and how many brothers and sisters I had.

'Right, Kathleen,' she said as soon as we got to the office. 'Sit down.'

I was starting to panic at this stage.

'Am I in trouble, Sister? Wha'ever it is, I didn't do it. I swear it wasn't me.'

'It's all right, Kathleen, there's nothing wrong.' She handed me this lovely red jumper. 'Now, try that on. I think it's your size. And here's some shoes and socks. Take those runners off, they're falling apart. Your poor feet are purple with the cold. After school, come back down to me. I'll have a parcel for you to bring home to your mother. Hurry along there and get down to your class as quick as you can.'

'Thanks, Sister,' I said. I ran down the corridor, somewhat confused in my mind as to what had just happened.

I thought I'd never get home to tell Ma. As soon as I got in from school, I handed her the parcel.

'How come tha' nun was so nice to me, Ma, and the others are so mean?'

'Isn't it obvious, Kathleen? It's as plain as the nose on yer face. She must be happy and contented with wha' she's doin' with her life. See the way she was able to stand back and have a look at yeh, and see tha' I needed a bit of help? Not like half of them other nuns. Miserable, they are. With their serious faces, lookin' like they hate themselves and everythin' around 'em. The likes of them should be tucked away behind closed doors in the convents, prayin', and not lookin' after little children.'

* * *

Down through the years, Sister Carmel often helped me and my sisters, giving us parcels of clothes or food to bring home to Ma.

About the rest of them, I think Ma was right. They were so strict and serious all the time. And the teachers weren't much better. It didn't have to be such a miserable time for us kids, but they were hell-bent on making it so. The school was ruled with an iron fist, which there was no need for. It could have been such a happy time in us kids' lives.

So, is it any wonder that every chance I got to avoid going there, I took it? If Ma wasn't keeping me out of school to help her with one thing or the other, I would be off mitching with my brother Phil. And believe me, he didn't need much coaxing. His school was across the road from mine. It was run by 'the Brothers', and they were even worse than the nuns.

Little did Ma realise the goings-on that we got up to behind her back. I remember the first time we scarpered off 'on the mitch'. It was a freezing cold day, in the depths of winter. There we were, rambling around the streets, in and out of the shops every now and then, trying to get a bit of heat, not knowing half the time where we were.

That's when we stumbled onto the dump for the first time. We couldn't believe our eyes. We were like two pickaroonies, rummaging through all the rubbish.

'Kathleen,' shouted Phil, 'would yeh have a look at this?' He held up a small truck with one of the wheels missing. 'De yeh know somethin'? I could fix this.'

I stood there laughing over at him, 'Did yeh see wha' I found?' I held up a doll with half a leg and one eye missing. 'Can yeh mend her for me, Phil?'

'For Jaysus' sake, Kathleen, can yeh not have another root there, and see if yeh can find somethin' a bit better.'

Which I did – a big lump of chocolate, and plenty more on the ground where I was standing. I didn't realise that the rats had probably been having a good piss on it before we got there.

'Come 'ere Phil. Yeh're not goin' to believe this.' I handed him some chocolate. 'De yeh think it's okay to eat?' I asked.

'Who gives a fuck, Kathleen, I'm starvin'.' He rubbed away at it with the sleeve of his jumper.

The two of us sat there in the middle of all this rubbish, eating away until we made ourselves sick, me screaming and jumping on top of Phil every time I saw a rat. We were green in the face when we finally decided to make our way back. On the way home, Phil came up with another one of his bright ideas. We were wondering where we were going to clean the chocolate and dirt off ourselves. Where did we go, only into the church, to the holy water font! We stood there, letting on to be saying a few prayers, dipping our hands in and out of the water, splashing our faces at every chance we got, hoping at the same time that the priest wouldn't catch us. We just about made it home in time, with Ma being none the wiser.

The dump was to be a hideout for all of us down through the years whenever we would scarper off on the mitch from school.

9

The Drink

There were seven of us kids now and another baby on the way. Ma was finding it very hard to make ends meet. Da would always make a few bob here and there, on bits of scrap and old furniture which were left outside the houses where he and the other Corporation workers went to collect the bins. He would then sell the various bits and pieces to the shops in and around Portobello Bridge. The money would be divided equally between them. He always gave his share to Ma, which just about helped us to keep our heads above water.

As soon as Da finished work, he would be home straight away. There was never a bother on him when he had to get in and help around the house. Be it cleaning or cooking, he would always get stuck in and give Ma a dig-out. His favourite part of the day would be when he was out the back garden, digging, weeding and planting his veg. He would spend hours out there, especially in the summer. We'd all be gathered around him. He'd have Phil digging the long trenches, getting it ready for his potatoes. He would show me and one or two of the younger kids how deep to make the hole for his veg.

Ma would sit there with the babies beside her, looking pleased with herself about the few shillings that Da had just given her. She never looked for much for herself. Neither did Da, for that matter. They lived from day to day, as most people did back then. Once the few bills were paid, and there was a bit of food each day, Ma was happy.

I remember Da coming home late one evening, which was very unusual for him; he was like a clock, always there at four on the dot.

'Don't be mindin' me bein' a bit late, Lil. I slipped in for a quick pint with the men. I can't keep sayin' no every time they ask me. They'd think I'm being stand-offish, not mixin'.'

'I suppose it's all right the odd time, Phil, once yeh keep it at tha'.'

* * *

Which, of course, he didn't. Da started coming home more than the odd day with a sup on him. Ma didn't say anything in the beginning, but you could see her giving 'the look'. None of us were any the wiser. I thought it was great when Da would start with the singing. He would break into a few of his usual pretend-opera songs with one or two of the little ones sitting on his lap. Then he would start with the storytelling. He had a few great classics, which he would tell over and over again, each of us asking for our favourites.

Slowly but surely, the 'odd day' became every second or third day, and in no time at all he was coming home with more than a sup on him. And into the bargain, he took to the gambling. Not only was he losing his own few shillings, but Ma's wages also.

Things went from bad to worse, so much so that Ma couldn't pay the bills. The lights were cut off, and the glimmerman wouldn't be too far away to knock off the gas. It was back to the candles again. The young kids thought it was great sitting in the dark. There would be a few candles on the mantelpiece, one or two over at the kitchen sink. We'd sit there for hours, telling ghost stories, frightening the shite out of one another, not realising the trauma that was going on around us.

That's when all the fighting started.

When Da won on the horses, he'd be in the front door singing his head off with a big bag filled with chips and a juicy fish for Ma, thinking that would make everything okay.

'Isn't this a grand supper I have for yiz all? And for yerself, Lil. There's the wage packet with an extra few bob to help yeh with yer bills.'

She'd snap it out of his hand. 'Wha' de yeh mean my bills? They're yer fuckin' bills as well.'

She was always so angry. Da thought that once he handed his money up his job was done. Even at that, it still wasn't enough to go around.

But when he lost money gambling, which was a lot of the time, he'd slip in the side gate and try to get up the stairs without Ma seeing him. Either way – upstairs, downstairs – it didn't matter; she'd be after him like a light. Her words were always the same.

'Is tha' you, Phil Doyle? Jaysus Christ, yeh're drunk again. De yeh not realise the kids are hungry? I'm waitin' all day on yeh to bring the few bob home. Where is it? Where's me money?'

That would be Friday, wages day. They were the worst.

Da would launch into how he was waiting on the last horse to come in.

'It was a cert, Lil, a sure winner. I could smell the money, it was nearly in me hands. The tip was tha' good, so it was.'

'It's in my hand I want the money, not yours, yeh bloody waster of a man.'

His excuses were always the same.

'Wha' am I to do, Phil? Wha's after happenin' to yeh? Yeh used to be such a good man. Don't yeh care any more? There's not a crust of bread in the house. If yeh keep this up, we'll be out on the street.'

We were often hungry for days on end, with very little food to go around.

She might as well have been talking to the wall. As soon as his head hit the pillow, he'd be out like a light, snoring away without a care in the world. If he stayed asleep, things wouldn't be too bad, but if he shouted back and called her 'woman', all hell would break loose.

One night in particular, Ma completely lost it. Da kept saying, 'Woman, get yer hands off me and leave me alone.' He was so drunk that night. I went upstairs to see if I could get them to stop fighting. When I went into the room, Ma was sitting on top of Da on the bed, shaking the living daylights out of him, screaming into his face at the one time, 'Yeh're only a drunken bastard, so y'are, de yeh hear me?' She gave him a fist in the face.

'Please, Ma,' I roared, 'come on down, leave him.'

'I'll leave him all right, Kathleen.'

Before I could say another word, she jumped up off the bed and pulled our one and only wardrobe down on top of Da. That soon woke him up. Well, you'd want to have heard the screams. The whole road must have heard him. 'Me nose is broke,' he kept roaring. I could see the blood pouring down the side of his face as I tried to move the wardrobe. My brother Phil flew up the stairs to help me, but with all our efforts, we couldn't get it to budge, it was so heavy.

'You stay here, Phil, I'll be back in a minute.'

'Right, Kathleen, but hurry, will ya?'

'Come on, Ma, please. Can yeh not hear the kids? They're upset. Come downstairs with me.'

'I can't take any more of this, Kathleen,' Ma screamed, holding on to her head with her two hands. 'Me brains is goin' to burst with the worry of everythin'. Look at him, he doesn't give two shites about us.'

'Leave it, Ma. Come on,' I said as I coaxed her back down to the kids.

In I went next door to get Mrs Kennedy's son, Peter. He was very good to us. He was always there with his little medicine box. If any of us fell, got a nosebleed or cut ourselves, he was there. We called him our chemist. A small man he was, very neat and tidy, his hair combed tight into his head with a half-jar of Brylcream in it. He always wore his braces out over his jumper. As for his shoes, you could nearly see your face in them, they were so clean. Ma always said, 'Peter Kennedy's a gentleman. He should have been a doctor; he has the gift, so he has.'

I knocked on the door, screaming in the letterbox at the same time.

'Peter, Peter, quick.'

When he opened the door, I was jumping up and down.

'Now, now, Kathleen, calm down. Wha's this all about?'

He spoke slowly and in a low voice; you really had to cock your ears to hear him.

'Ma's after smashin' the wardrobe on top of Da; there's blood everywhere. Quick, quick!'

'Hold on now, Kathleen, wait a minute until I get me little box.'

I ran back into the house with Peter right behind me. Ma was still in the kitchen with the kids. They were crying; she was crying. I followed Peter up the stairs. Phil was still struggling with the wardrobe.

'It won't move, Peter. I've tried everythin'. I can't get it to budge.'

'Stand back there, the two of yiz. I'll manage it on me own.'

Up he pushed it, back against the wall. Then he brought Da into the toilet.

'Wha' have yeh been up to, Phil, for Lil to get all fired up and do this to yeh?'

'A few drinks, Peter, tha's all I had, a few drinks.'

Da was lying through his teeth. We knew it and so did Peter.

'Me nose is broke. Would yeh have a look at the size of it?

It's all over me face.'

'Now, now, Phil, stay quiet and let me have a look.'

He cleaned the blood off first. Then he pressed around his face. Da let out an unmerciful roar.

'Jaysus, Peter, will yeh take it easy, yeh're killin' me.'

'Well now, Phil, yeh're a lucky man. It's just a bad nosebleed, tha's all. But I tell yeh one thing, yeh're goin' to have two nice black eyes over the next few days. Just to be on the safe side, when yeh go into work tomorrow, get the Corporation doctor to have a look.'

'How can I go into work lookin' like this? I'd be the laughin' stock of the place. No, I'll take some of me sick leave, tha's wha' I'll do. Tha's a mad woman I'm married to, Peter, mad so she is.'

Peter wasn't having any of it. He didn't half let Da have it right, left and centre. There was no way he was letting Da say anything about Ma. Raising his voice slightly, he told him, 'Now, yeh listen to me, Phil Doyle. Tha's a fine woman yeh have down there and yeh want to start takin' care of her, de yeh hear me now?'

Da just stood there. He couldn't believe his ears – quiet Peter lashing out at him like that.

'Yer best bet now is to sleep them few drinks off and sort things out with Lil tomorrow. I'll be on me way now. Kathleen, come on down with me, make yer Ma a cup of tea and help her settle them kids down.'

When we got to the end of the stairs, Ma was standing there.

'Peter, I'm sorry for all this trouble we're givin' yeh, but the man is breakin' me heart. I don't know where to turn to any more.'

'Now, now, Lil, try and talk to Phil tomorrow, when he's sober. He's not a bad man.'

'I know tha', Peter. It's a curse, the drink, it'll be the ruination of us all.'

'De yeh want me to come in and have a chat with him? Maybe I can get him to take the pledge and keep him away from the stuff altogether. Wha' de yeh think, Lil?'

'Would yeh, Peter? Tha' would be great, if yeh could do tha' for me.'

'Right then, I'll be off now – and, Lil, leave the wardrobe where I left it, standin' against the wall. See yeh tomorrow.'

'Thanks again, Peter.'

Ma turned to me. 'Kathleen, get Phil; yeh'll have to go in and ask tha' oul crank of a Granda of yers for a lend of a few pound. Tell him yer Da lost me wages on the horses again. I'll try and pay him back when I get me children's allowance.'

'Please, Ma, don't ask me to go in there. He screams and shouts. He frightens me.'

'De yeh think I like sendin' yeh in to tha' oul fuck? Wha' am I to do, Kathleen? The kids are hungry. I know he's a crank but there's nothin' I can do. Yiz have to go. Now hurry up and get yer coats on. Carmel, ask Mrs Kennedy for a loan of the bus fare. Tell her I'll give it back tomorrow.'

Carmel was gone and back in two seconds.

'Mrs Kennedy says yeh're not to worry, Ma, it'll do when yeh have it.'

'Tha's grand. Off yiz go. Try and get back as quick as yeh can before the shop closes. I'll give Mr Green a few bob off me bill. Hopefully, he'll give me enough messages for a few days anyway.'

'Ma, wha' if Granda doesn't give us the money? Wha' will we do?'

'Just tell Mariah things are really bad and don't leave until youse get somethin' off him. I'm dependin' on yeh, Kathleen. I've nobody else.'

* * *

We got off the bus at Christ Church and walked down the Hill towards the tenements, where Granda Phil and Granny Mariah lived.

'You can ask him, Kathleen. I'm not. I asked the last two times.'

'Phil, tha's not fair.'

'I don't give two fucks. I'm not askin' him for anythin'. I'll go in with yeh, and stand there, but I won't be sayin' nothin'. I hate tha' oul' shitebag.'

When we got to the door, I gave a little knock, half-hoping they wouldn't hear us, but Phil soon fixed that. He gave the door a right bang with the back of his hand.

Gran answered the door, as usual. Granda never did; he was always sick. There was only one room, so as soon as you walked in, there he'd be in your face. You wouldn't have time to take a breath.

Coughing and choking, he let out a roar, 'Who's tha'?'

'It's young Phil and Kathleen. They've come all the way in from the country to see us.'

He was still coughing, waving his hand in the air for us to come over. I looked up at Gran, half-afraid to move.

'I suppose yeh're hungry. I'll get yeh some bread and sugar. His chest is very bad today, Kathleen,' she whispered in a low voice. 'Go on over and sit beside the fire, get yerselves a bit of heat.'

Granda was turning purple at this stage. He picked up this metal bowl and started choking and spitting in it. My stomach was turning inside out at the sight of it; I felt sick.

'Well now,' said Gran. 'How's tha' son of mine, yer father?'

'Drunk,' Phil said, real cheeky-like.

'Yeh mean he has a sup on him. A man's entitled to a drink after a hard day's work.' She never wanted to believe that Da, her only son, would do anything bad. She looked at Phil, and gave him the bad look, and then turned around to me. 'Right, Kathleen, now tell me wha's goin' on out in tha' God-forsaken place.'

80

I said in a low voice: 'Ma has no money to buy food, the kids are starvin', the lights were turned off and the glimmerman is on his way, Gran.'

She put her hands up to her forehead and blessed herself.

'Holy Mother of God, wha' way is me son livin'?'

Granda finally got his breath and sat up in the bed. He was very small and thin – as Ma would say, 'a bag of bones, tha' oul' fella, so he is.'

'I heard tha', Mariah. Spent the wages again, did he? Wha' did I tell yeh? A bad crowd tha' son of yours got himself in with, and tha' Lil wan out there havin' all them children. Is it any wonder they're starvin'? Yeh'd need a job in the government to be able to keep all them goin'. I suppose it's money yeh're in for, the pair of yeh? Well, yeh won't be gettin' any, so off with yiz now!' He pointed over to the door.

'Now, oul' Phil, don't be gettin' yerself all worked up like tha'. Somethin' must have happened. Phil wouldn't do such a thing.'

'Would yeh stop and listen to yerself, Mariah? Always makin' excuses for him. Why don't yeh face it, yer son is after turnin' into a waster. Now, you two get yerselves home. Yeh'll be gettin' no money offa me. And tell tha' mother of yours, she's not to send yiz in here again.' With that, he went into another frenzy of coughing and spitting.

It took all my strength to hold onto Phil and stop him from running out the door on me. I wanted so much to shout at Granda, 'Yer only an oul' fuck and I hate yeh.' But I knew Mariah would have a heart attack and Ma really needed the money, so we stood there and let him go on and on and on.

'Come here, the pair of yiz,' said Mariah, 'an' get yer coats on. Wait at the end of the stairs, I'll talk to him.'

'Will yeh, Gran? Thanks.'

We made our way out of the room. We sat there listening to him ranting and raving, with Gran trying to make the peace.

She came out after a while with some messages in a bag and the money.

'Why does he always do tha', Gran? He frightens the shite out of us, and then he gives the money. Why?'

'Don't be mindin' him, Kathleen, he's sick and old. Now run along and get home before it gets dark. Tell yer mother to send tha' money in as soon as she gets her allowance or I'll have to listen to him. I'll be out to see yiz next week. Tell yer father I said so.'

'Right, Gran, thanks,' I said, as we went running up the Hill.

* * *

Just as we got to the top, I heard a familiar voice. I turned around and who was it – only Maisie, Ma's best friend.

'Would yeh have a look at the two of yiz? When I saw tha' head of blond hair, and them long black plaits, I knew, I just knew yeh were Lil's kids. The pair of yiz have got so big.'

She rubbed Phil's hair, tossing it like mad.

'Jaysus, Phil, the last time I put me fingers through yer hair it was like chasin' a herd of buffaloes, the fleas were tha' big.'

'Wha' de yeh mean? There nothin' in me head.' He walked off, all annoyed with Maisie for saying that.

'Cranky little fucker, isn't he, Kathleen?'

'Ah, he didn't mean it, Maisie, he's just a bit upset.'

'Anyway, wha' are yiz doin' in here? How is yer Ma? I haven't seen her in ages.'

'She's at home with the kids.'

'Jaysus, Kathleen, let me see yer face. Were yeh cryin'? Wha's after happenin'? Is Lil all right?'

I told Maisie everything. 'I tried to tell Granda how bad things are at home, but he wouldn't listen and told us to get out.'

'Don't mind tha' oul' fuck, Kathleen. He's on his last legs, tha's wha's wrong with him. I hope he dies roarin'. Men, they're all the same – a shower of bastards, so they are. Look at me with tha' Jojo Murphy, the life he's after givin' me, the pig. I never thought I'd see the day tha' Phil Doyle would turn to the drink. Come on, luv, I'll walk yiz up to the bus stop. Tell yer Ma I'm goin' to make me way out to see her. I don't care if it's in the arsehole of the country. God help her, she must be in an awful state.'

'Will yeh really come out, Maisie? She'd love tha'.'

'I give yeh me word, Kathleen. I'm goin' straight up to the church now and light a candle to our Blessed Lady askin' her to help yer Ma get back on her feet.'

With that, Phil made his way back over to us.

'Don't you be so touchy, Phil, de yeh hear me?' She tossed his hair again. 'Sure, I'm only windin' yeh up. Yeh should know me by now. I was just havin' a bit of a laugh with yeh, tha's all.'

Phil stood there with a sulky face on him, mumbling under his breath, 'Sorry, Maisie.'

Just then the bus came. Maisie hugged and kissed us. She stood there waving and shouting. 'Tell yer Ma I'll be out to see her as soon as I can.'

We were halfway up Thomas Street and could still hear her voice.

* * *

As soon as we got off the bus, we ran all the way to Mr Green's shop. He was getting ready to close. Phil asked him would he hold on because Ma was on her way. I fell in the front door, gasping for breath.

'Quick, Ma, here's the money. Mr Green has the gates on the shop and all – hurry up, he's closin'!'

'Kathleen, you stay here and watch the kids, make sure they don't go near any of them candles.'

'Okay, Ma.'

She stood there and looked at me for a second.

'Yeh're a good girl, Kathleen.'

83

Hearing her say that made it all worthwhile. Those few words meant so much to me.

It wasn't long before Ma was back in the house with Phil and herself carrying a right load of messages.

'Tha's great, Ma, yeh made it in time.'

'Just about, Kathleen. The only thing is, the glimmerman was here when yiz were in town. The gas was cut off.'

'Wha' are we goin' to do now, Ma?'

'The same as always, Kathleen.'

'Ah Jaysus, Ma, not out the back yard again! We'll freeze to death and to top it off, it's lashin' rain out.'

'Wha' else can I do? Yiz have to be fed. Come on, yeh all know the drill. Young Phil, gather the big rocks I have out there against the wall.'

Ma made a circle with the rocks, filled it up with turf and sticks and got a right blazing fire going. She took one of the grids from inside the oven, placed it on top of the rocks to make sure the pots wouldn't tip over. She sat there muttering to herself, 'Typical timin'; fuck tha' glimmerman anyway, me with all these mouths to feed.'

I stood over her with a big umbrella while dinner was cooked.

Sometimes that went on for a few days, or maybe for a week or two depending on how quick things could be sorted out. Although we didn't know it at the time, I suppose we were one of the first families around Crumlin to have our own barbeque.

* * *

Da was in a bad way the next day. He had pains everywhere. We were all sitting around the table when he came down. Noel started laughing first, then Phil, and that got them all going. Ma just glared at everybody, which soon put a stop to the laughing.

'Jaysus, Lil, wha' did yeh do to me last night? I'm in bits.'

'Yeh pushed me too far this time, so yeh did, Phil Doyle.'

You could hear a pin drop. There wasn't a sound out of any of us. We all knew that if Ma gave the look and used the second name, there was big trouble on the way.

'Yeh left me with not a penny in me pocket, and me havin' to send them two kids into tha' oul' fella of yer's, beggin' for a few shillin's, so tha' I could feed them, and him treatin' them like dirt.'

She was really screaming loud at this stage. There was a plate of fried bread in one of her hands and a jam jar of tea in the other. I thought she was going to throw them at Da. Instead, she bashed them on the table. The bread and the tea went everywhere. None of us moved. She stood face to face with Da. He never said a word.

'I'm not puttin' up with yeh any more. De yeh hear me?' She pushed her fist into his face. 'Yeh can go back to yer oul' wan. I'm sure she'll be glad to have her precious son back. I'll get help somewhere. A waster yeh're turnin' into – and you were a man of the cloth for years. Yeh should be ashamed of yerself.'

Da said nothing. He just got himself a cup of tea and sat by the fire, thinking, knowing full well that Ma was right.

* * *

Peter came in that evening and Da went up to the church with him and took the pledge. He promised Ma the sun, moon and stars, and swore that he would never set foot inside a pub or bookies ever again, and that he really meant it this time. That's the way things went over the years with Da: on and off the drink, in and out of the bookies. He tried really hard, but he always fell off the wagon. For him it wasn't worth it. He always came out the worse in the end. Ma made sure of that.

'From now on, Phil Doyle, Kathleen and young Phil will be at the wages office every Friday, bang on the dot of four. As soon as yeh get paid, yeh can take yer own few bob first. Then yeh'll be handin' them over me wages.'

Da jumped up off the chair. 'There's no way I'm standin' for this, Lil – sendin' the kids down to the yard, makin' a show of me! Yeh're not doin' tha', I don't care. I'm off the drink, for God's sake, Lil. Wha' more de yeh want?'

'No! I heard all tha' before. Tha's all I ever get, just words tha' mean nothin', broken promises. I'll be takin' no more chances. Yeh won't put me through this ever again. The next time yeh hit the bottle, at least I'll have me few bob to get me through.'

'Jaysus Christ, woman!'

'Don't *woman* me! It's either the kids or me goin' down to the yard, and by Jaysus, Phil Doyle, if yeh make me go down to tha' Corporation yard, and go down I will, yeh won't hold yer head up for a long time. I'll go crazy mad, so I will.'

Da wasn't long backing off. He knew better.

* * *

The first wages day came. Ma had her plan all ready to go into action.

'Kathleen, take tha' dress off yeh. Go upstairs and put on a skirt and jumper.'

'Why, Ma?'

'Just do wha' yeh're told. I have me reasons. Hurry up now, and come straight back down.'

I was up and down the stairs in a jiffy. Ma was sitting by the fire pushing the pram, trying to get Jacinta asleep.

'Pull yer jumper up, Kathleen.'

'For wha', Ma?'

'Just watch, listen and learn.'

She had one of the baby's big nappy pins in her hand and fastened it to the top of my knickers.

'Wha' are yeh doin' tha' for, Ma?'

'Kathleen, when yeh get to the yard and get the wage packet off yer Da, turn around and face the wall. Have young Phil standin' beside yeh. Make sure nobody is lookin'. Put the wage packet inside yer knickers and pin it to them; tha' way there won't be a chance in hell of yeh losin' it, or for tha' matter gettin' robbed. Now, when yiz get on the bus tell the bus conductor to let yeh off at Rathmines, beside the big buildin' with the clock on the top. There's gates at the side of it; go through them, and tha's were yer Da will be standing with all the men, waitin' for the wages office to open. Just go and stand over at the wall, smile and give a big wave to make sure yer Da sees yiz. He should come over to yiz. Now, if it's a thin' tha' he doesn't come near yiz, tha's when I want yeh to call his name out. Scream and keep screamin' until he does. Tha'll soon put a stop to him sneakin' off. Are yeh listenin' to me?'

'Ma, will Da not get annoyed with us?'

'Fuck 'im, Kathleen, he doesn't be worried if I'm annoyed when he's spendin' his wages. Kathleen, I'm dependin' on yeh to do this for me. I've nobody else.'

Those words were said to me so many times over the years.

'Yeah, Ma, I know wha' to do.'

'Take Clare with yeh. She's a cheeky little bitch. There'll be no problem for her to scream her brains out if she has to.'

As soon as we got to the yard, I stood at the wall with my brother Phil and sister Clare, all the while keeping an eye on Da. You could see he was uneasy as he walked up and down, fidgeting with his hands while he spoke to the other men. Phil gave a little wave over, making sure Da saw us.

'Tha's lettin' him know we're here, Kathleen.'

'I think he already knows tha', Phil. Shuss . . . say nothin'. Here he is over.'

Da was fuming as he made his way across to us.

'Did the three of yiz have to come down? Would one of yiz not have been enough? Tha' mother of yours is hell-bent on makin' a show of me. I'll be the talk of the yard tomorrow. There's no need for this. No need at all.'

The three of us stood there, not moving, waiting on Da to hand over the wage package.

'I'm sorry, Da, Ma says we're to stay here until yeh give us the money.'

That's when Clare got her spoke in. 'Will I scream now, Kathleen, will I?'

'Stay quiet, Clare, I'm talkin' to Da. Please, Da?' I put my hand out.

He gave a quick look around, checking to see if anyone was watching him as he slipped the wage package into my hand. Then he walked away from us without another word spoken. He was all agitated and annoyed. I watched him make his way down through the yard, all the while keeping his head down as he passed by the other men, not knowing for sure if any of them saw what was going on over at the wall.

* * *

Ma never had to go without her part of the wages, ever again. Every Friday on the dot of four, there would be two of us standing at the wall to meet Da. She always had to be two steps ahead just to get by. And get by she did.

But Da never gave up the drink.

10

Ma Starts Work

There seemed to be no end to Ma having babies. They kept arriving, one after another. Thomas was less than two when Jacinta arrived and then, two years later, there was Patricia. I never seemed to get a chance to mix with the other kids or to play outside. By the time I was twelve, there were nine of us kids.

Ma was finding it very hard to make ends meet and was on Da's back all the time to hand up more wages. But there was no way he was handing over his drink money. They seemed to be at one another's throats all the time. I would sit there listening to them going on and on, Da lying through his teeth, Ma giving out about this and that, which she had every right to.

As a child I longed for a happy home. I was always daydreaming, letting myself get lost in my thoughts, wishing and hoping things would be different. I wouldn't be long being pulled back from my dreams with the roars of Ma.

'How in the name of Jaysus am I supposed to manage on seven pound a week, Phil? I've too many mouths to feed now. If yeh're not goin' to give me more money, I'll have to get meself a job.'

'Yeh can't go to work, Lil. Who'll mind the kids?'

'*You* will, Phil.'

'Are yeh mad? *I can't mind babies!*' he roared.

'Well, yeh better start learnin', because if we don't do somethin' soon we'll be out on the street. I haven't paid the rent in six months.' She handed Da a letter. 'There, read it yerself. It came this mornin'. Tha's the final warnin'. If we don't give a few bob soon, they're goin' to evict us.'

'Good God, Lil! Why didn't yeh say somethin' sooner? Yeh shouldn't have let it get to this.'

'And would it have made any difference? *Would it?*' she screamed into his face, one of her mad rages coming on. 'Yeh'd only be tellin' me I'm naggin' yeh again. I'm robbin' Peter to pay Paul. Every time I try to give a few bob off the rent, one of the kids needs somethin'. If it's not them, it's the gas or the lights. Can yeh not see wha's goin' on around here, Phil? Ah, maybe it's easier for yeh to turn a blind eye.' She went over to pick up one of the babies.

'Lil, de yeh have to keep puttin' me down all the time in front of the kids? I'm not tha' bad.'

'So tha's wha' yeh think I'm doin'? Right then! Have a look at this. Come 'ere, Noel, Phil, Carmel, Clare! Show yer father yer shoes. Go on! Lift yer feet up.'

One by one, the kids showed Da their shoes.

'Jaysus, Phil, will yeh have a look and open yer eyes, *for God's sake!* Look, a bit of plastic and cardboard in the soles of the shoes. There's tha' many holes in them I have to try and do somethin' to keep the rain out. They haven't got a pair of stockin's between them.'

Da stood there, looking at each and every one of us, not saying a word. How could he? Ma was right and he knew it.

'I'm borrowin' a few bob all the time just to keep them in food. Somethin' has to be done, Phil.'

'Lil, we'll talk about this later.' He was trying to gloss things over as usual. It was always the same with Da, putting everything on the long finger. He wouldn't face up to his responsibilities, leaving it all up to Ma.

'No, Phil, it's gettin' sorted out now, once and for all. Me mind's made up. Mrs Reilly up the top of the road – she works in O'Connell Street in some fancy restaurant called the Paradiso. They're lookin' for a woman in the evenin's to take over when she's finished work, for washin' up and keepin' the kitchen clean. It's from five in the evening until three in the mornin'. She's goin' to put in a good word for me. Tha' way I'll have a good chance of gettin' the job and, if I do, *I'm takin' it*.'

'And how are yeh supposed to get home at tha' hour of the mornin', Lil?'

'I have it all worked out, Phil, and don't yeh be tryin' to put obstacles in me way. It's happenin', so yeh better get used to it. One of the women tha' does nights all the time has a friend who owns a taxi. He collects a few of the women every night and drops yeh straight to yer door. He gets ten shillin's for the week off each of them. If I get the job, he said tha' he'd squeeze one more in. I'll be left with three pound after tha' and, by God, tha'll go a long way to helpin' me with everythin' around here.'

'But, Lil . . .'

'There's no buts about it, Phil Doyle! Did yeh not hear a word I said? They're goin' to kick us out on the fuckin' street. Is it not sinkin' into tha' head of yers?' she shouted.

'I'm sorry, Lil, I'll change me ways. I promise I will.' Da would really mean what he said at that moment in time, but he never changed. They were only words.

'Yeh'll have to, Phil, there's no two ways about it. I'm at me wit's end.'

In the middle of all this mayhem, Ma took out a small white clay pipe.

'Wha's tha', Lil?'

'Can't yeh see it's a fuckin' pipe! Tha's wha yeh drove me to.

I have to do somethin' to settle me nerves. Me father gave this to me today. I'm not able to buy me few Woodbines, I'm not like you. I wouldn't spend me last few shillings on meself knowin' tha' I needed it for the kids and the house. Yeh're a fuckin' waster of a man, tha's wha' yeh are. No good at all.'

'For God's sake, would yeh ever cut yer language out, Lil? There's no need for it, no need at all.'

'Is there not now? Well fuck, fuck and fuck again. Wha' de yeh think of tha'? Ah, me arse. Don't be annoyin' me, would yeh. The only thing I have to keep me sane is me few cigarettes and I can't even have them now.'

'Yeh're not goin' to start smokin' tha' pipe. Yeh'll be makin' a holy show of me altogether. Wha' will people think if they see yeh?'

'If tha's all yeh have to worry about now, Phil Doyle, yeh can count yerself lucky. Anyway, I don't give two shites wha' you or anybody else thinks. As a matter of fact, I'll start smokin' right now. Where's tha' bit of tobacco me father gave me?' She rummaged through her pockets. 'Ah, here it is.' And up she lit the pipe. She was puffing and puffing for a few minutes before she got it going. After that, she was away in a hack. Da just shook his head and started reading his paper. The kids all thought it was great.

'Hey, Ma,' Clare laughed, 'yeh're like one of them Indians out of the cowboy pictures.'

'Tha's right, Clare. They used to smoke their pipes before the war, or was it after the war? I'm not too sure. Isn't tha' right, Phil?' She raised her voice once more.

Da just sat there, shaking his head and not answering.

'Phil, I want yeh to listen to me. Take yer face out of tha' paper when I'm talkin' to yeh.'

'Jesus, Lil, I heard yeh the first time. I *am* listenin'.'

'I'm goin' to make me way down to Mr O'Keeffe, the councillor. He has a shop down Sundrive Road. Mrs Reilly told me she got into a bit of bother with her rent. He went into the

Corporation with her and got an arrangement set up.'

Da wasn't long putting the paper down and cocking up his ears to what Ma was saying.

'Tha' would be great if he could do tha' for us, Lil. Go on, go ahead, meself and Kathleen will watch the kids.'

'Oh, so I have yer attention now, have I?' She made her way out the door.

* * *

Ma saw Mr O'Keeffe that night. I was walking the floor with Patricia, who was going mad for the diddy, when Ma finally got back.

'Yeh were gone ages, Ma. The baby is starvin'.'

'I know, I know, Kathleen, give her over here to me, quick! Me diddies is burstin'. Tha's a filthy night out there. I'm soaked into the skin. Grab tha' towel Carmel and dry me feet before I catch me death of cold. Clare, make me a cup of tea, I'm gaspin'.'

'Well, Lil, how did it go? Did yeh get to see him?'

'I did, Phil, I did. The nicest man you could ever meet. You want to see all the women down there. Tha's why I was so long. All as bad as meself, not a shillin' between any of us. I showed him the letter and told him how bad things were. He said if the Corporation agree and yeh let them take the rent out of the wage packet and a few pennies of the arrears every week, tha'll settle it. I've to meet him at twelve o'clock tomorrow outside the rent office.'

Da didn't say much but you could see the relief on his face. He was well pleased with the news.

The rent was taken out of Da's wage packet every week and sent into the Corporation. From that day on, Ma never again had to worry about being put out on the street.

Ma kept up the pipe over the years after that when the money was scarce. You always knew she had an extra few shillings when you saw her smoking the Woodbines again.

* * *

A few days later Mrs Reilly dropped in to see Ma on her way home from work.

'I've good news for yeh, Lil – I got yeh the job.'

I thought Ma was going to burst out crying. 'The blessin's of God on yeh,' she said, nearly taking the hands off Mrs Reilly, she shook them that much. 'Come in, come in. Sit down there. Kathleen, make a cup of tea for Mrs Reilly. I'm prayin' to the Virgin Mary herself every night, askin' her to help me. Now me prayers is answered. She never lets me down. I'll be lightin' a candle first thing in the mornin'. Thankin' herself.'

'Does Phil mind yeh goin' to work, Lil?'

'Don't yeh know he does, Mrs Reilly? Mind you now, when it comes to them kids, he's an awful worrier. He'd never leave them on their own once he knows I won't be here. I won't let yeh down. I give yeh me word and tha's me bond.'

'I'll have to run now, Lil, so I'll tell me boss tha' yeh'll start at five o'clock tomorrow. I'll drop in in a day or two to see how yeh're gettin' on. Cheerio now and the best of luck to yeh!' Off she went.

Ma was thrilled with herself. As well as making the extra money, you could see she was looking forward to getting out of the house. Even though the work was going to be hard and the hours long, she didn't seem to mind.

'Yeh know wha', Kathleen? This could be the makin's of yer father.'

'How de yeh mean, Ma?'

'He'll have no time to go to the pub and I have to say, when he has an extra few bob and not spendin' it on the drink, he's very good to me. Things could be startin' to take a turn for the best around here.'

'I hope so Ma. I really do.'

'I'll start gettin' a bit of dinner ready now. Kathleen, gather them small ones up and put them sittin' down at the table. When tha's done, tell Carmel to call the others in. A half an egg, a slice of bread with a few chips will have to do; tha's all I have. Things is really bad this week.'

The kids would be all trying to get the plate that Ma cut the eggs on. That way yeh got the extra bit of yellow to dip yer last bit of crust in.

'Phil, run upstairs and tell yer father to leave readin' tha' paper. There's a bit of dinner ready. He's to come down straight away or there won't be a chip left on the plate. Every time I turn me head there's a few more chips gone. I can't catch which one of the kids is takin' them.'

Da came over and sat down beside me. Thomas jumped onto his lap. I had Jacinta in my arms and Patricia was asleep in the pram. Phil, Carmel, Clare, Marion and Noel were finished their dinner and were getting ready to go upstairs, when Ma called out.

'Hold on there a minute, I've somethin' to say.'

Clare jumped. 'It wasn't me, it was him,' she said, pointing over at Noel.

'Yeh're a liar, Clare! You went into the garden first,' Noel answered.

'You robbed Mrs Kennedy's apples first.'

'No, I didn't.'

'Yes, yeh did.'

The two of them started scrapping, Clare spitting and kicking, Noel pushing and shoving.

Bloody eejits, I thought. *I keep telling them, always wait and listen to what's going to be said and say nothing. But do they listen? Never!*

Ma put her hands on her hips. 'So tha's wha' yeh're up to when me back's turned. I'll sort you two out later.'

'No, Lil, it'll be done now.' Da got Noel by the ear. 'Kathleen, grab Clare and follow me, before she runs off. In yeh go, the two of yeh, and tell Mrs Kennedy yeh're sorry. I wouldn't mind but yeh only have to ask the woman and she'd give yeh any amount of apples yeh want.'

We marched them in next door to Mrs Kennedy's. I stood there holding onto Clare while Mrs Kennedy told Da, 'I know Clare is only a skinny little thing, Phil. But yeh'd want to see her climbin' the tree. She does be like a little monkey, swingin' with one hand and throwin' the apples over to yer garden with the other. Tha's a wild one yeh have there.'

'Sure, don't I know it? We'll have to keep an eye on her, Mrs Kennedy. Tha's for sure.'

It wasn't long before we were back in our own house with a big bag full to the top with the loveliest apples you ever saw, all red and shiny.

'It's the tree Mrs Kennedy is worried about, Lil, in case they break any of the branches.'

'Right, right, Phil. Tha's enough about the apples. Are yiz all here? Now listen to wha' I have to say.'

'Lil, wha's so important tha' yeh have us all gathered here like the twelve apostles at the Last Supper?'

'I said, are yiz all listenin'? Right then, I got the job.'

Da's face dropped but he said nothing, because he knew it had to be done. The kids just stood there listening, not really understanding what this was all about. Not that it would change much for any of them. They'd just carry on as usual. It was up to myself and Da to look after things from now on.

'Phil, yeh have to make sure yeh're home every day at four o'clock. I have to start at five. Tha'll give me plenty of time to get into town. Mrs Reilly told me tha' they're very strict about being late, so yeh can't let me down.'

Da just nodded his head. I think he was still in shock.

'Kathleen, you'll have to take over the two small ones. Make sure they're fed and yeh change their nappies. Yer Da's no good at tha', but he'll help yeh with feedin' the rest of the kids. Young Phil, you make sure the others give themselves a wash every night.'

That's a joke, I thought. *Phil can't wash himself right, never mind look after the kids. That'll be left to me as well.*

'Everybody has to pull their weight around here now. I can't do this on me own. There's no two ways about it. This has to be done.'

* * *

There was loads of hustle and bustle the next day, with Ma trying to get everything sorted before she started her first day at work. I never saw her in such a tizzy, rushing all over the place: 'Do this . . . fix tha' . . . hold him . . . feed her.'

'Ma, will yeh sit down for a minute? I'll make yeh a cup of tea. I want to ask yeh somethin'.'

'Wha', Kathleen, wha' is it? I haven't got time to sit. We have to get the washin' done and then there's the dinner.'

'It's about Patricia, Ma. Wha' am I goin' to do when she's hungry and lookin' for the diddy, and yeh're not here?'

'I know, I know. I've already thought about tha'. I've two old baby bottles here. I'll squeeze me milk into them through the day and I'll feed her just before I go. But yeh have to make sure she gets her last feed before eleven, because me diddies will be burstin' with milk and I'll need her nice and hungry to empty them out. Now, de yeh understand tha', Kathleen?'

'I think so Ma,' I said, not realising I'd be walking the floor every night with Patricia screaming with the hunger, waiting for Ma to come home.

'Kathleen, look after the little ones there. I'll try and get a bit of dinner started before yer father comes home. Come 'ere, Carmel, take Clare with yeh and go down to Mr Hogg the butcher, tell him I sent yeh. Ask him will he give yeh a pound of rashers and two pound of sausages. Can he put them on me bill? I'll give him a few shillin's at the weekend. Then, go over to the corner shop. I have a half a crown here. Give it to Mr Green off me bill and say yer Ma is sorry it took so long to pay.

KATHLEEN DOYLE

Then ask could yeh have a few messages until next week. Tell him I got meself a job and tha' I'll be in as soon as I get me first wage packet. They know me word is good. Tha's grand, Kathleen. As soon as they get back, I'll make a coddle. Tha'll be easy for yiz. Yer father just has to heat it up when he comes home.'

Ma was running around like I don't know what, half talking to me and half talking to herself.

She was so excited her first day, heading off to work. I stood at the front door with little Patricia in my arms and Da standing beside me, waving and waving until she got lost in the distance, thinking to myself, *Will we be able to manage?*

* * *

The following morning, Ma was up bright and early, making the breakfast. She was really on a roll, talking and talking like I never saw before. We were all gathered around the table when she started launching into the goings-on of her first night at work. 'The nicest people yeh could meet. They made me very welcome, so they did. I was only in the door when the chef came over to me, fillin' me in on wha' me jobs were, and I can tell yeh, there was a lot for me to do. I never stopped from the minute I went in, washin' delph, cleanin' pots and scrubbin' floors. I had the kitchen gleamin' in no time. Yeh'd want to see the amount of food tha' goes to waste in there. Some of the plates had half of the dinners still on them, and me havin' to scrape it out into the bin. I could have fed the lot of yiz today with wha' I had to throw out. A mortal sin, tha's wha' it is.'

'Ma, why didn't yeh ask if yeh could bring all the bits home to us?' I asked.

'Jaysus, Kathleen, I couldn't do tha'. Well, not on me first night anyway. Let me get meself in there for a little while first.'

And no better woman to ask, which she did after a few days. And it wasn't a problem. Anything that was left on the

98

plates, Ma could have. Believe me, that went a long way with us kids. There would be pieces of chicken, halves of chops, bits of meat, rashers and sausages, all heated up together to make a dinner the following day.

* * *

Ma settled really well into her job and seemed to be happy in herself, heading off every day to do her ten-hour shift in the restaurant while I got ready to do mine.

Da was great the first couple of weeks. He was on time every day, but wasn't long slipping back into his old ways. Each day he got later and later. Ma would have herself in a right state, she'd be walking the floor, fucking and blinding, waiting on him to come in.

'You go ahead, Ma,' I would say. 'Yeh're only gone out the door when he gets here.'

'Are yeh sure about tha', Kathleen? Yeh wouldn't be tellin' me lies now, tryin' to keep yer father out of trouble?'

'I'd never do tha', Ma. Honest, I swear.' I made the sign of the cross on my chest. Once I did that Ma would believe me, or pretend to. I had got so tired of all the fighting between Ma and Da that it was easier to tell a few lies; it made life a bit better for everyone.

Most days I would manage the kids with the help of my brother Phil, and Carmel was starting to get a bit of cop-on, so she gave a dig-out as well. But there were days when I would be frantic and up the walls with worry, especially when baby Patricia was teething and crying all the time. And little Jacinta missed Ma terribly at first. It took me all my time to comfort her, but after a while she settled in with the rest of the kids. We all looked after one another. That's the way it had to be.

Da would always go on with one yarn or another as to why he was late. And no matter how much of a sup he had on him, he'd always say, 'Now, Kathleen, I don't think yer Mother needs to know tha' I fell a little bit behind with the time. We don't want her gettin' all fired up now, do we? I'll give yeh me word tha' I'll be here on the dot of four tomorrow.'

'Of course yeh will, Da,' I would say, as Phil and myself would help him up the stairs to sleep it off, knowing full well that not a word of what he was saying was true.

* * *

That was the start of Ma working for many years to come, and me taking on an even bigger role in rearing the family.

11

Maisie and Ma

A good few months went by before Maisie finally made her way out to see Ma. I was in the garden with a couple of the kids when I heard a scream.

'Kathleen, Phil! One of yiz come down here to me and give me a hand with these heavy bags.'

When I looked down the end of our road, there she was.

'Ma, quick, look who's comin'!'

Ma rushed out to the front door. 'Wha' the hell are yeh gettin' yerself all worked up over, Kathleen?'

When she looked down the road, she let out such a roar. 'I don't believe it – Maisie, Maisie!' Ma ran down the road to her. The two of them just kept crying and hugging each other. 'After all this time, yeh finally came out to see me, Maisie.'

'Holy Jaysus, Lil, how in the name of God de yeh live out here in this God-forsaken place? It's in the middle of nowhere.'

'Would yeh stop, Maisie, it's not tha' bad. Yeh don't be long gettin' get used to it. All the kids love the open space. They can go mad up in the fields. It's great for them, and it gives me a grand break.'

'All the same, Lil, there was no stoppin' yeh once yeh got goin'. Yeh can make babies quicker than anybody I know.'

'Didn't I tell yeh before, Maisie? Phil Doyle only has to hang his trousers at the end of the bed and I'm gone again. Every time he knocks he gets an answer,' she said, giving Maisie a nod and a wink.

'Yeh're a mad thing, Lil, de yeh know tha'? Jojo Murphy could be bangin' the door down all night long and he wouldn't be gettin' any answers off me, I can tell yeh tha' for nothin'. Put the teapot on there, Lil. Me mouth is dried up to nothin' here. And we'll have a smoke.'

'I haven't got one to me name. I only have me oul' clay pipe.'

'Ah for fuck's sake, yeh're not smokin' a pipe?'

'I do, Maisie. When I've no smokes I put a bit of turf in the pipe and have a few puffs.'

'Here yeh are, Lil, I picked up a few loose Woodbines in Meath Street before I got the bus. And there's a few messages. It'll make a bit of dinner for yiz. So, fill me in on wha's happenin' with yeh.'

'I wouldn't know where to start, there's tha' much gone wrong in me life.'

'I'm not rushin' anywhere, and if I make me mind up and if yeh have somewhere for me to put me head down, I'll stay the night. We might even go to the pictures, wha' de yeh say?'

'Would yeh really stay, Maisie? Wha' about Jojo?'

'Fuck him. And the kids are big and hairy enough to look after themselves.'

'Yeh can sleep in the bed with me, Maisie.'

'With yerself and Phil? No, thank yeh very much. He might get himself all confused and throw his leg over the wrong way. I swear, Lil, I'd piss on meself with the fright, so I would. I'll stay in with the kids, if tha's okay with yeh.'

'No, yeh won't, I'll push the two chairs together. Phil can sleep there. It won't do him any harm for one night. Anyway, I'm dyin' to tell yeh, Maisie – I got meself a job. Tha's how I haven't been able to come in and see yeh for so long.'

'And I thought yeh just forgot about me, Lil.'

'Never in a million years, Maisie, would I ever forget yeh.'

'Tha's it, Lil, we're definitely goin' to the pictures tonight. This calls for a celebration.'

'I haven't got a shillin' to spare, Maisie, never mind go out.'

'Don't yeh worry about tha', I have a few bob. I rifled Jojo's pockets last night when he was asleep.'

'Jaysus, Maisie, yeh never!'

'I did; I do it all the time, Lil. Sure he wouldn't know. He'd think he was after spendin' it on the drink the night before. Yeh learn a few tricks as the years go by. Fellas like Jojo only think of themselves and tha's wha' I'm doin' from now on, lookin' after me. The only way I know how. Yeh're as strong as an ox, Lil, and well able to take care of yerself, but me with me six and a half stone, if a gust of wind blew up now, it would pick me up and fuck me through tha' winda in seconds. It would, Lil, I swear it would.'

'Yeh're a scream, Maisie. I haven't laughed this much in years.'

'Lil, would yeh ever give us another drop of tea? Me throat feels like I'm after swallowin' half of Sandymount Beach.'

'I don't like the sound of tha', Maisie. Yeh want to go to the doctor and get tha' checked out.'

'Would yeh stop yer fussin', Lil, it's just a few swollen glands – nothin' to worry about. Kathleen, come 'ere, I have somethin' for yeh. Take tha'.' It was a big green pound note. 'Yerself and young Phil go down to tha' chip shop at the bus stop and get about ten singles of chips and two nice fresh fish for meself and yer Ma.'

'Jaysus, Maisie, yeh don't have to do tha'. It's too much.'

'I know I don't have to. The thing is, I *want* to. Isn't tha' wha' friends are for? Now, run along the pair of yiz and wha'ever change is left, pick up a few sweets for later on.'

I chatted away to Phil as we made our way down the road. 'Wouldn't it be great if Maisie lived out here all the time? Did yeh see the way Ma is all happy in herself? She's laughin', messin' and actin' the eejit since she arrived.'

'Well now, Kathleen. She hasn't exactly got much to be laughin' about with Da comin' in most of the time mouldy drunk and hardly ever a shillin' in her pocket, scrimpin' and scrapin' all the time.'

'Yeh don't have to tell me, Phil, I know all tha'. I'm only sayin', tha's wha' I would love.' I was getting myself all worked up.

'Ah for Jaysus' sake, Kathleen, will yeh not be gettin' yer knickers in a knot. The way I see it, everythin' is okay tonight, so enjoy it when it's goin'. Now, come on, let's get the chips, I'm starvin'. Maybe we'll fiddle an extra single in and eat it on the way back. Wha' de yeh say?'

'Ah, I suppose yeh're right, Phil. Don't be mindin' me. I do be just daydreamin'. We'd better hurry.'

* * *

We were only in the door with the fish and chips when the front door opened again.

'Maisie, here's Phil comin' in. He's after been in with his mother. He goes in every Sunday to see herself and his three sisters. Him being the only brother, they think there's no one like him. Now, sayin' tha', they're all very good to me. He never comes home without a few messages and somethin' thrown in for the kids. Credit where it's due, Maisie.'

'Shush . . . say nothin', Maisie, here he is.'

In came Da. 'Well, well. I haven't seen yeh in years, Maisie. Wha' brings yeh out to this neck of the woods?'

'I had a bit of time on me hands and I thought, who better than Lil and yerself to visit? It's well yeh're lookin', Phil.'

Da looked at the table full of food. 'Wha's this, Lil?'

'Maisie's treat, Phil.'

'Tha's right, a few of me numbers came up on the bingo last night, isn't tha' right, Lil?'

The pair of them laughed themselves silly, not letting Da know the truth.

We all sat there, delighted with ourselves, getting a full bag of chips for our tea instead of a slice of bread and dripping, and there were a few sweets for afterwards. To us it was like having a party.

* * *

Maisie and Ma went out to the pictures while I minded the kids with Da. And by the sound of them when they came home, they had the best night ever. They fell in the door laughing.

'You'll never believe wha' happened to us, Phil,' said Maisie.

'Well, by the sound of the pair of yiz, it was a good night.'

'Kathleen, love, get me a cup of tea there 'til I get meself together and fill yer father in with the goin's-on of the night. There was this fella sittin' next to me and when it was comin' near to the end of the film, he went and offered me a few sweets. I didn't want to be rude, him bein' so nice and all, so I went and put me hand into the bag, which was on his lap. There's me thinkin' I was takin' a few sweets for meself and Lil, and wha' de yeh think was in the bag? Yeh're never goin' to believe me, Phil. He had "down below" sittin' there, waitin' on me hand to come in! A heart attack I thought I was goin' to have. The whole picture house heard me screams – *and* his. I jabbed me favourite hat pin straight into the top of his leg. He was up and gone like Flash Gordon before the lights were put back on.'

Da looked over at Ma, saying, 'Lil, the kids. Yiz have to watch wha' you're sayin'.'

Ma was still laughing away at Maisie, saying to Da, 'Give it over, Phil. They don't know wha' we're talkin' about.'

I didn't, but as I looked over at my brother Phil, with a sly grin on his face, *he knew*.

'Phil, wha' is Maisie talkin' about?' I whispered.

'I'm not sayin', Kathleen. Ma would kill me if she knew I talked about stuff like tha'.'

'Ah, go on, tell me. I swear I won't say anythin'. I'm dyin' to know wha' they're laughin' at.'

'Right then, yeh'd better not say I told you. Yer man is one of them dirty fuckers Ma is always warnin' us about. They sometimes call them flashers. They open their coat real fast and show off their mickey and run. Don't ask me why they do it, I don't know. Well, tha's wha' yer man was doin' with Maisie, only *his mickey* was in the bag.'

That soon took the smile off my face and stopped me asking any more questions.

* * *

Maisie stayed the night and slept in with Ma. You could hear the two of them talking and laughing away into the early hours of the morning. Da slept on the two chairs and didn't mind a bit.

Maisie visited Ma a few times after that day and always had her laughing. From the time she walked in, Ma would be at her happiest. Until one day she told Ma the bad news.

'This will be me last time comin' out to see yeh, Lil. The bus run is gettin' a bit too much for me now.'

'Holy Mother of God, yeh don't look well, Maisie, wha's wrong with yeh? Sit down, sit down.'

'It's me oul' glands again. A bit of an infection went astray, Lil.'

'Didn't I tell yeh to get tha' checked months ago? Maisie, I told yeh.'

'I did, Lil. It was already gone too far. The doctor said a couple of months at the most. Sure I already knew meself.'

Ma burst out crying, she was so upset. I had never seen her like that before.

'Yeh should have said. Why didn't yeh tell me, Maisie?' She

was crying and hugging her like she never wanted to let her go.

'And have yeh cryin' every time yeh looked at me? Sure, look at yeh now. It's a bit of laughin' I need, Lil, not cryin'. Tha's why I made it me business to come out to yeh. We had some great times over the years.'

'We did, Maisie, we did.'

'Go on, Lil. Put the teapot on and we'll have a smoke and an oul' yap.'

They sat there for hours crying, laughing and smoking, both of them going back down memory lane.

* * *

That was the last time I saw Maisie. But Ma made sure she got in to see her as often as she could in those last few months.

I'll never forget the day the news arrived.

Da had been in to see Granny Mariah and when he came home, he was pale in the face and had such a worried look on him.

'Sit down there, Lil. I have something to tell yeh. I didn't want to be the bearer of bad news, but I suppose it's best tha' I be the one to tell yeh. Poor Maisie died early this morning.'

I got such a fright when I heard those words. The tears flowed down my face as I watched Ma fall to pieces in front of me. She cried and cried. You could have filled a river with the tears she shed.

Da took the day off work to look after the kids so that I could go to the funeral with Ma. She never spoke the whole time we were there – not that there were many people to talk to, with only a handful having turned up.

Ma put me sitting to one side as she stood by the coffin. I felt sad that Maisie was gone but I was more upset looking over at Ma saying her last goodbye to her one and only friend.

* * *

Ma wasn't herself for a long, long time after. All the life seemed to go out of her. She went into herself, barely speaking to anyone, just going through the motions of looking after us kids. She'd sit there in the chair, feeding the babies, staring out the window, not minding anyone or anything around her. I didn't know how to comfort her, being too young to understand the hurt and loss she was feeling inside.

One day, on my way down to the shops I bumped into Mrs Kearney. I told her about Maisie dying and Ma not being herself.

'Don't worry, Kathleen. It'll be all right. I'll talk to yer Ma. She'll be fine. Wait and see.'

Mrs Kearney was so good; she dropped in every day after that. She'd sit there for hours on end trying to cheer Ma up. Slowly but surely, Ma started to come round and get back to her old self again.

12

The Cane

Because Ma had been sick, I had been out of school for months on end and I really hated going back. I was so far behind the rest of the class, there was no way I could keep up with them. I used to feel such a fool, sitting there knowing nothing. I suppose if I had been in all the time and knew some of the lessons, it might not have been so bad. The odd time that I was sent to school I was always late, so straight away I was in trouble.

Ma got free milk from the clinic because she had so many kids. I had to collect the milk every morning before I went to school. The clinic didn't open until half past nine, so by the time I had queued and got the milk, it would be nearly ten o'clock by the time I reached school. I'd be falling up the long marble corridor with my schoolbag over my back and ten bottles of milk banging and clattering all over the place. No matter how hard I tried to sneak in as quietly as possible, I always got caught.

One morning, I was nearly at the classroom when a voice called out. I knew it was one of the nuns. I could hear the sound of heavy rosary beads swishing against her black habit. I was so afraid of those nuns!

'Kathleen Doyle, is that you again? What did I tell you about being late and bringing that milk into the school? Do you ever take any notice of what's been said to you, child?'

I looked around and there was Sister Norma, the ugliest woman you ever saw on two feet. She had a big fat face pushed out from under the veil on her head, and this big red lump of flesh hanging under her chin in what passed for a neck. I swear, the cock Ma had out in the backyard with the chickens was better looking than that nun.

'Sorry, Sister. There was loads of people on the queue. I hadn't time to go home with the milk. I would have been more later.'

'And what time do you call this, you God-forsaken child?' I bit my lip and said nothing. 'I'll be giving you a note. And tell your mother I want to see her about you not being in school. The inspector will be giving her a visit.'

I wanted to say, *I don't care and I don't want to be here, so fuck you, Sister, and fuck Speckie the Inspector*, but instead I stood there listening to her go on and on about how close I was to being put into a home for not going to school.

When she was finished giving out to me, I smiled and asked, with a sly grin on my face, 'Sister, can I bring the milk down to me Ma on the lunch break? She'll be waitin' on it for the babies.'

'This is the last time, do you hear me, Kathleen Doyle? Now get into your classroom before I change my mind about letting you go home with that milk.'

I was trying to slip into the classroom unnoticed, but the noise of the bloody milk bottles gave me away. The teacher turned around and caught me. Twitchy Maher. That was her nickname and it suited her so well. She had a face like a rabbit; if she wasn't twitching her nose, she was picking and flicking it.

'Well now, Miss Doyle, you've decided to make your entrance, have you?'

'Sorry I'm late, Miss,' I said, thinking to myself, *for fuck's sake, tha's twice I'm after gettin' the second name, first off Sister, now Twitchy.* I knew, I just knew it – there was going to be big trouble for me today.

'Who do you think you are, Miss Doyle? You seem to think that you can wander in and out of school when you feel like it. Do you think you know more than the rest of the class?' Her voice rose into a high-pitched squeak.

'Sorry, Miss. I don't. It's just tha' me Ma . . .'

'Be quiet, child, when I speak to you.' She banged her fist on the desk.

Good Jaysus! Now she's callin' me 'child' as well. Tha's it, I'm dead. She's goin' to fuckin' kill me.

'Get up to the blackboard and let's see if you can do that sum. Then we can all see how smart you are.' A few of the kids giggled. 'Be quiet down there!' she roared at the top of her voice.

I was shitting myself walking past her. I stood there with the chalk in my hand, shaking. I hadn't got a clue what to do and she knew it.

'Sorry, Miss, I don't know it. I'm sorry.'

She pulled me by the plaits over to where she kept her long skinny bamboo cane, which had tiny pieces of wire wrapped around it. She swished the cane up and down, banging it off the desk, getting ready to give me a good lash.

'Hands out, you good-for-nothing child!'

I slowly stretched my hand out with fear. Down came the cane, with an unbearable sting to follow.

'That's for being late, Kathleen Doyle. Now, out with the other one.' I looked and stepped back. 'I said the other one!' She lashed out in temper and the full force of the cane came down, again and again. 'That's for answering me back.'

'But, Miss, I didn't . . . I wasn't . . .'

'More cheek, is it, from you? Hands out again!' she roared. I stretched my hands out once more.

'Now, tell the class you're sorry for all this delay.'

I was very stubborn and wouldn't say sorry; so she just kept slapping me. She wasn't about to let me get the better of her in front of the class. You could hear a pin drop as the kids watched in horror. I lost count of how many times the cane came down. I could feel the blood drain from my face and my legs starting to wobble.

'I'm goin' to be sick, Miss.'

'You're a weakling as well as stupid! Now get outside of my class and sit on the bench until I say you can come back in.'

When I got outside, I cried and cried from the pain and the stinging in my hands. Every finger was cut and bleeding. *Tha's it! I'm gettin' outta here. Tha' fuckin' bitch is mad. She'll kill me before the day's over with the mood she's in.* I was down the stairs and heading for home before I knew it.

When I got to the house and Ma saw my hands, she went crazy mad. She ran out to the back yard, roaring up the gardens for Mrs Kearney.

'Mrs Kearney, quick! Quick, come down here to me. Would yeh have a bandage and a bit of cream?'

'Give me a minute and I'll be down, Lil.'

There was no way you could call Mrs Kearney by her first name; you had to give her the full title. She was very tall and thin, with long red hair all wavy and curly. She spoke real posh and always had her full make-up on. She was a really kind person and very good to Ma.

Ma lit a Woodbine and put the kettle on, pacing up and down in one of her mad rages.

Mrs Kearney made her way into the kitchen. 'Now, Lil, what's this all about?'

'Kathleen, come'ere! Look wha' she's done, look at her hands.'

'Who, Lil, who are we talking about here?'

'Tha' fuckin' teacher, tha's who. I'm goin' to fuckin' kill the baster'n' bitch when I get me hands on her.'

'Now, Lil, stop that cursing in front of the children. Come over to me, Kathleen. Oh my God, look at the state of your little hands, you poor child. There is no need for this, no need at all. They're not allowed to do the likes of this to any child.' She put some cream and bandages on my hands. 'Right, Lil, get your coat; we are not letting this go, but you have to promise me one thing.'

'Wha's tha', Mrs Kearney?'

'You'll keep that temper of yours under control.'

That was like asking for a miracle. You could see Ma was getting all riled up more and more as the minutes went by.

'I'll ask Mrs Kennedy next door to watch the children for you until we get back, Lil.'

Up to the school the three of us went. We were only in the door when we met two of the nuns, one of them being Sister Norma. She stood there with her chicken neck hanging out, looking down on us.

'Can I help you, ma'am?'

'Yeah, just tell me where tha' Twitchy Maher wan is,' said Ma.

'I beg your pardon? Twitchy? Twitchy who?'

'Twitchy fuckin' Maher. Are yeh deaf or wha'?'

I tipped Ma. 'Ma, it's tha' room at the top of the stairs, just up there.'

She took the stairs in twos, with the nuns running after her.

'Lil, come back,' Mrs Kearney shouted. 'You promised to keep your temper.'

Ma banged and kicked the door as she screamed for Twitchy to come out. I thought it was going to come off the hinges.

'What on earth is going on here?' Twitchy said, opening the door. She only had the words out of her mouth when Ma gave her the fist straight in the face. Twitchy fell to the floor. Ma was on top of her, pulling the hair out of her head.

'Beat my Kathleen, would yeh, yeh fuckin' bitch? No

wonder he left yeh standin' at the altar – with a face like tha' any man would run a mile.'

Sister Norma eventually managed to pull Ma up off Twitchy.

'Take yer hands off me! I'm warnin' yeh! You're just as bad for lettin' this happen, and don't pretend yeh don't know wha's goin' on around here! Why don't yeh get up off yer big fat arse and see wha's goin' on in this school, and the world out there for tha' matter. Yeh frustrated oul' fuck.'

Sister nearly fainted when she heard what was coming out of Ma's mouth. 'Mrs Doyle, how dare you speak to me in that manner!'

'Don't "Mrs Doyle" me, I'm tellin' yeh!' Sister couldn't get a word in edgeways; Ma was on a roll. 'Everybody around and in the school knows, Twitchy Maher's fella went off with another wan.' Ma roared into Sister's face. 'And tha's why she's a moody fucker. She won't be takin' her moods out on my child. I'll kill her first. Did yeh see wha' she done to my Kathleen?' She took the bandages off my hands.

When Sister Norma saw my hands, her face changed colour. She didn't know what to say or where to look. Then she tried to switch the blame from Twitchy to Ma.

'Now, Mrs Doyle, this is all down to you keeping Kathleen out of school and coming in late, upsetting the class and teacher.'

'I'm tellin' yeh, tha' Twitchy wan will never lay a finger on my Kathleen again or she'll have me to answer to.'

Ma just gave the look and shook her head, as she took me by the hand to bring me home.

* * *

Da was only in the door when Ma launched into the goings-on of the day. The first thing out of his mouth was, 'Lil, yeh didn't make a show of me in front of the nuns, did yeh?' The priests and nuns could do no wrong in Da's eyes.

'Fuck yeh, Phil Doyle, and them nuns – look at the state of Kathleen.' She held my hands out. He wasn't long pulling his words back.

Da brought me to school after a few days. He spoke to the Principal about what happened. He said the matter would be dealt with and there would be no charges brought against Mrs Doyle for attacking the teacher.

I was put back into Twitchy's class. Ma tried to send me to school as much as she could, which wasn't very often, but it didn't make any difference. Twitchy put me down the back of the class and taught me nothing. I never said anything to Ma or Da. It wouldn't have made any difference anyway – Da always had a sup on him and Ma was too busy with the babies. Sure, I thought, it was great not having to worry about doing schoolwork.

I'd take out a book the odd time and try to read it and sometimes I'd put up my hand in class to answer a question, but Twitchy would just pass me by, giving me the sly grin. That was her way of getting her own back on me for the day Ma went crazy mad.

Ma might have won the fight that day, but in the end Twitchy really won because when I left school I had little or no education at all. I couldn't read and was just about able to write my name. But what I did have, which Ma instilled in every one of us, was an inner strength and determination to make something of myself in life and never, ever to be as poor as I was as a child.

13

The Swimming Pool

Little Patricia was nearly a year old and not a bit of trouble. She'd sit in the pram, laughing and farting out at everyone. She always had a smile. Unlike Jacinta – you could see that she was going to be wild.

It was summer. I was sitting on the steps outside the front door rocking Jacinta in my arms trying to get her asleep. She was two years old and a desperate whinger. You wouldn't have a minute's peace, between her eating muck, climbing the garden walls and demolishing the few flowers we had left in the garden. You couldn't watch her.

I can't believe this, I thought. *It's bad enough that Clare is as mad as a hatter, but I now have another wild one to mind, one more to drive me nuts altogether, and it won't be too long before Patricia is handed over to me as well.*

Ma called out to me. 'Kathleen, I'm goin' out to do a bit of shoppin', see if I can pick up a few bargains. I'm takin' Patricia with me.'

'Sure, that's grand, Ma.' *You take the quiet one with you, and leave me with all the head-bangers.*

'I've to go down to the clinic. Patricia has to get one of her needles, so I'll be gone a while. Keep an eye on the rest of the kids and don't let them carry on. They're not to *move* outside tha' gate! De yeh hear me, Kathleen? I'm dependin' on yeh to look after things for me. I've to get all this done before I get meself off to work.'

'Right, Ma, wha'ever yeh say.'

'Oh, Kathleen, I nearly forgot. There's some drippin' in the dish in the oven for when they get hungry. Get Carmel to put it on some bread. Tha'll keep yiz goin' until I get home.' *That's right, Ma, give Carmel the easy job to do. Don't ask her to do anything. Leave it all to me. Why can you not depend on her for a change, or Phil for that matter?*

Off Ma went with not a notion of what was going on inside my head. I was still giving out like mad to myself. *Dripping again,* I thought. *Jaysus, will we ever see a bit of real butter in this house? God, what's wrong with me? I'm doing nothing but giving out since this morning. I'm starting to sound like Ma. I'll have to stop.*

It was really hot that day. The kids were running around in their knickers out in the back garden. The two basins and buckets from the kitchen were brim full of water and the kids were having great fun splashing and trying to drown one another. After a while, they started whispering and giggling. I always knew when they were getting up to something.

'Wha' are yiz up to?' I shouted out at them.

'We were just sayin', Kathleen . . .' piped up Marion.

'I'm sorry I asked. Whatever it is, I don't want to know!'

'Will yeh just listen to us?' the rest of them shouted in.

'Right then. Go on. I'm listenin'.'

'Wouldn't it be great to have our own swimmin' pool, Kathleen?' says Clare, trying to suck up to me.

'Don't be stupid, Clare; only rich people have things like tha'.'

'We could make our own,' Marion and Noel roared at me.

'Are yiz nuts? Will yeh get away and leave me alone, the lot of yiz,' I shouted back.

I wasn't in any humour to listen to them. I was fed up; I wanted to go out, swing on the lamp-post and play with the rest of the kids on the street, playing beds, skipping, marbles, all the things they were doing. I didn't want to be always looking after babies.

Just then Phil came in. 'De yeh hear wha' them eejits are sayin', Phil? They're talkin' about makin' a swimmin' pool. Did yeh ever hear anythin' so stupid?'

'Wha' have yiz got in mind? I could do with a dip meself. I'm sweatin',' said Phil.

'We could get loads of clothes and block around the doors in the kitchen, then fill the room up with water,' said Clare and Noel.

That got Phil thinking: 'Could be done, Kathleen, could be done.'

'Are yiz all gone mad? Ma' would kill us stone dead. It's not goin' to happen, go away.'

I stood up and went into the kitchen with Jacinta in my arms, the rest of them all trailing behind me.

'Ah, go on, Kathleen,' they chimed in. 'Let's do it.'

'No, no, forget it, it's not happenin'.'

'Yeh're just like Ma,' says Clare. 'We're never let do anythin'.'

'No, I'm not like her! I'm me, I'm meself, I'm Kathleen.'

'Yeh are, yeh are,' they all roared.

'Fuck off, the lot of yiz, and leave me alone.'

'See. Yeh even curse like her,' said Carmel.

Phil took up the cry. 'Why don't yeh prove it then and let them? Ma does be gone for ages when she goes to the clinic. Sure we'll have it all brushed out the back yard by the time she comes home,' he added reassuringly. 'Come on, Kathleen, do it. Let yerself go for a change.'

Thomas was going mad, jumping up and down at the thought of a swimming pool. In fact, I must have gone a bit mad myself that day, because they finally got around me and I said 'yes'.

Before I knew it, they had blankets, coats, sheets and anything else they could get their hands on blocking every door in the kitchen. All the furniture was pushed into one corner of the room and then the basins and buckets were filled up right to the top with water, which was lashed all over the floor. We all took turns blocking the doors by lying against the coats and blankets, doing our best to keep the water in. We didn't get up off the floor until the water was way up past the skirting boards.

I got stripped down to my vest and knickers, and then stripped little Jacinta, leaving her with only a nappy on. We all jumped around like lunatics, while Phil kept lashing the buckets of water onto the floor. I was laughing and playing with the kids for a change and it felt good instead of giving out and always telling them what to do, which shouldn't have been left up to me. It wasn't fair.

Next thing, Noel got the kitchen table, tilted it against the wall and made a slide. We put the youngest ones onto the top of the table and then pushed them into the water. You'd want to have heard the screams of us! We had a great laugh, the best fun ever. The whole road must have been listening to us.

'Kathleen, yeh know the way yeh're always sayin' some day yeh're goin' to have a lovely bubble bath all to yerself?' asked Clare.

'Yeah. So? Wha's tha' got to do with all this?'

'Well, yeh're goin' to have one with all of us now!' she screamed, wheezing with the laughter. Then, before I could open my mouth, she shook half a box of washing powder into the water.

'Right, Marion, will yeh splash? Thomas, come over here and start kicking the water to make the bubbles.'

I couldn't stop them. They were all at it. Within minutes, the bubbles were nearly up to the ceiling. We couldn't even see one another. *Holy Jaysus. What am I after getting myself into?*

'Yeh stupid little fuck, Clare Doyle, we'll never get rid of these bubbles. Tha's it, we're all dead. Ma will be back soon. She'll kill us all first and then we'll be put in a home.'

Jacinta started crying. The suds had got into her eyes. Then the rest of them started whingeing. 'Me eyes, me eyes! They're burnin' me.'

With that, there was a big bang on the front door and everybody went really quiet.

'Who's that?' I asked.

'It's Mrs Kearney, Kathleen,' she called out in her posh accent. 'What is going on? Is Lil there? I can hear you from my garden. You're all being very boisterous.'

I opened the window. 'Ma brought Patricia to the clinic for her needles, Mrs Kearney.' I whispered in a low voice, 'Jacinta is asleep.' I was hoping she would just leave and not hear the mayhem going on behind me.

'You must have a burst pipe or something, Kathleen. There's water pouring down the three steps out here. Open the door. I'll get Jack to have a look.'

Oh Jaysus, how did the water get out the front? 'Ah, it's okay, Mrs Kearney, one of the kids knocked over a bucket of water.'

'There's a lot of water out here, Kathleen. Are you sure it was just a bucketful?'

As I kept Mrs Kearney distracted, the older kids were trying to get as much of the water out to the back yard as quickly as they could. But it was very hard, having only the one brush to do the job. Phil came up behind me.

'It's no good, Kathleen. The more I brush, the worse it's gettin'. Tha' tick Noel was dyin' to have a shite. Wha' does he only go an' do? Open the kitchen door to make a dart up to the toilet and now the suds are all over the hall.' By now, I was hanging out the window, smiling down at Mrs Kearney while Phil was roaring in my ear: 'Did yeh hear me, Kathleen?'

'Shut the fuck up until she goes,' I snarled at Phil over my shoulder.

Mrs Kearney was droning on. 'Make sure you dry that lino well, now. If a drop of water gets underneath, it will smell something terrible. And we can't have that, Kathleen, now can we?'

'No, Mrs Kearney. Thanks for knockin'.' I gave her a big smile.

Just as she turned to walk out the gate, I looked down the road and there was Ma puffing on her Woodbines, pushing the pram with one hand and waving to Mrs Kearney with the other. I ran into the kitchen shouting, 'Ma's at the corner.' There were suds and bubbles everywhere, bursting out all over the hall, on into the kitchen and out into the back yard.

'Wha'll we do? Wha'll we do, Kathleen?' the kids kept saying, looking at me and hoping I was going to fix the problem.

'I'm outta here,' said Clare.

She went to make a run for it but I grabbed her by the plaits. 'No, yeh're not, yeh little bitch. Now, get them towels off the line and start dryin' yerselves, de yeh hear me? Phil, the hall is burstin' with water. Wha'll we do?' I was frantic at this stage.

'Well, Kathleen, there's no two ways about it. We'll just have to open the front door, whether we like it or not. There's no other way.'

We tried to pull the door inwards to open it, but it wouldn't move. Phil took Noel and Thomas around to the front of the house so that they could help him push the door in while myself and Carmel pulled on the other side.

'Are yeh ready, Kathleen?' said Phil. 'Pull the door when I tell yeh to. Are yiz pullin'?'

'We are, Phil, but we keep slippin'.'

'Push, yiz lazy bastards. Noel, get yer fat arse up against the fuckin' door and push.'

'I am pushin' and don't call me fat.'

'Yeh are fat.'

By now, I was screaming through the letterbox at the lot of

them, telling them to stop fighting. All I could see was Noel's face going purple with temper. Phil knew how touchy Noel was and could get him going in no time. Phil kept up the stream of abuse: 'Yeh're just a big heap of shite, Noel. I've more strength in me little finger.'

'You fuck off, Phil Doyle.' Noel was like a bull, pushing like mad, and in seconds the door was open.

The water gushed down the three steps and out the front gate. Phil turned to Noel, giving him a good pat on the head and saying, 'Sure, I didn't doubt yeh for a minute, Noel. I knew once I got yeh goin' with tha' temper of yours, yeh would do all the work for me in no time.'

Phil didn't keep the grin on his face for long. I tipped him on the back and gave him the nod to look. When he turned around, there was Ma standing at the gate, the water gushing down through her sandals.

I was covered in suds and green in the face with fright. Carmel and Noel had vanished. Phil's face was as white as a sheet. We just stood there. Everything was quiet for a few seconds and it seemed to take ages for Ma to react. She looked at Phil and then back at me. We were sick in the pits of our stomachs. Mrs Kearney was standing beside Ma, saying, 'Now, Lil, let's not lose control here,' knowing full well the mad temper Ma had.

Ma looked down at her sandals and then straight back at us again. I must have suddenly gone deaf because I could see her mouth moving, but I could hear no sounds coming from her. I could feel Phil pulling at my vest, trying to get me to run with him. I was stuck to the ground. My feet wouldn't move; it was like Ma was moving in slow motion, coming towards us. Phil didn't run.

Mrs Kearney tried to pull Ma back, yanking at her cardigan. As Ma's arms came out of their sleeves, Mrs Kearney went flying back and landed on her arse. Ma didn't even notice that she had fallen as she charged at us, screaming. I jumped out of her way and landed on the only rose bush in the garden. That soon brought my hearing back! I was still in my vest and knickers, and now I had cuts all over me, with thorns stuck everywhere.

Phil went flying in the other direction and landed on the big black pram, or 'the bus', as we used to call it. As the two front wheels collapsed, all I could hear from Phil were the words 'holy fuck'. Within seconds, he too had gone missing with the rest of the kids. I got such a box in the head off Ma as she made her way into the house. As I pulled myself from the thorn bush, I could see Mrs Kearney struggling on the ground.

'Oh, Kathleen, love, come over here and help me up before anyone sees me,' said Mrs Kearney.

'Look at the pram. Ma uses tha' at night for the babies. She'll really go crazy mad when she sees the state of it. She'll kill us, Mrs Kearney, she will, I know she will.' I stood there trembling with fright.

'And what do you call that, Kathleen? Just listen to her. If that's not your mother going mad, I don't know what to say. You have really pushed her too far this time.'

Ma stood in the kitchen, screaming out the window. 'Bad cess ta yiz. When I get me hands on yiz I'm goin' to fuckin' kill yiz all. Me house is ruined. Wha's tha' on the floor? Me blankets, yeh shower of bastards! Holy Jaysus – wha's this? The only coat I have to me name. It's all tha' keeps me warm in the winter. Ah for Jaysus' sake, will yeh have a look at the bit of fur on the collar? It's like a dead fuckin' rat, so it is.'

I quickly went around the side of the house to see where the rest of the kids were hiding; they were up Mrs Tully's big tree, which was at the end of our back garden.

Ma ran out of the kitchen and spotted them in the tree. Mustering up every ounce of strength that she had, she started throwing stones, bricks and anything she could get her hands on. I didn't know if I was safer on the ground or up in the tree with the rest of them.

All the saints and scholars, popes and any statue that had a name in the Catholic Church got a mention that day. Then, after all the shouting and roaring, Ma walked up the garden, tears rolling down her face. Finally, after five or ten minutes, she remembered that she had left Patricia in the pram around the front of the house. Only now did she finally get around to spotting the unfortunate Mrs Kearney sitting on the steps, her two hands cut to bits.

'Holy Mother of God, Mrs Kearney. Wha' happened to yeh? Are yeh all right?'

'You knocked me flying in the air with that temper of yours, Lil Doyle!'

Ma starting crying again. 'I'm sorry, I'm sorry. Let me get yer hands cleaned up.'

Just then, Phil popped his head around the corner. 'Ah, Ma, I'm really sorry.' Ma would neither look at him nor answer him.

Mrs Kearney stepped in straight away.

'They're a wild bunch, Lil, there's no doubt about that. Now, I know the house is ruined, but if we all get stuck in, we'll have it back to normal in no time.'

Mrs Kearney stared straight at Phil, trying to get his attention.

'Phil, go up to my house and get Jack. Tell him to come down here and check the plugs. Lil, it's just to make sure it's safe to go back into your kitchen.' It wasn't long before Phil was up and back with Mr Kearney.

'Sorry, Ma. Sorry, Ma,' I kept saying.

But she wasn't having any of it. She just sat there with a stern look on her face, telling me that since I was the one who had been left in charge, I should have had more sense. I wanted to tell her that I didn't want sense. I wanted to be just like the rest of the kids. I didn't want to be in charge, I didn't want to be a Ma. But no time was ever the right time to say that to her.

Mrs Kearney asked for a glass of water and a damp cloth to wrap her cut hands in.

Well, you never saw Phil run as quick. He was in that kitchen and back to her in a flash, and was in there straight away, licking up to Ma.

'There yeh are, Mrs Kearney. We've no glasses, will a jam jar do? And one for yerself, Ma.' He smiled from ear to ear.

Mrs Kearney sat with Ma for ages, trying to keep her calm as she wrapped her hands in the sheet that Phil tore up in the kitchen. The rest of the kids slowly made their way down the garden to see if it was safe, one after the other mumbling, 'Sorry, Ma', 'Sorry, Ma'.

Ma sat there with the stern look still on her face, saying nothing.

* * *

Da was home early that day, with not a sup on him, thank God, and was in shock when he saw the state of the house. He stood there listening to Ma telling him all about what we kids had got up to. When she mentioned how there was a swimming pool made in the kitchen, he tried hard to keep a straight face. He knew that Ma was after giving all of us a lash and there was no point in him starting on us, because that would only get Ma going again. Instead, he tried to fix the situation, telling Ma not to be getting herself into a state. Amazingly, he wasn't long sorting things out. I stood there and listened to Da and thought to myself, *Why can't you be like this all the time? Then maybe things would be different for all of us.*

'Phil, lift this pram into the house with me, then get yerself and Noel out to the back yard and bring me in them two concrete blocks and put them under the pram. When I'm down in the scrap-yard tomorrow I'll pick up a couple of wheels. Now, hurry up. There's a lot to do. Kathleen, get yerself dressed and make yer mother and Mrs Kearney a cup of tea while I sort out this house.' He gave me a wink while Ma wasn't looking. I felt a bit better. 'The rest of youse girls get them coats and blankets, give them a good twist and throw them over the clothesline. Lil, the lino will have to be taken up off the floor. There's no savin' it.'

Ma looked at Da. 'Jaysus Christ, Phil! We're back to bare floorboards again!'

'It can't be helped, Lil. It'll stink us out of the house if I don't take it up.'

Ma glared at us kids and all she could say was 'Bad cess ta yiz all.'

'Come on now, Lil,' said Da, 'don't be keepin' it up. Wha's done is done. Anyway, yeh're runnin' late for work as it is. Yeh best be on yer way.'

'Phil is right, Lil,' says Mrs Kearney. 'You run along. I'll give a hand here.'

'Right then, Phil, I'll leave it to yiz. I'll only end up goin' crazy mad again if I stay here.'

Usually I would be giving out like mad to myself about having to mind all the kids when Ma went to work, but I was never as happy to see her head off that day, knowing that by tomorrow she would have calmed herself down, as she always did.

* * *

It took days for the coats and blankets to dry. The weather was good, so every door and window was open for a week to air the house. Da asked Mr Kearney to rig up a hose out in the back yard.

'Thanks, Jack. If it keeps them mad kids of mine happy and it stops me house floatin' down the road like Noah's Ark, sure wouldn't it be worth it, Jack, to give them a hose each?' said Ma, once again giving us kids the stern look.

You wouldn't even have the word 'warm' or 'sweating' out of your mouth when one of the kids would turn on the hose and drown you. We all made sure to be on our best behaviour, for a few days anyway, and nobody mentioned the word 'swimming pool' again.

Well, not for a long time anyway. We all knew better.

14

Chocolate and Turf

'Kathleen, go out the back yard and bring me in two heads of cabbage. I'm after gettin' a lovely bit of bacon and two sheets of ribs. Carmel, come 'ere.'

'Wha', Ma?'

'Put them bloody dolls away and start peelin' tha' small sack of spuds there. I'll try and get this dinner done before I get meself off to work. Tha' should keep yiz goin' until tomorrow. Kathleen, make sure when yeh're washin' tha' cabbage yeh check it well for maggots and flies. Tha's only fresh ou' o' the ground. It'll be crawlin' alive with them.'

'Did yeh have to say tha' Ma? Yeh'll be puttin' me off me dinner before I get it, for God's sake.'

'Don't be so bloody squeamish.'

'Oh God! There's loads of them. I'm not eatin' any of this.'

'Hold on a minute there, Kathleen. Who's tha' after comin' in?'

She caught Noel and Clare sneaking up the stairs.

Gobshites, I thought, *if they charged in like they always do, she wouldn't take any notice, but when they sneaked in she smelled a rat.*

'Wha' are yiz up ta?' she roared. 'Come down here, you two.'

'Hold on, Ma,' Noel said. 'I'm doin' me toilet.'

'I'll give yiz two seconds to get yer arses down here. If I have to go up them stairs after yeh, it's the back of me hand yeh'll be gettin'.'

The two of them made their way down and walked into the kitchen.

'Holy divine Jaysus! Would yeh have a look at the cut of them, Kathleen?'

I had to put my hand up to my face to stop myself laughing or Ma would end up killing us all.

Noel was around seven years of age by this time. He was a big heavy young fella, with slanty eyes, his hair shaved, skin tight into his head. 'Jap-head', we used to call him. Clare was a year younger, as skinny as ever, with her long black plaits and the biggest green eyes you ever saw. She was trying to hide behind Noel, but he kept pushing her to the front. They were covered from head to toe in muck, except for their faces; that was full of chocolate.

'Yiz were up in tha' dump again!' shouted Ma, running at the two of them. Noel got a right box in the head. Clare must have run around the table a dozen times. Ma couldn't catch her; she was like lightning.

'Wha' did I tell yiz about goin' up to tha' fuckin' place? A disease yeh'll get! Tha' chocolate's dumped because it's gone off. There's rats pissin' and shitin' all over it. Can I not get tha' into tha' tick skull of yers?' She gave Noel another box. 'As for you, Clare, yeh skinny little fuck, if I get me hands on yeh, I'll redden the arse off yeh for not listenin' to me.'

Clare was like a hare, running around the table, in and out the back yard before Ma could catch her. She dragged the pair of them by the scruff of the neck up the stairs.

'Yiz'll be eatin' soap for a week by the time I'm finished with the two of yiz. I'll be the talk of the road with this carry-on; makin' a holy show of me, so yiz are.'

I'm sure the people at the top of the road could hear the

roars of them and Ma as she scrubbed them in a bath of ice-cold water.

'I haven't got time to start molly-coddlin' yiz, heatin' pots of water. *Think* the next time. This is wha' yiz'll have to face, if yeh go near tha' dump again. Are yiz listenin'?' And the pair of them got another box.

Ma made her way down the stairs, breathless from all the running around.

'Tha's the two of yeh sorted out. Now sit at the fire, the pair of yiz, and heat yerselves up there before yeh freeze to death. Right then, Kathleen, is them spuds and cabbage done?'

'They are, Ma.'

Carmel always took half the day to do anything, but by God those spuds were peeled in record time.

'I hope the rest of yiz don't go near tha' dump.' She looked over at me.

'No, Ma. We wouldn't do tha'. Would we, Carmel?'

'Never, Ma, honest to God. We don't.'

'*Hmm* . . . I hope not.'

If she only knew the lies I told for them; the half of what they got up to when her back was turned! Not a day went by that two or three of them weren't up in that dump, rooting out old bits of scrap, never mind the chocolate. They got cute and stopped eating the chocolate themselves, copping on that it was giving them the shites; but they didn't care who else ate it or what state their arse ended up being in. They'd clean it and break it up into squares, put it into a bit of paper, pretending that one of our aunties worked in a sweet factory, and sell two or three pieces for a penny. Any bits of scrap would be brought around to Wally around the corner. He'd buy anything for a shilling or two.

In the middle of all this mayhem, Phil walked in with a smile stretching from ear to ear.

'There yeh are, Ma. There's a few shillings. Help yeh with the messages.'

'Where did this money come from, Phil?'

'Sure, I was up helpin' Paddy load the turf into his van, up there in the turf depot.'

'Who's this Paddy fella?'

'Yeh know him. He lives down Sundrive Road. Everybody knows Paddy, Ma. He's always up there gettin' the turf for the old folks. Isn't tha' right Noel, Clare? Tell 'er, didn't yeh see me?'

'Yeah Ma, I did.'

'I can't place him at the minute but he sounds like a good man. Phil, I hope yeh thanked him now.'

'Course I did, Ma.'

'I'll go out meself tomorrow and tell him any time he needs a bit of help, just knock here. There's always one or two of yiz around to give him a hand.'

You could see the panic on Phil's face, knowing he'd been lying through his teeth to Ma; he had really been up in the dump with the other two. They didn't know where to look. Noel wouldn't look at Phil, because they'd start laughing, and then Ma would smell a rat once more, so they just kept looking at me. I just gave them a little grin, thinking: *Nice one – I'll have these in me grip for a little while anyway. They'll jump any time I need a bit of work done.*

Phil chimed in, 'No, Ma, don't do tha'; don't go out to him. I want him to think I'm all grown-up and can get me own work.'

She thought for a minute. 'Hmm . . . right then, I'll leave it with yeh.'

He was nearly fourteen and just about ready to start work anyway.

* * *

Phil was outside the turf depot as soon as he got in from school the next day, waiting on Paddy to come along. And, sure enough, he got himself a job.

When Phil came home that evening after finishing work with Paddy, he was telling Ma all about how he was able to lift the sacks of turf onto his back and carry them into the back yards for the old people.

'You'd want to see the money tha' he makes! A wad of notes in his pocket, he had.'

Ma sat there and listened, taking it all in and saying nothing.

The next morning we were all eating our breakfast when Ma turned around to us.

'I want yiz all to listen to wha' I have to say.'

Everyone looked at one another with panic on their faces, wondering if they were after getting caught for whatever they'd been up to the day before.

'I got a bit of a brainstorm last night after listenin' to yeh, Phil, about all the money yer man Paddy is makin'. I wonder, does he deliver the turf around here?'

'I'm way ahead of yeh, Ma. No he doesn't, I already asked him tha'. He goes all around Sundrive, Walkinstown, Drimnagh and Kimmage, he said. He never does around here; the houses are too close to the turf depot and it wouldn't pay him.'

'Right then, tha's all I wanted to hear.' She rubbed her two hands together. 'When yiz come home from school today I want a couple of yiz bigger ones to go knockin' on the doors. Start with Mrs Kennedy next door and every house after tha', right up to the top of the road, all the houses at the back of us and right down onto Cashel Road. Ask around and see if they would like the turf delivered for as little as a shillin'. No roarin' and shoutin' when yeh knock. See wha' they have to say – and one more thing, make sure yeh smile. Yeh're bound to get a few jobs outta tha'.'

The kids were all tryin' to get their spoke in.

'I want to get the turf, let me go.'

'Ma, how are we goin' to get the turf to the people?' Phil asked.

Ma put her hand on the big black pram. 'I'm goin' to give yiz the bus. I think it's seen its day as far as puttin' me babies into it goes. There's nothin' only tears and rips everywhere. But the frame is still very strong. It'll do the job.'

I was so happy when I heard Ma say that. *Could this mean she's finished having babies? I hope so.*

* * *

It didn't take long for us to build up a turf round. People were well pleased with the price and so was Ma with the extra money. Phil was great; as soon as they were old enough, he taught all of the kids how to lift the sacks and tip them into the back yards. When they would be standing there waiting to get paid, he would be twisting the ear of whoever was with him.

'Remember now wha' Ma said – show yer pearly whites and smile. Yeh never know, we might get an extra penny.'

As Ma always said, a smile never cost anything but could make you plenty in life. She was right; it always did.

That was the start of the turf round. It was handed down to each and every one of us and went on to make a few shillings for Ma.

15

The Rat and the Sword

Da stayed off the drink for a good few months this time. He got himself back into the garden. There were rows of cabbages, spuds, lettuce, onions and scallions. You name it, he planted it. The back garden was very big and he would spend hours out there in the summer. Ma even made herself a few bob, selling the vegetables to some of the neighbours.

Ma was standing at the back door with Jacinta in her arms, as proud as punch. It was great to see her smile and be happy for a change.

'Would yeh look out there at yer father, Kathleen. He's as happy as Larry, diggin' and weedin'. I swear tha' man has green fingers. Look at the size of them heads of cabbage; yeh could feed an army, they're tha' big.'

I thought to myself, *Wouldn't it be great if things stayed like this forever?*

But that wasn't to be.

Word got around the road: the best of veg at number fifty-one. When any of the neighbours knocked, they would get a right load of stuff for little or nothing.

'How much do I owe yeh, Lil?' they would ask.

'Just give me a few bob when yeh get yer allowance, and

don't forget now. God is good – isn't he keepin' tha' man of mine busy and off the drink.'

'It's a curse, Lil, a bloody curse!'

Peter next door and Mrs Kearney up the road never had to knock. Every week Ma would make up a parcel for each of them with everything that Da grew. Ma always told whichever one of us was bringing the bag into them not to take a penny, no matter what they said, because they were very good to us. Ma drilled it into each and every one of us. 'When yeh can, it's nice to be able to give and not always be takin'.'

* * *

In the summer Ma would have all of us up from early morning. She would never let any of us stay in the bed.

'It's not good for yeh, makes yer brain lazy. There'll be no wasters in my house, not if I have anythin' to do with it.'

Ma would call once, then twice, and if you were not halfway down the stairs the third time you would get a box in the back of the head or a good root up your arse.

'Phil, Kathleen, Carmel! Get yerselves washed first, you go first, Phil; as soon as yeh're finished, get back down here and start dishin' out the porridge with Clare. Kathleen and Carmel, start cleanin' out the bedrooms while yeh're waitin' to get washed. Open all the windows, pull back the blankets and check and see if anyone pissed in the bed last night. And when yeh're at it, give them blankets a good bang and shake – make sure there's no hoppers in them. Shake the DDT powder in – tha'll kill the little fuckers.'

There was a double bed in the back bedroom for Ma and Da, and a cot for the new baby, Patricia.

'Wha' are yeh doin' Carmel?'

'I'm checkin' the beds, like Ma said.'

'Carmel, don't be such a gobshite. Yeh hardly think Ma and Da piss on themselves, for Jaysus' sake! She was talkin' about the two beds in our room.'

The four girls slept in one double and the three boys slept in the other. I pulled the blankets off the bed and as usual it was always the girls' bed with the pissy stains. I took the sheet off, went down to the kitchen and slipped it in the washing machine.

Ma was feeding little Patricia. 'Wet again, Kathleen.'

'Just a bit, Ma.'

I went over to the table where Marion and Clare were sitting, stuffing their mouths with porridge.

'Right, which one of yiz is pissin' in the bed? I'm sick of wakin' up every morning with a smell on me. It's not me or Carmel so it has to be one of yiz.

Clare jumped up with embarrassment. 'How de yeh know it's not one of them?' She pointed at Phil, Noel and Thomas, who were laughing and whispering to one another. 'They could easily come over in the middle of the night and do a sneaky piss. Phil Doyle would make them do it for a laugh.'

Before I could say anything, the three boys started singing, 'Smelly knickers, Clare, piss in the bed Marion, pissy, pissy, pissy!'

Marion started crying. Clare made a run at them. Phil jumped out of her way. Thomas was only four, so she left him alone. She knew Ma would kill her if she punched him, so she dived on Noel. She was a wild little bitch and afraid of nobody.

'Kathleen, wha's goin' on? The noise of yiz!'

'Ma, they're only messin'.'

'Well, let them get out the back yard and do their messin'; I'm tryin' to get the child asleep.'

Noel shouted, 'Get her off me, Kathleen, she's a head-banger.'

'Clare, will yeh stop, for God's sake.'

'They started it, Kathleen.'

'I don't care who started it. It's bad enough I have to drag Ma off Da when she's all roused up without me havin' to do it with yiz as well. Now stop it!'

Carmel just sauntered out to the yard, not giving too shites who was killing who. Phil was sitting on the kitchen sink, turning blue he was laughing that much, and Thomas was dancing on the table, cheering.

'Clare won, Clare won.'

Noel stretched out and gave Thomas a right kick in the leg.

'Shut the fuck, yeh little turncoat.'

'Right! Out the back yard, all of yiz, before Ma comes in.'

Marion was still sitting by herself, crying. 'It's me, Kathleen, wettin' in me knickers. It just happens, I don't know I'm doin' it. I'm sorry – don't tell Ma.'

'Marion, it's okay, Ma won't fight with yeh. She'll get yeh checked and make sure yeh're all right.'

Clare came over. 'Don't cry, Marion.'

'I told her it was me wettin' the bed.'

'De yeh want me to batter Noel again? I will, I'll kill him for yeh.'

Marion just laughed, she was an oul' softy. Clare always looked after her; they were great pals. 'You two go in and clean the kitchen, I'll talk to Ma.'

Tha's them sorted for a while, anyway, I thought.

* * *

Every morning Da pulled up outside our house in the bin truck, ten o'clock on the dot, for a cup of tea with the other men. There was Ronnie the driver, Jembo, Blinkie and Mickey. They'd all worked together for years and were the best of friends.

During the summer holidays, us kids loved to see them stopping for the cup of tea. They would have a right load of sandwiches with them. I think they used to get their wives to put an extra bit in just for us. The minute they sat down we'd all stand around the table looking into their faces to see what we could get from them.

'You lot get yerselves out the back yard and play! Yeh're makin' a show of me,' Ma shouted.

Ronnie laughed, 'Not at all, Lil, sure I think tha' woman of mine thinks I'm eatin' for half the Corporation.'

Blinkie and Mickey chimed in with the same response: 'Mine too, Lil.'

'Lil, it will only be thrown out. And anyway, sure don't yeh make us our tea every mornin'? We all live too far to go home for a break.'

'Ah, here now, yeh can't be throwin' out good food like tha', and I couldn't let yeh sit out in tha' smelly bin truck now, could I, Mickey?'

Ma was a very proud woman and tried to hide how bad things really were at times, which was most of the time for her. As soon as Da and the men would leave to go back to work, Ma would call us in.

'Sit down at the table, the lot of yeh, and we'll see wha' we have here.'

The sandwiches would be cut to a finger size; Ma made sure every one of us got a taste. Sometimes if we were lucky we would get two or three each. There could be a bit of egg in one, cheese in another, but the ones we all loved the best were the sausage and rasher sandwiches; your mouth would be watering and you'd wish you had more.

* * *

One day, it was only nine o'clock when the bin truck pulled up.

I was sitting on the front steps, with Patricia in my arms, trying to get her asleep.

'Kathleen, is tha' yer father I hear out there?'

'Yeah, Ma, they're early today.'

Ma came out to see what was going on.

'Holy Jaysus, wha's after happenin' to yeh, Phil?'

Da was limping up the garden path; he had only one boot on and one of the legs of his trousers was ripped right up to his waist.

'Lil, yeh'd never believe wha's after happenin' to me. I'm lucky to be standin' here alive. Isn't tha' righ', Blinkie?'

'He's not tellin' a word of a lie, Lil, I was nearly a goner meself.'

'Hold on a minute until I put the teapot on.'

'Are yeh listenin', Lil? Wha' are yeh doin'?'

'I'm lookin' for me Woodbines, Phil, will yeh hold on. Righ', I have them – go on now, tell me wha' happened.'

'We went down to the flats our usual time, eight o'clock. I was pullin' out one of the large bins from the chute. It was full to the brim, overflowin' with rubbish, so it was, when I felt somethin' runnin' up me leg. I let out such a scream then, I couldn't talk. I just stood there with me mouth open, holdin' the top of me trousers, pointin' down between me legs.'

'Ronnie roared over, "Jaysus, Phil, wha's wrong with yeh? Yeh're gone an awful bad colour – are yeh alrigh'?"'

'"It's . . . it's . . . it's a fuckin' rat! It's between me legs. Get it out, get the fuckin' thing out!" I was roarin' all over the place.'

'Phil, yeh never said "fuck" – you don't curse! I don't believe yeh,' Ma said.

'Believe him, Lil, the whole of the flats heard him screamin'.'

'Such a day I'm after havin', Lil.'

'Did it bite yeh?'

'How the hell do I know if it bit me or not? Wasn't I bangin' and punchin' down there tha' hard, I don't know whether the rat or meself done the most damage.'

'Well, yeh better keep yerself to yerself, Phil Doyle, and not be comin' near me until the doctor has a look at yeh.'

Ma was laughing and giving the men a wink.

'Will yeh watch wha' yeh're sayin' in front of the men, for God's sake, Lil.'

'Don't be so fuckin' serious, Phil, will yeh!' She walked into the kitchen to make the tea for the men. 'I'm afraid yeh'll have to settle for yer tea in jam jars today. There's not a cup left in the house with them kids.'

'We don't mind, Lil, a cup of tea out of a jam jar is the tastiest yeh'll get,' Jembo answered.

'Lil, are yeh goin' to stay quiet and let me finish?'

'Go on, go on, Phil, I'm listenin'.'

'Ronnie put me lyin' down on me back while Mickey pulled me boot off. He had to slit the leg of me trousers with his penknife. He grabbed the rat by the throat and choked it to death there and then, right in front of me.'

Ma screamed with fright. 'For fuck's sake, Mickey, yeh didn't! How could yeh do tha'?'

'I did, Lil, I did. There's nothin' to it. I live along the canal and the rats come up to the bins all the time. Mind you now, yeh have to be very fast – grab and twist the little fuckers' necks or yeh'd never catch them.'

'Mickey, will yeh stop, for Jaysus' sake, yeh're makin' me sick.' She lit another Woodbine.

'I swear, Lil, it was the size of a cat. Jembo, back me up, tell 'er.'

'Phil's not tellin' a word of a lie.'

'There's more, Lil,' Da went on, getting more worked up by the minute. 'I hadn't even got the colour back in me face when this fella hangs out over the top balcony of the flats and starts threatenin' us. "Will yeh ever keep quiet down there," says he. "I'm tryin' to get some sleep up here! Now, fuck off or I'll come down and sort yiz all out."

'"Who the hell de yeh think yeh're talkin' to?" Ronnie roars up at him. "Yeh'll be sortin' nobody out – an' serve yeh better to get up off yer arse and get yerself a job, yeh lazy heap o' shite."'

Ronnie was well over six foot tall and as broad as an ox; he had a big porter belly. Ma was forever slagging him. 'I don't know who looks like they're havin' the babies around here, Ronnie, you or me.' Ma was the only one who could get away with sayin' things like that to him.

Da went on. 'I was bendin' down, Lil, just about to put me boot back on, when yer man from the top flat comes chargin' down at us with a samurai sword. "I'll show yiz who's a heap of shite," he roared as he swung the sword all over the place. "Talk to me like tha', will yiz, with the wife and kids listenin'? I'll fuckin' kill one of yiz first." He was lashin' the sword against the walls, and takin' lumps out of the bin truck at the one time. There was no talkin' to him, Lil. He was full of the whiskey – yeh could smell it a mile away.'

Ronnie took up the story. 'I meself like a sup now and again, but yeh never saw the likes of it, Lil. His eyes were roarin' red in his head. He was out for blue murder, so he was. I'm afraid of no man, I'd take the best of them on. I think yeh know tha' yerself, Lil.'

'I do, Ronnie, no better man than yerself.'

'But a man with a sword, now tha's a different kettle of fish altogether. We were runnin' all around the flats, up and down the stairs, tryin' to get away from him. He was out of control. I thought he was goin' to take Blinkie's head off. He missed him by an inch – am I right there, men?'

'Yeh are, Ronnie, not a word of a lie.'

'Only Mickey jumped over the railin's, run and got the police, God only knows wha' would have happened,' said Da. 'It took us all our strength to hold him down until he was taken away in the police wagon. Sure, look at me, I hadn't even got time to get me other boot back on, Lil.'

'It sounds like yiz were lucky to get out in one piece, Phil.'

'I'm tellin' yeh, it was touch and go there for a while. I tell yeh one thing for nothin', Lil, yeh won't be seein' me in them flats again, not unless tha' maniac is sorted out. I'll give the job up first, and we'll be sayin' the same,' said Ronnie. 'The funny thing about all this, Lil, when he sobers up tomorrow he won't remember a thing and one of us could have been lyin' in the city morgue, dead as a dodo.'

'I know somebody like tha', Ronnie.' Ma looked straight over at Da. 'Remembers only wha' he wants to, when it suits him. Isn't tha' right, Phil Doyle?'

'For God's sake, Lil, I've had a bad enough day without yeh rubbin' and clippin' at me and in front of the men.'

'Hurry up and get changed, Phil,' Ronnie said, giving Da the eye. 'Yeh'll have to get yerself looked over by the doctor, and we've to get the bin truck back to the yard to be checked and tell the foreman wha' happened. Thanks for the tea, Lil.'

After they'd left, Ma sighed. 'Isn't tha' terrible, Kathleen?'

'Wha's tha', Ma?'

'The men didn't have time to even open their sandwiches, and all over tha' gobshite in the flats carryin' on like a madman.'

'They'll be able to have them later on, Ma.'

'Tha's not wha' I mean, Kathleen. I was dependin' on them few bits they leave me every day to make some lunch later for yiz. There's hardly anythin' to eat. Ah well, nothin' I can do about it now.'

* * *

Da came home early that day.

'Wha's wrong now, Phil Doyle, was there trouble over this mornin'? Is yer job safe?'

'Will yeh stop worryin' all the time, Lil. I'm home because the doctor said so. He gave me a shot in the arse.'

'Why's tha', Phil?'

'Tha' bastard of a rat gave me a nick down there. I was screamin' and bangin' meself tha' much I didn't feel it. He gave me a sick note for a few days; he said I'll be rightly swollen by tomorrow.'

'Phil, wha' de yeh mean "down there"? Is it yer leg or wha'?'

'Yeh know wha' I mean, Lil.' He rolled his eyes in the air, getting himself more worked up by the minute.

'Oh, I see, yeh mean yer balls, Phil, is tha' wha' yeh're tryin' to say?'

'Jaysus, Lil, will yeh watch yer mouth in front of the kids? It's a bar of carbolic soap yeh need to clean out tha' mouth of yours.'

'Are yeh goin' to tell me or wha', Phil? Yeh're turnin' yer eyes crossways in yer head. I don't know wha' yeh mean.'

'Right then, it seems yeh're goin' to keep it up until I tell yeh. Yes, yes, yes, I'll say it – balls, balls, balls – me balls! Is tha' enough for yeh, Lil? Are yeh happy now tha' I said it. I can't get a bit of privacy around here with yeh. I'm goin' upstairs.' He slammed the door behind him.

Ma roared up the stairs after him. 'Yeh're a cranky fuck, Phil Doyle, tha's wha' yeh are. I was only askin' wha' happened.'

'Well, now yeh know, Lil. Are yeh happy? Yeh'd bring out the worst in anybody, so yeh would.'

I was in shock when I heard Da roaring and cursing, as you would never hear him speak like that or be rude to anybody.

'Ma, Da's real annoyed, I never saw him like tha' before.'

'Never mind yer father, Kathleen, he can be a bloody crank at times. Gather the kids up and put them sittin' down at the table. A half an egg and a slice of bread will have to do; tha's all I have. We missed out on our sandwiches today.' She mumbled to herself as she cooked the eggs.

'Are yeh talkin' to yerself again, Ma?'

'Well then, I'll say it out loud and clear for yeh. There's just one thing I have to say about the goin's-on of the day, Kathleen.'

'And wha's tha', Ma?'

'Fuck yer man with tha' sword, and fuck tha' rat.'

* * *

Da was out of work for the next two weeks because 'down below' was swollen so bad and he had himself in a terrible mood with Ma because she had made him say 'balls' in front of us kids. He kept himself busy out the back garden, digging, weeding, and planting a few seeds, keeping out of Ma's way. And the pubs, for that matter. For a little while anyway. Da thought he would never get himself back to work quickly enough, away from Ma's watchful eye, so he could get back to his old ways again.

I loved my Da so much, but I would get so angry with him at times, but only ever in my thoughts. *Does he care about us?* I would wonder. *If I can see what is happening, why can he not?* I should have said something. Why didn't I speak out and try to make him see sense? But they weren't the ways back then. Children were seen and not heard: that's what we were told. Speak only when you're spoken to, and never answer back.

16

Fish and Chips

'Kathleen, where are yeh?'

'I'm upstairs, Ma.'

'Come down here, I want yeh to do somethin' for me. I was talkin' to one of the Caffola sisters down there in the chip shop earlier on. I want yeh to go down around three o'clock, take one or two of the kids with yeh. She was tellin' me tha' she does have bits of broken fish left over from the night before and, if I'd like, she'd keep them for me. Now, when yeh go into the shop, tell 'er Lil sent yeh and don't forget to use yer manners. Oh, and another thing – make sure to give her a big smile. Tha' way she might throw in a few chips. If she does, don't touch even one, or I'll take the hand off yeh, de yeh hear me now, Kathleen? Tha'll help me make a bit of dinner for tonight with a few mash potatoes.'

I arrived on the dot of three with Carmel and Clare, calling across the tall counter: 'Hello Missus, me Ma Lil sent us for the bits of fish and a few chips.'

Carmel nudged me. 'Kathleen, yeh were only supposed to ask for fish.'

'Shut up, will yeh, or she'll hear yeh! Tha's wha' Ma meant

when she told us to smile. Have yeh not got any cop-on at all, Carmel?'

The three of us stood there with smiles on our faces the length of the shop, hoping that she would put more than a few chips in the bag, so we could nick one or two on the way home and, to our surprise, she did. On top of all that, she handed each of us a chip bag full to the top with all the bits of crisps that she had taken from the bottom of the pan. We were over the moon.

'Now, girls, tell your mother to send you down every day to me and I'll keep any bits I have for her.'

There was no end to the smiles on our faces as we left the shop and Ma was well pleased with the news.

We went down to the chip shop over the following weeks and were standing outside one day waiting for the queue to empty, when this woman on her way out of the shop put a bag of chips into one of my hands and a shilling in the other. I stood there and looked at her, not knowing what to say or do.

'Share them with the other two little ones and bring that money home to your mother.' And off she went about her business with not another word spoken, leaving me standing there with my mouth open, not understanding what it was all about.

'Kathleen, why did tha' woman give yeh money and chips?' Clare and Carmel asked.

'How do I know? I don't know everythin', do I! We'll ask when we go home. Now, come on, we'll go in and get the bits of fish for Ma.'

The three of us devoured the bag of chips on the way home, only telling Ma about the shilling.

'Now why did tha' woman give yiz this shillin'? Wha' were yiz doin' when she handed it to yeh, Kathleen?'

'Nothin', Ma, we were just standin' there, I swear.'

She stood back and looked at the three of us. Then out of the blue she burst out crying.

'I'm sorry, Ma. I thought yeh'd be glad. I promise I won't take money off anyone again.'

'It's not tha' Kathleen, I'm only glad of the shillin'. Tha'll get me a loaf of bread and a drop of milk. I'm cryin' over the fact tha' yiz look so poor. Is it any wonder the woman gave yeh money? Look at the three of yiz – yer dresses are fallin' apart, and the shoes on yer feet are barely holdin' together. Pity tha's wha' it was, pity.' She broke down crying again.

The three of us stood there looking at one another, not knowing what to do or say.

'This is not the life I wanted for any o' yiz, but it's the best I can do for now.'

None of us cared or took much notice of what state our clothes or shoes were in. The only thing that would have been on my mind from day to day was whether we were going to get any dinner or would it be bread and dripping again.

Ma finally calmed herself down and got on with checking out what was in the bag, hoping there would be enough to go around all of us. It wouldn't matter how little you got; she always made sure everybody got a taste.

* * *

I was dying for Phil to come home so that I could tell him what had happened and to see what he thought. He stood there listening to me, taking it all in.

'Well, wha' de yeh think, Phil?'

'We could be on to a good thing here, Kathleen.'

'How can it be a good thing? Ma was real upset and all.'

'Yeh're an awful gobshite at times, de yeh know tha'? Can yeh not see further than yer nose? We could make ourselves a few shillin's out of this.'

'But how, Phil, wha' de yeh mean?'

'I'll go down with yiz the next time. If yer wan thought yiz looked bad, wait 'til she sees me. Would yeh have a look at the state of me shoes? And with not an elbow left in me jumper, sure they'll be throwin' the money at me.'

I looked down at Phil's feet and, right enough, his stockings were sticking out from the toes of his shoes and his jumper was in a bad way.

Sure enough, Phil was standing outside the chip shop the following day when I arrived with Clare.

'Right then, Kathleen, show me wha' yiz were doin' just before tha' wan gave yeh the money.'

'We were doin' nothin', only standin' like the way we are now. I told yeh all this last night, so wha' are yeh shitin' out of yeh for?'

'Wha' I'm tryin' to find out off yeh is, were yiz jumpin' around laughin' and playin', or were yiz standin' there all serious and miserable.'

'We were talkin', tha's all, I keep tellin' yeh.'

'Good, tha's wha' I wanted to hear. Tha' means yeh were a bit serious. Right — are yeh listenin' to me, Kathleen? — if yeh see anybody goin' to pass by us, put a real sad face on, tha' way they might pity us and give us a few pennies, or maybe a shillin' or two.'

'Phil, if we do get money, how are we goin' to give it to Ma? We can't say somebody gave it to us; she'd smell a rat, or get upset and start cryin' again.'

'Kathleen, don't yeh know I always have a back-up plan? I'll tell her the turf round is doin' well and she'll be none the wiser. And I have another little scheme goin' around in me head if this doesn't work.'

I was soon to learn Phil's other little scheme. Myself and Phil, with a couple of the little ones, would stand at the bus stop, lying through our teeth, telling people as they got off the bus that we lived in Walkinstown, which was a good distance from Crumlin, too far for the small ones to walk, and that we'd lost our bus fare. That got us loads of pity and plenty of pennies in our pockets. Outside the chip shop didn't work too well, so it was the bus stop every time, until one day we were standing there with our sad faces on us when Mrs Kearney tipped me on the shoulder. I nearly wet my knickers with the fright. Phil scarpered and left me to face her on my own.

'Kathleen Doyle, before you start telling me a string of lies, I have been standing over by the chemist for the past ten minutes, watching you and Phil. Do you realise what you are doing? You are begging, that's what you are doing – begging!'

'No, we're not, Mrs Kearney. The people are real nice; they were just givin' us a few pennies.' I hoped I could pull the wool over her eyes, but she wasn't having any of it.

'Well then, Kathleen, you won't mind me telling your mother how kind all these people have been to you.'

'No, no, Mrs Kearney, please don't! We're tryin' to make some money for Ma. Things are really bad; some days there's not enough money to buy any messages. Ma thinks we're makin' extra money on the turf round. Please don't tell her, she'll get all upset and cry, then she'll kill us.'

Her voice softened. 'Do you not think I know that? I have no intentions of telling on you. Your mother is a very proud woman and if she got the slightest inkling of this it would kill her, never mind all of you. Now, Kathleen, I want you to promise me that none of you will ever do this again.'

'I swear we won't.' I made the sign of the cross, knowing Mrs Kearney was really religious, hoping that she'd believe me even more.

'Right then, Kathleen, we'll leave it at that; but I will still be keeping an eye on you, so pass that message on to young Phil.'

I was so glad it was Mrs Kearney who tipped me on the shoulder that day and not Ma. We still went down to the chip shop for the bits of fish, but we didn't hang around there too long, and the only time after that day we went near a bus stop was to get on a bus.

* * *

Phil wasn't long coming up with another of his little schemes.

'Kathleen, come 'ere, I want to talk to yeh.'

'Fuck off, Phil; wha'ever it is, I'm sayin' no. I don't care, yeh do nothin' only get me into trouble. Yeh left me standin' on me own with Mrs Kearney the other day at the bus stop, scampered off, so yeh did. She gave me a right mouthful, yeh know wha' she's like; there was no end to the threats I got from 'er.'

'Would yeh give it over, Kathleen, yeh're well able to handle her and anyone else around the road. Anyway, never mind all tha' shite, tha's over and done with. It's now we have to worry about. Did yeh see the few scrappin's tha' Ma was tryin' to make a dinner from? There's not enough food to go around. Wha' she has will have to do the little ones. Come on with me, Kathleen, we'll have to do somethin'. Get yer coat and while yeh're in the house grab the net bag Ma gets the messages in. Tell 'er yeh're comin' with me to deliver a few sacks of turf; tha' way she won't smell a rat.'

We weren't long dropping the turf off to a couple of houses on Cashel Road, making ourselves a shilling or two. Phil left the big pram at the side of one of his customers' houses, saying he would pick it up on the way back. Off we headed down towards the Old County Road shops, with Phil filling me in on his plan as he tied the net bag on the belt around his trousers, which was well covered up with his jacket.

'Kathleen, before we go into the shop, take this shillin'. Now, wha' I want yeh to do is pick somethin' out to buy, then change yer mind a few times. Tha'll get up yer wan's back tha's servin' yeh and have her all annoyed and worked up. Now when yeh're doin' tha', first chance I get, I'll grab anythin' I can tha' we can eat. I'll give yeh the eye and the nod tha' I'm finished, but wha'ever yeh do, don't leave the shop without buyin' somethin'. Tha' way we won't look too sussie. And whatever yeh do, get somethin' we can eat – don't go spendin' the shillin' on soap or powder. Yeh know wha' a cleanin' freak yeh've turned into, always moppin' up around yeh.'

'Oh, I don't know, Phil, robbin' out of the shops! No, I'm too afraid, I can't do it. Anyway, it's a sin and I'd never be able to tell the priest I was out robbin'.'

'For Jaysus' sake, just say an extra few Hail Marys tonight when yeh're sayin' yer prayers! Now, will yeh give it over, I need yeh to keep nicks for me.'

I still wasn't moving.

'Right then, don't help me. I'll do it on me own, but if I get caught it'll be all yer fault. Anyway, it's Ma yeh should be thinkin' about, not yer bloody sins.'

'Okay, okay, I'll do it. But yeh have to promise me, Phil, yeh'll say nothin' to nobody, ever.'

'I don't think this is somethin' I'll be goin' around braggin' about. Now, will yeh shut the fuck up, Kathleen, and get into the shop.'

'There's just one more thing, Phil. If we're goin' to be robbin', will yeh try and get a bit of real butter? It's so long since we had some.'

'Tha's more like it, Kathleen.'

He gave me a sly grin, pushing me into the shop ahead of him. I got the poor woman behind the counter so confused she was nearly tearing her hair out by the time I was finished, giving Phil enough time to get as much as he could into the net bag.

Ma couldn't believe her eyes when we handed her the bag of messages. Of course, the first thing she did was to ask where the money came from. As always, Phil had all the answers, telling Ma that he collected bits of scrap and copper off the people while he was doing the turf round and selling it on to Wally, a scrap merchant down the road. Ma looked down at the bag checking out all that we had 'bought'.

'Yeh must have had a right load of scrap to be able to buy all of this.'

As she looked at the two of us, I kept my head down, trying not to look her straight in the eye. The rest of the shite that came out of Phil's mouth was a string of lies – and Ma knew it. He came up with one of his classic stories as usual.

'Sure, haven't I been savin' it up for the past few weeks? How else would I be able to get the few messages for yeh? I wanted to surprise yeh, Ma.' He smiled, showing off his pearly whites.

'Hmm . . . I see then . . . and you were there when he was sellin' the scrap, Kathleen?'

'I was, Ma.' I was still too afraid to look at her.

'Tha's okay, then. The blessin's of God on the pair of yiz; the Holy Mother herself is lookin' after me again.'

And that's all that was said on the matter.

* * *

As kids, each and every one of us would always be scheming, coming up with one idea after another. If we weren't out robbing from the shops, living next door to the turf depot came in very handy. We'd be up there after it was closed, filling the sacks up and selling it on cheap the next day; or Phil would be out with me or one of the other kids as soon as it got dark, a screwdriver in his pocket, unhinging any wooden side gates he could get his hand on. Himself and Noel would chop them up, making up bundles of sticks, selling them on the following day with the turf. If the truth be known, some of the neighbours were actually buying back their own side doors.

I would say an extra few Hail Marys every night, trying to convince myself it was okay to do what we were doing. Back then, we weren't thinking about doing harm or wrong. In our minds, we were helping our Ma, and that's all that mattered to us. She never would have survived otherwise.

That's the way things went, on and off, over the next two years, until Phil went out and got himself a proper job, delivering messages for the local shops, passing the turf round on to Noel, teaching him all the tricks he had learned. He would drill it into his head how important the big smile was. That's when we decided to give up the robbing.

'Kathleen, me face will be too well known around here now. We best stop while we're ahead.'

'Oh, thank God! I'm only too happy to stop.'

For once I didn't argue with Phil.

* * *

Before I knew it, I was thirteen years old and Ma was getting ready to have her tenth baby – my little sister Mary. Although I didn't realise it at the time, it was to cause so much sorrow and heartache for Ma.

Granny Kitty and Fanny the Donkey

Granny Kitty and Granda John

Da and Ma on a rare day out in town

Ma and Da having a good day

Carmel, Phil and Kathleen

Da and Carmel

The little ones, Patricia and Jacinta

Dad, Noel and Phil with Jacinta and Patricia

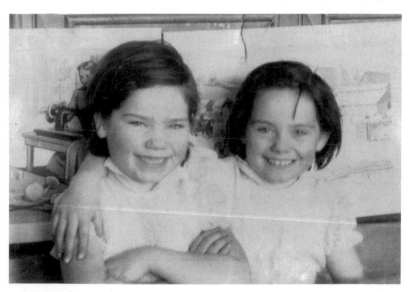

Marion and Clare, the best of buddies

Clare – the dog lover of the family

Phil Doyle, All-Ireland
Middle-Weight Champion

Patricia, Clare and Jacinta

Alan and Kathleen (sweet sixteen)

Thomas and Speedy the dog

Kathleen and Alan – at the Hop

Alan and Kathleen at their first dinner-dance

Kathleen and Alan on a date

Alan and Kathleen on their Wedding Day

Ma, Patricia and baby Paul

Mano and Paul, last of the babies

Da and Ma with Mano and Paul

17

Baby Mary

At this stage I definitely knew that babies were not delivered in Santy's bag, or found in a head of cabbage, or that the stork dropped one in on his way to Africa. I was as usual out of school, cleaning and looking after the kids.

'Kathleen, will yeh go upstairs and get the sheets off the beds, and any other bits lyin' around, and bring them down to me. I have to try and keep the washin' down before I go away for a few days.'

I knew what she meant: into the hospital. The rest of the kids had been told that Ma would be going to the Isle of Man to do a bit of shopping with the other women on the road, for the Christmas clothes.

The local nurse had just been in to see Ma on one of her routine visits. She was one large woman, with her arms crossed under her diddies, pushing them nearly up into her mouth. As for her arse, it was so big, I thought when she sat on the chair that the legs were going to fold in.

'Lil, you'll have to have this child in hospital; you're not getting any younger.'

Ma had had the first seven of us at home and the rest in hospital. She wanted to have this baby at home, but the nurse wasn't having any of it.

'There are too many children in this house anyway. You can't be jumping up a few hours after the birth – and knowing you, Lil, that's what you will be doing. Your husband is well able to make babies, so he should be well able to mind them for a few days.'

Ma would usually have put up a fight and not let anybody tell her what to do. But she looked so drained and tired, she just sat there and said nothing. I think she was glad to be getting a bit of a break for a few days away from all the mayhem and worry that surrounded her.

After the nurse left, we were sorting out the washing. Ma was telling me all the things I was to do while she was away. She had this little electric washing machine which had a mangle attached; it was great for squeezing the heavy water out of the clothes.

'Kathleen, yeh know yer Da hates doin' the washin'. He'll do anythin' else, but don't ask him to wash. Now, where's tha' Carmel wan? She should be in from school by now.'

'She's out the back yard, Ma.'

'Tell her to peel the spuds for the dinner.'

Carmel? Tha's a joke, I thought to myself. *Ten years of age and all she wants to do is play with her dolls. She lives in her own little world.*

'And when yeh're finished there, Kathleen, go up the road and see if Clare is on her way home. Check with one of the other kids and see if she was in school today. Yeh know her, she's a little fuck on the mitch, any chance she gets. Yeh'll have to keep an eye on her for me as well.'

'Right, okay, Ma.'

I was glad to get out of the house for a while, even if it was only to look for Clare. I would get so fed up; there was always something for me to do or someone for me to mind.

I laughed to myself while I walked up the road; as if any of the kids would tell on Clare! She'd kick the living daylights out of them.

There she was, running down the road, a skinny little

156

thing and black as the ace of spades, covered in muck.

Oh my God! Look at the dirt of her. She's making a holy show of us. 'Clare Doyle! Look at the cut of yeh. Have yeh been up in tha' dump again? Ma will fuckin' kill yeh. She told yeh if yeh went on the mitch again wha' she'd do to yeh. It's bad enough Speckie the Inspector knockin' on the door for me. If he finds out yeh're not in school, he'll fuck the two of us in tha' home for them delinquent young wans.'

Clare was like a gypsy, always rooting out old bits of things, fixing them and trying to sell them on to the other kids on the road.

She tried to suck up to me now. 'Look wha' I found, Kathleen.'

I gave it a quick look. 'Wha' is it, Clare?'

'It's a brooch, Kathleen. Wha' de ye think?'

'Tha's no good, Clare; the pin is gone off the back.'

'Sure, I'll get a small safety pin and put it through the holes. Teresa Kearney said she'd give me three pence for it. I'll give yeh half, if yeh don't tell Ma . . . ah, Kathleen, don't tell, she'll kill me. One more chance, please?'

'I swear this is me last time, Clare. I'm not coverin' up for yeh any more.'

'Ah, thanks, Kathleen.'

'Right then, get yer arse down tha' road. When yeh get to the house, slip in the side gate and, quick as yeh can, wash tha' dirt off yeh. I'll tell Ma one of the young wans up the road is helpin' yeh with a few sums. Now whether she believes me or not is another thing, but I'll try anyway.'

Ma asked as soon as I walked in the door. 'Kathleen did yeh find Clare?'

'Yeah, Ma. She'll be here in a minute; she's doin' a bit of homework with one of her friends.'

'Jaysus, tha' has to be a first, Clare doin' homework without bein' made to. Are yeh sure, Kathleen?' She gave a bit of a stern look.

'I am, Ma, I am.'

* * *

Noel and Marion were running around the kitchen playing chasing. Jacinta was out the back yard making muck pies with Thomas. Patricia was asleep on the chair and Phil was delivering the messages for the shops down the road.

'Kathleen, help me hang the sheets on the line. I'm not able to stretch.'

We were just about finished with the washing when Noel roared out with panic. 'Ma, Ma, quick, there's fire comin' outta the wall.'

'Holy Jaysus, let me in.' Ma pushed past me, nearly knocking me to the ground.

The kids were running around like lunatics, screaming, 'The house is on fire, the house is on fire! Wha' will we do, Ma?'

Ma ran over to the washing machine. I could see the plug sparking and smoke coming from the socket. Ma wrapped a small cloth around her hand, not realising it was wet, and pulled the plug out. She got a terrible shock and fell to the ground.

All the kids just stood there. I was hysterical. I ran up the road to Mrs Kearney. I tried to keep myself calm but I couldn't.

'Quick, quick, Mrs Kearney! Ma needs yeh. She's on the floor, she's bad, she's really bad.'

When we walked back into the kitchen, I got the fright of my life. Ma was as white as snow and out cold. I thought she was dead. I didn't know what to do. The kids were all crying. Noel and Marion kept saying, 'Ma is dead, Ma is dead, Kathleen, she's dead!'

Mrs Kearney bent down and felt Ma's wrist. 'Lil, Lil!' she called out as she stroked her face.

Ma started to move and slowly came around.

'Noel, quick, go upstairs and get me a pillow for your mother, and bring down a blanket as well. Kathleen, try and settle down the children. They have themselves in an awful state.'

I got them all to sit on the floor and be quiet. It all happened so fast I didn't know what to be doing.

With all the commotion going on, a few neighbours had gathered outside. One of the women got the ambulance; somebody else sent for the ESB. Ma was taken straight to the hospital. Word was sent down to the yard where Da worked to come home urgently. Mrs Kearney stayed with us until Da came home.

In the meantime the men from the electricity board had arrived and they told Da, 'The wires were live; your wife is lucky to be alive.' I'll never forget the look on his face when they said that to him. He turned green with fright and went straight to the hospital, not knowing what to expect when he got there.

Mrs Kearney turned to me. 'Kathleen, I'll have to go home to make Jack's dinner, he'll be in soon. Will you be all right? I'll check with you later, to make sure you are all okay and to talk to your father to see how Lil is.'

'Thanks, Mrs Kearney, we'll be fine. I'll take care of things here.'

Phil came in and helped me with the kids. Jacinta was pulling at the end of my dress. 'I'm hungry, Kathleen.' That started them all off.

'Carmel, butter some bread. Tha'll keep them quiet for a while. The spuds are peeled, so we'll fry a few sausages. Clare, go down to the corner shop with Noel, ask Mrs Green will she give us a few messages on the bill. Tell her Ma is sick. She'll pay her back next week, when Da gets paid.'

If I hadn't sounded like Ma before, I certainly did now.

When they'd all finished eating, we got the younger kids washed and up to bed while the rest of us waited on Da to come home from the hospital. I was sitting there giving Patricia a bottle of tea, when he walked in. I knew something was wrong. His eyes were all red and swollen. He'd been crying.

'Where's Ma? Where's Ma? Is she with yeh?' the kids asked.

He sat down. I could see that his lip was trembling, as he tried not to cry. I thought my heart was going to burst.

'Yer mother is all right. She'll be home in a few days. She just got a bit of a fright.' He looked over at Phil and myself with sadness in his eyes and shook his head.

The kids were jumping up and down. 'Ma's okay, Ma's okay!'

'Will yeh have a cup of tea, Da?' I asked.

'Tha'll be grand, Kathleen.'

Phil jumped up. 'I'll get it. Yeh're lookin' after Patricia.'

When the rest of them fell asleep, Da told us what happened.

'Yer mother had a little baby girl, but the shock went through her and she died; her little heart gave in. The doctor said yer mother was a very strong woman; they don't know how she is still alive.'

I couldn't believe or understand the words that were coming out of Da's mouth. *How can this be? Ma's baby, my little sister, dead. Why did this happen? WHY?*

* * *

Da took a few days off work to help with the kids and go up to the hospital. The next day Phil and Carmel minded the kids. I went up with Da to see Ma.

We were only in the door when she told him, 'Phil, I'm goin' to call our little baby Mary. I want yeh to get the priest and make sure she gets the blessin' and when yeh're there ask if they'll let yeh see her. Yeh can tell me who see looks like.'

Back in those days, when your baby died, you weren't shown or allowed to hold her. It was wrong, but that was how it was.

'Jesus, Lil, please don't ask me to tha'. It'll kill me. I can't, please.'

'I swear, Phil Doyle, 'til the end of me days, if yeh don't do this for me, I'll never forgive yeh.'

Da wasn't very good at dealing with anything like this but he went along with Ma's wishes. The whole time Da was gone, Ma sat in the bed, crying her heart out, not saying a word. All I could do was hold her hand.

When Da came back up to the ward, he looked so distressed his lip was trembling as he spoke; he told us she was lovely.

'She has a head of black hair, just like you, Kathleen.' Ma got so upset when he said that and so did I. 'Lil, the sister said it would be cheaper to get her buried from the hospital, costing only a few shillings. She would be taken to the Holy Angels in Glasnevin.'

Mrs Kearney came down to the house the day before Ma came home. She told me to go upstairs and see if there were any new clothes put by for the baby. I found a little brown parcel in the back of the press. In it were two vests, two cardigans, three little blankets and a half-dozen nappies. I cried as I came down the stairs with the parcel.

'Give that to me, Kathleen. It's better not to have them in the house; your mother will only break her heart every time she looks at them. And not a word about the baby when she comes home. You're a big girl now, Kathleen, you understand?'

I wanted to scream out loud: 'No, Mrs Kearney, I don't understand. All this is grown-up stuff. I don't want to know. Why can I not talk about my little sister?' But no, as usual I just kept my thoughts to myself and said nothing. I worried so much that it was all my fault, because I was always giving out about minding babies.

Ma was home the following day. She was so quiet for such a long time. All the kids thought it was great, her not chasing them around or getting a dig for one thing or another, but I knew the truth. I wanted so much to ask her, 'Are yeh all right, Ma? They should have let yeh see little Mary.' I wanted so much to speak out, to say how I was feeling, but I never did.

That wasn't the way back then.

Nobody spoke about little Mary ever again.

* * *

The next year seemed to take for ever to go by. Ma slowly started to come around and get back to her old self. I wasn't sure if that was a good thing; then again, it was better than looking at her being so sad all the time.

18

Going to the Hop

The day finally came when I officially left school and was off Speckie the School Inspector's list. At least now I would be able to go down to the shops and not have to look over my shoulder for Speckie, who used to come up behind me on his bike, stop and tell me I was going to be sent away to a home for delinquent girls.

He was one tall man. He must have been about six foot three and not a bit of flesh on him. I don't know how he used to ride that bike with those long legs. I think he must have been deaf as well, because he was always screaming into my face. 'Speak up girl,' he would roar. I would be shitting myself, telling him all the lies under the sun as to why I wasn't in school.

I suppose he wasn't all that bad, especially when I think back on all the lies Ma used to tell him too. According to her, I had every sickness going. He probably took one look at Ma and her clatter of kids and felt sorry for her. Or maybe giving out just made him feel better.

I was only fourteen and dying to get out into the big world. After all the years being stuck in the house, minding kids, I was raring to go.

'Ma, I want to go out today and get meself a job.'

'Tha's right, Kathleen. Yeh're a big girl now. It's time yeh started makin' a few shillin's for me and start earnin' yer keep.'

Jaysus, Ma, I thought, *haven't I always been a big girl as far back as I can remember? And I think I well earned my keep.*

'Well now, Kathleen, wha' would yeh like to work at?'

'I want to be a hairdresser, Ma.'

I was always messing about with the kids' hair, trying all sorts of hair-dos out on them and on myself. I was really good at it. But it wasn't to be.

'Jaysus, Kathleen, they don't get paid hardly any money. Yeh'd be better off gettin' yerself a job in one of the factories. Just go around and see wha' wages they offer yeh.'

I went around a few hairdressers. The most they were paying was ten shillings a week, so that was hairdressing out the window. The factories, on the other hand, were paying three pounds five shillings a week. Ma was delighted when I told her. But I wasn't.

'Tha's great money, Kathleen. I know yer brother Phil is workin', but yeh wouldn't see wha' he brings in, with him servin' his time at the paintin'. Tha' takes seven years. Sure he'll nearly be a married man himself by the time he gets a decent wage. So, you'll have to go where the money is. I don't know how I'm goin' to keep up with everything. These kids are eatin' me outta house and home.' And that was that. I had no say in the matter, as usual.

* * *

My first job was in a sewing factory but I didn't last long at that because I was afraid of my life of the needle.

I ended up in a sweet factory in Tallaght called Urneys. When I brought my first wage packet home, Ma was well pleased, handing me back five shillings for myself.

'Now, Kathleen, outta tha' yeh have to pay yer bus fare.

And whatever else yeh have left, yeh have to put by and try to dress yerself because the rest has to go on food and bills.'

Talk about trying to perform a miracle! But that is exactly what I did. I saved every penny and if it took me six months to get myself a skirt or a jumper, I wouldn't touch a penny of it in the meantime.

* * *

I was on my way home from work one day when I heard a shout.

'Is tha' you, Kathleen Doyle?'

I looked across the other side of the road. It was Breda Murphy. She was as blind as a bat; you'd nearly have to be right on top of her before she could see you. She was much taller than me and had a waxy white face. Her hair was a coal-black fuzz-ball; you'd think somebody was after putting a plug up her arse and giving her an electric shock. If you saw her in the dark, you'd get the fright of your life.

I made my way over to her. 'Yes, Breda. It's me, Kathleen. Wha' de yeh want?'

'There's a hop on Sunday night up in the boys' school. Are yeh comin'?'

My ears cocked up when I heard that. 'I'd love to Breda, but I'll have to ask me Ma and Da.'

'Tell them I'll mind yeh and tha' the Brothers do be walkin' around and all, makin' sure nobody does be wearin' or anythin'.'

'Yeh mean kissin'?' I thought I was real grown-up saying that to her.

'Nobody says kissin' any more, Kathleen. Tha's real old fashioned. It's a wear, righ'?'

'Okay, Breda. I'll come up to yer house and let yeh know if I can go. See yeh.'

It was Friday night and I always had a few bags of broken chocolate for the kids. I used to buy them for five pennies in the factory. I needn't tell you, they would be sitting in the garden watching out for me to come up the road. You'd want to have heard the screams and shouts of them whenever they saw me coming!

'I knew tha' was you, Kathleen, as soon as I heard them kids roarin'. I says to young Phil, so I did, "here she is with the sweets",' Ma said as she shared out the chocolate. 'Yer Auntie Mary was here today, Kathleen. She left a bag of clothes. Have a look and see if there is anythin' there to fit yeh.'

Auntie Mary was very good to us. She was always bringing stuff down – food, clothes, shoes, bed sheets, you name it. Anything her family was finished with and didn't want, we got it.

Da also sometimes brought us home parcels of clothes. He worked all around Rathgar and Rathmines, lovely big houses, really posh areas. If you lived there you had money. All the ladies thought Da was a proper gentleman – and he was, only for the drink. He always wore a cap, a heavy tweed one in the winter and a light beige cotton one in the summer. He knew everyone from working the streets; he'd pass nobody by without tipping the peak of his cap and wishing them all a good morning.

One day one of the ladies whispered to Da, so as not to let any of the other neighbours hear her, 'Philip, could I have a word with you if you don't mind?' He always got his full title off them, and he loved that. 'Would you be very offended if I left a parcel of clothes out now and then for you? I know you have lots of children and it is such a shame to throw them in the bin. Some of the clothes are practically new.'

'Jaysus, missus, yeh can offend me anytime yeh like. The wife will be delighted.'

The word got around that Da wasn't offended, and so a couple of times a year when the posh ladies would be kitting out their kids with all new clothes, we'd get the old ones. We used to be like vultures; Da would only be in the door with the brown parcel under his arm and not a crease in the paper, tied real neat with a bit of twine and a proper bow. We would kill one another fighting over who got what. Ma always made sure that everyone got something out of each parcel.

Anyway, I had a good root through Auntie Mary's bag that day.

'Ma, would yeh have a look at this? Sure it's nearly new.'

'Let's see, Kathleen. Jaysus, tha's lovely. Go on upstairs and try it on.'

It was a tight green skirt with a waistcoat and brown polo neck jumper. *I could wear this to the hop,* I thought to myself. Up the stairs I went and tried it on, with Ma following behind me.

'Tha' looks nice, Kathleen, but I think it's a bit too tight around yer rear end.'

'No, Ma, it's not. Tha's the way they all wear them now – skin tight. It's all the fashion.'

I was poured into the skirt; my arse was bursting at the seams. But I didn't care. I thought I was lovely. I was definitely keeping this for myself.

'Ma, I met Breda Murphy when I got off the bus tonight. She asked me to go the school with her on Sunday night. There's a hop on.'

'Hop wha', Kathleen?'

'Jaysus, Ma. Tha' means they play music and all.'

'Yeh mean a band?'

'No, Ma, records! So can I go?'

'Oh, I don't know, Kathleen. Wha' time is it on 'til?'

'Ten o'clock, Ma. The Christian Brothers and all will be there. Ah, go on, Ma. Let us go, please! I never go out anywhere. It'll be me first dance.'

'Hmm . . .' she thought for a few moments. 'I suppose tha's true, Kathleen. Right then. Yeh can go. Once yer father hears tha' the Brothers are keepin' an eye on yiz, he won't mind.'

I jumped up with excitement and threw my arms around

Ma, with no response back, of course. 'Would yeh give over yer molly-coddlin', for God's sake, Kathleen.' She got herself together and went back downstairs.

* * *

I thought Sunday would never come. I had my rollers in all day. I cleaned the house from top to bottom and helped get the kids washed and ready for bed. I didn't want anything to stop me from going to that hop.

I went upstairs to get ready. Phil and Noel were lying on one bed, Carmel, Clare and Marion on the other. Jacinta and Patricia were asleep on the chair downstairs and Thomas was in the kitchen playing with his soldiers. The girls thought it was great, me going to my first dance. As usual, Phil had to start with his messing and getting my back up.

'Noel, would yeh have a look at the state of her! Kathleen, I'm tellin' Ma yeh're puttin' lipstick on.' I ignored him and tried to give him the look, just like Ma did when she was raging.

'Wha' will yeh do if yeh're asked up to dance?' asked Marion.

'I'll get up and dance, tha's wha' I'll do.' I was showing off because I knew Phil was listening. With that, he burst out laughing.

'Who'd ask yeh up to dance? With tha' big fat arse on yeh and yer smelly breath.'

'Wha' de mean? There's nothin' wrong with me breath.'

'Yeah, there is, Kathleen, it's rotten. Yeh wouldn't know if yeh were talkin' to yer face or yer arse half the time.'

Phil was nearly on his knees with laughing, with Noel joining in, as they watched me getting myself into a state, knowing full well I'd lash back at him.

'Tha's it. I'm goin' to fuckin' kill yeh, Phil Doyle,' I roared.

I was on top of him like a flash, beating the head off him with my hairbrush. The bastard pulled every roller out of my hair, and me after spending ages putting them in. The girls were all jumping up and down on the bed, cheering me on to win the fight. With that, didn't the bed only go and collapse, and that soon put a stop to our fighting.

Ma was up the stairs in seconds.

'In the name of Jaysus, wha's goin' on up here? Yiz are like somethin' out of a madhouse with the carry on of yiz. Yeh're after wakin' up the little ones – and look at the bed, look at the fuckin' bed.' She was screaming her brains out. 'Who started all this?'

'It was Phil, Ma. He wouldn't leave Kathleen alone.' The girls took up for me straight away.

I was sitting on the bed with my hair standing to attention, not a curl left in sight, lipstick all over my face, with a hole in the knee of the stockings I had only bought the other week.

'I have a good mind not to let yeh go out tonight, Kathleen.'

'Ah, Ma! I didn't do anythin'. It was Phil. He started it.'

There were tears and snots running down my face. Phil was standing behind Ma, laughing and sticking out his tongue at me. With that, Ma turned around and gave him such a box in the head I thought he was going to go flying out the bedroom window.

'Get down them stairs, yeh long skinny fuck. I caught yeh. Laugh at me when me back's turned, would yeh? I keep tellin' yiz, I have eyes in the back of me head.'

He nearly died on the spot. *Jaysus,* I thought, *Ma hit Phil!* I couldn't believe it; it was a first, her hitting her blue-eyed boy like that.

'Kathleen, get yerself ready before I change me mind. Look at the state of the bed. I'll have to wait until yer Da comes home from yer Gran's to see if he can fix it. If not, the four of yiz will have to sleep on the floor until I get a new spring, and God only knows when tha'll be.'

I didn't give two shits who was sleeping on the floor and for how long, once she let me go to the hop. I ran into the toilet like a light to fix the mess I was in. I back-combed my hair, smoothing it out, trying to make some sort of a flick.

'Run downstairs, Clare, an' see is me bottle of lacquer in the press.'

She roared back up to me, 'Kathleen, it's empty!'

'Wha' am I goin' to do, Ma?'

'Don't worry, Kathleen, I'll make yeh some lacquer.'

'How, Ma? Out of wha'?'

'Come down and watch this.'

She filled the empty bottle with warm water and poured in some sugar.

'Now, Kathleen, let tha' cool down for a few minutes. Tha'll keep yer hair in for a week. The only thing is the flies, they like the sugar.'

'Wha' de yeh mean, Ma?'

'Well, if yeh see any flies around the top of yer head, yeh'd better run because if one of them gets into tha' nest on yer head, we'll have to shave all yer hair off.'

I looked at Ma, then at the bottle, then back at her. I wasn't sure if I was supposed to laugh or not. With that, all the kids started laughing like mad.

'Kathleen, yeh're an awful gobshite at times. Yeh'd believe anythin'.'

It wouldn't be very often Ma would crack a joke or for that matter say anything that you would giggle about.

I ran back up to get ready. Just then there was a knock on the door. It was Breda Murphy.

'Is tha' you, Breda?' I roared down. 'Come on up.' I gave her a little twirl in my green suit. 'Well, wha' de yeh think?'

'Kathleen, tha's a massive suit. Where did yeh get it?'

'Me cousin Marie gave it to me. Yeh don't think it's a bit tight? Me Ma said it was.'

'Don't mind yer Ma, sure wha' would she know.'

'Ah Jaysus, Breda, look at me stockin'. The hole is gettin' bigger. Wha' am I goin' to do?'

'No worries, Kathleen, I'll fix tha'.'

'How, Breda? There's no time.'

'With nail varnish, of course. Yeh just put a bit around the hole – tha' stops the ladder goin' up yer leg. I do it all the time. There's some up in me house. I'll go and get it. I'll be back in a few minutes.'

I gave my hair a little tip up with my steel-tail comb, sprayed on the sugary water and made my grand entrance into the kitchen. All the kids started cheering and clapping.

Ma gave me a little smile. I thought, *this is great – Ma's in good form.*

'Enjoy yerself, Kathleen, and make sure yeh come straight home, as soon as the dance or wha'ever it's called is over.'

'I will, thanks, Ma.'

Breda came back with the nail varnish, fixed my stocking, and off we went to the hop. When we got there we went straight to the toilets to put on our lipstick.

'De yeh want some eyeliner, Kathleen?'

'Sure, I don't know how to put it on, Breda.'

'I'm great at doin' it – now hold yer head back.'

Good God, she'll blind me, I thought, *she can't see a fuckin' thing.* 'I'll leave it alone, Breda. It's okay.'

'Would ye give it over, Kathleen. Yeh have to have a bit of eyeliner. Now, hold yer head back against the mirror and close yer eyes.' She began painting my eyes. 'Good Jaysus, Kathleen, wha' have yeh got in yer hair? It's like a rock. Yeh're nearly after crackin' the glass.'

'Me Ma made it out of water and sugar because I didn't have any lacquer.'

'Wha' did she do? Put the whole bag of sugar in? Tell her yeh only have to put in one or two spoonfuls in the water. Tha's wha' my Ma does. Now. Wha' de yeh think, Kathleen?'

I stood back and looked in the mirror, hardly recognising myself. 'Oh, I don't know, Breda. Does it not look like I've two black eyes?'

'Would yeh go 'way, Kathleen. It's all the fashion. Sure doesn't Dusty Springfield have her eyes like tha'?'

'And who is she?'

'Jaysus, Kathleen, de yeh not listen to the radio or anythin'? She's real famous. She sings an' all. Oh, I keep forgettin' – yeh're only fourteen and I'm sixteen, I know much more than you do. Now stand back and let's have a look at yeh. God, yeh're very flat. Have yeh not got on a bra?'

'I have, but me diddies is not growin'. Every night I pray to the holy statue in me Ma's room and ask her to make 'em bigger. But I think she's gettin' herself all mixed up and puttin' them in me arse instead of me chest.'

'Kathleen, didn't I tell yeh I know everythin'? Come 'ere, watch this.'

She took some toilet paper and stuffed it into my bra.

'Now. Yeh look better already. Yeh haven't got a big arse, Kathleen. It's just when yer diddies are small it makes yer arse look big.'

'Are yeh sure, Breda? It's just tha' Phil said . . .'

'Don't mind him. He's a fuckin' eejit.'

As we were walking down the corridor to the big hall, I could see a few fellas standing around, smoking on the sly. I saw one or two of them nudging each other as we passed by. I looked over and gave them a little grin. Breda pushed me and gave me a thump in the back.

'Wha' did yeh do tha' for?'

'Yeh never look at them, Kathleen!'

'Why not, Breda?'

'Because they'll think tha' yer interested in them, tha's why. I know wha' I'm talkin' about. I've been here a few times and tha's wha' all the girls do. Yeh just give them a look.'

I thought, *I don't want to give them 'the look'. I get enough of tha' at home with Ma.*

'Now, when we get into the hall, and if a young fella asks yeh up, yeh're to say no and turn away.'

'Why, Breda? I want to dance. I've been practising ever since yeh asked me to come to the hop.'

'Will yeh listen to me, Kathleen? If yeh smile and get up straight away, they'll think yeh're real easy.'

'Easy for wha', Breda?'

'Yeh know wha', Kathleen Doyle, yeh're a fuckin' eejit! De yeh not know anythin'? First of all, they'll be lookin' for a wear. Then, they'll ask yeh to go outside. Make sure tha' yeh don't do tha' because if yeh go outside with them, before yeh know it they'll be pullin' the diddies out of yeh and feelin' yer arse. Now, de yeh see wha' I mean? Are yeh takin' all this in? Me Ma always says yeh have to play hard to get.'

'Well, Breda, me Ma said tha' I was to have a great time and tha's wha' I'm goin' to do. And if any young fella tries to feel me diddies he'll be in for a shock because I've none, only toilet paper. So I don't care – the first one who asks me up, I'm gettin' up. So there.'

'Suit yerself then, Kathleen Doyle, but I'm tellin' yeh, they'll all think yeh're real easy.'

So Breda was standing there giving the looks and turning away with her head in the air, but whenever she wasn't minding me I was smiling and showing my teeth to the whole hall. I wasn't leaving that hop without a dance, and that was that. That's when a slow dance came on. All the Christian Brothers started walking around in between the couples, making sure that they weren't standing too close to one another or trying to get a wear. It was just as well Phil told me what a wear meant. Breda would have really killed me because I would have thought it meant something to do with wearing my clothes.

'Kathleen,' said Breda, 'we're standin' here long enough. If anybody comes over now we'll get up.'

She was making faces and rolling the eyes in the air all the time, so it wasn't any wonder nobody was coming near us. Just then, I saw two young fellas looking across at us. I tipped Breda.

'Breda, Breda, there's one on his way over.'

'Wha's he like?'

Her being half blind and all, he could have looked like something from Mars but she wouldn't have known that until he was nearly on top of her.

'Kathleen, I said wha's he like?'

'He's about yer size; wait, hold on. Oh Jaysus, Breda, he has millions of pimples.'

'At this stage I don't give two fucks, Kathleen. The night is nearly over.'

Before I could say anything, she pushed me out of her way and stood in front of me, grabbed his hand and started dancing. She was one sly bitch.

I stood there mumbling and fucking to myself. Then I turned around, and there he was.

The love of my life.

Alan.

'De yeh want to dance?' he asked.

He was the same height as myself, small and stocky, with dark blond curly hair combed back with a half tub of Brylcream in it, with a kiss curl flicked down on his forehead. Just then, 'Jailhouse Rock' came on and he gave me this big smile.

'Can yeh jive?' he asked as he took my hand.

'I can a bit.'

My brother Phil had shown me a few steps that he learned from some young wans he was hanging around with, so I wasn't too bad. I was on that floor like Flash Gordon. After a few minutes we were flying. He was doing backhanders, side-steps and double twirls – you name it, he was great. After the first dance he told me his name was Alan and that he was from Walkinstown.

I was shitting myself, my voice shaking with excitement. 'I'm Kathleen. I live down the road from here.'

He gave me that big smile again. The next song came on. It

was a slow set, so I didn't know what to do – Phil had only shown me how to jive. Alan just slid his hand around my waist, put my right arm around his shoulders, and held my left arm against his chest. I pulled back real quick.

'Wha's wrong?' he asked.

'Ah, it's just the Christian Brothers. They'll give out if yeh stand too close.'

To tell you the truth, I didn't give two fucks about the Christian Brothers. I was just worried that the toilet roll would make a dinge in my bra and Alan would know that I had no diddies.

'Well, Kathleen, are yeh still in school?'

'No, I left a month ago. I'm workin' in a sweet factory.'

'So how old are yeh, then?'

'I'm fourteen.'

'I'm fifteen and I work for me Da. He has a shoe repair shop.'

And it went on like that. We seemed to be talking for ages.

'Can I walk yeh home, then?'

I was just about to say 'yes' when Breda pushed my coat in between Alan and myself.

'Are yeh righ', Kathleen? Come on. We're goin' home.'

'Wha's wrong, Breda?'

Alan was still standing there.

'Kathleen, yeh know the fella with the pimples? Well, I went outside for a bit of fresh air and before I knew it, he was like a lizard. He stuck his tongue so far down me throat I nearly choked.'

'Just wait a minute, Breda, I won't be long.'

'I said we're goin', Kathleen, *now*, come on.'

With that, she stormed off.

I turned to Alan. 'Will yeh wait?'

'Yes,' he said, giving a big laugh.

'Breda, come 'ere. I thought yeh said not to go outside.'

'I know, I know. I was just standin' outside the door. I didn't go around the back of the hall.'

'Why, Breda? Wha's around the back of the hall?'

'I was just gettin' a wear, Kathleen, but the fucker wanted more.'

'More! More of wha', Breda?'

'Jaysus! De yeh know anythin', Kathleen Doyle? Yeh're as tick as shite. Ah, yeh're gettin' on me nerves. I'm goin' home.'

Off she went, leaving me standing by myself. Just then, Alan came over to me.

'Are yeh all righ', Kathleen?'

'Breda said tha' fella tried to choke her.'

'Don't mind her. Tha's me pal. He was just tellin' me he was only tryin' to give her a French kiss, tha's all.'

'Wha' does tha' mean? Is he from France?'

Alan fell around the hall laughing.

'Yeh're very funny, Kathleen.' He went on to explain to me that it was a new way of kissing. I thought my face was going to burst it got so red.

'I feel really stupid. I'm an awful tick, Alan.'

'No, yeh're not. We only found out about it last week. Tommy found a magazine under his Da's bed. It was all about kissin' and other stuff.'

Little did he know, I didn't even know how to kiss the old way, never mind the new way. And now, as I was discovering, there were other things as well!

When we got to the end of the road, Breda was standing there with a big serious puss on her.

'Yeh're a real sleeveen, Kathleen Doyle, lettin' me walk down tha' road on me own.'

'No, I'm not, Breda – yeh ran off on me.'

'Well, yeh should have run after me!'

I wanted to punch the head off her, she was making such a show of me. I was trying to be real nice in front of Alan but at the same time, I had to keep licking up to the bitch because I had no one else to go to the hop with, and Ma wouldn't let me go on my own.

'Breda, this is Alan.'

'Hello,' she said, rolling her eyes in the air and turning to walk away. 'Are yeh comin' or wha', Kathleen?'

'Walk on up, Breda, I'll be with yeh in a minute.' *Yeh bitch,* I thought to myself as I smiled at Alan. 'I'd better go, Alan, she's already annoyed.'

'De yeh want to go out tomorrow night? Maybe we can go and see a film.'

'I'd love to.'

'The Star picture house is just up the road from where yeh live. So, I'll be across the road, at the candy corner shop at half-past seven, if tha's all right with yeh, Kathleen?'

'Okay, I'll meet yeh there, Alan.'

He bent over towards me. *Oh Jaysus, he's going to kiss me,* I thought. I held my mouth closed real tight in case it was one of those French ones. I opened one eye and caught him laughing.

He just kissed me on the cheek and off he went. Breda was still giving out when I caught up with her. She went on and on and on . . . but I didn't care.

I was on cloud nine.

I had a date with Alan.

19

The Date

I was up bright and early the next morning. I stuck a few rollers in my hair. As a factory worker, I had to wear a turban on my head for hygiene reasons; so nobody ever noticed my rollers.

'Is tha' you, Kathleen?' Da whispered up the stairs.

'Yeah, Da.' I slipped out of the room, stepping over the four kids sleeping on the floor. It was only half past six, far too early for them to get up.

'Pour yerself a cup of tea. I have the fire lightin'. Will yeh have a bit of toast?'

I sat down with my cup of tea while Da knelt in front of the fire with the fork stuck in the bread, holding it against the flames.

'Yer mother told me wha' happened last night. Phil should have more sense. He should keep his fightin' for the boxin' ring and not his sister. I'll talk to him tonight.'

'Sorry about the bed, Da. I just lost me temper with Phil.'

'Well now, Kathleen, yeh didn't lick it off a stone; yeh take after yer mother for all tha'. There's one or two scrap-yards on me route today. I'll drop in and see if they have an oul' spring lyin' around. Tha'll solve the problem.'

'Da, can I ask yeh somethin'?'

'Course yeh can, wha' is it?'

'Ma said, if it's all right with yeh, I could go out tonight to the pictures. I met this lovely fella; I've a date with him. His name's Alan.'

'And how old is this young fella?'

'He's fifteen and he's from Walkinstown.'

Da looked at me for a minute, thinking to himself, but before he could say anything else, I got in there straight away. 'He has a job working for his Da, mending shoes.'

I had my coat and scarf on by the time I told him everything and was nearly out the door, rushing for the bus, with still no answer.

'Ah, Da, go on, let us go, please?' I put my arm around him. 'Go on, Ma will let me go if yeh say yes.'

'Are yeh sure yer mother said it's okay?'

'I swear, Da, on the Holy Bible she did.' I blessed myself.

'Now, yeh wouldn't say tha' if it wasn't true, would yeh, Kathleen?' He looked at me with a little grin. 'Right then, yeh can go. I'll see yer mother when she gets up.'

I gave him a big hug. 'Thanks, Da.'

* * *

The bus was just pulling up to the stop when I got to the corner. I fell onto the seat soaked to the skin; the heavens were open and me with not an umbrella. I kept saying that I'd buy one, but I never seemed to have the money.

My friend Rosie Delaney got on the bus at Walkinstown. I'd met her the first day I started work; she came over to me in the locker room and told me not to be nervous. She sat beside me on the bus every morning from then on and we'd be chatting all the way up the Greenhills Road.

'I was dyin' to see yeh, Kathleen. How did yeh get on with yer first hop?'

I launched in, telling her all about Breda and the fella with the tongue. She nearly fell off her seat laughing. She was seventeen and probably knew all about these things. I let on I knew too.

Then I told her about Alan.

'Yeh mean Alan McGrath?'

'De yeh know him, Rosie?'

'Yes I do, Kathleen, he lives up the road from me house, so he does. He's a really nice young fella.'

'Well, I have a date with him. We're goin' to the pictures tonight. Look, I have me rollers in and all.'

'Tha's great Kathleen. The only thing is . . . Molly O'Brien . . . she's a bitch, she works in the factory too.'

'*Who's she?*'

'Her and Alan were goin' together for about six months and they only broke up about two weeks ago. I'd say she'll go mad when she finds out he's goin' out with somebody else already.'

'Oh, maybe I won't go then.'

'No, don't be stupid, Kathleen, you go. Serves her right anyway; she used to treat him like dirt and he was mad about her, always buyin' her presents and things.'

We were outside the factory before I knew it.

'Rosie, wha' does tha' Molly wan look like? Tell me before I go in.'

'Don't be worryin' yerself, Kathleen, yeh won't even see her. She works up in Dolly's room – tha's miles away, yeh're at the other end of the factory. Jaysus, look at the time! It's nearly eight o'clock, we'll be late for clockin' in. I'll meet yeh on the bus on the way home; see yeh later.'

I made myself sick worrying and looking over my shoulder all day. Every girl that passed by, I jumped. I thought the day would never end so I could see Rosie and find out if she'd heard any news. She was on the bus before me and had plenty to say.

'Kathleen, I'm up here! I kept a seat for yeh,' she shouted down to me. When I went upstairs, Rosie was sitting on the front seat waving and shouting. 'I've loads to tell yeh. Molly heard all about yeh.'

The blood started to drain from my face. 'Oh shite, did she? Who told her?'

'Well, it wasn't me, I can tell yeh tha'. Sure wasn't half of Walkinstown at the hop Sunday night, Kathleen. Girls, they're all the same, they're right bitches. I was watchin' them all day, fillin' Molly in on everythin'.'

'Does she know I have a date with Alan?'

'Yeah, she does, Kathleen. Yeh know tha' young fella you were tellin' me about – Tommy, with the tongue.'

'Oh yeah, I forgot about him.'

'Well, his sister works with Molly; Alan told Tommy, and he told her, and tha's how the word got around. Are yeh with me, Kathleen?'

'For fuck's sake, Rosie, me head's all over the place. I can't think straight.'

'Yeh'd want to see the face on Molly. She was real sick, jealous as anythin'.' She glanced behind her. 'Oh' shite, Kathleen, I'm scarleh! She's at the back of the bus!'

'Good Jaysus, Rosie, wha' will I do? I'm dyin' to turn around.'

'No, don't turn around, Kathleen. Tha's why she came up the top of the bus – she wants to see wha' yeh look like. I'll be gettin' off at the same time as her. I bet yeh she comes over and tries to pick out of me. Don't worry, I won't tell her anythin'.'

'Wha' de yeh think I should do, Rosie? Will I not go?'

'Don't mind her, Kathleen, just go out tonight with Alan and have a great time and stop worryin'. Right then, here's me stop. See yeh in the mornin'.'

I turned around as Rosie walked towards the back of the bus, two girls looked down at me, nudging each other. I still didn't know who Molly was but she knew me now. I was in such a trance, wondering what I was going to do, that I nearly missed my stop.

I was halfway up the road when I saw Breda Murphy. She called out to me, 'Is tha' you, Kathleen Doyle?'

'Yeah, Breda, it's me.'

I wasn't in any humour for her and I didn't feel like listening to a load of scutter and shite; that's all you'd ever get out of her.

'Well, wha' happened? Did yeh get a wear or wha'?'

'*No, I didn't.*'

'Wha' are yeh lyin' for, Kathleen? I saw yeh; he was standin' real close and all.'

Yeh blind fuck, yeh can't see the hand in front of yeh, never mind me standin' down at the corner. 'He just gave me a kiss on the cheek, Breda, tha's all. He's real nice.'

'Kiss on the cheek, me arse, Kathleen Doyle, yeh fuckin' liar.'

I could feel my temper starting to rise. 'I have to go, Breda, I'm in a hurry. I have a date with Alan.'

'Yeh're not serious? With tha' teddy boy – sure they're all real slags. The first fella asks yeh out and yeh go runnin' after him. Yeh're an awful tick, so yeh are.'

'Don't be sayin' tha', Breda, he's not a teddy boy or a slag.'

'Yes, he is – did yeh see him when "Jailhouse Rock" came on? He was like a ravin' lunatic, dancin' and jumpin' around like a mad thing. I thought at one stage he was goin' to fuck yeh out the top window, he was liftin' yeh up in the air tha' much. And one other thing, every time the dance was over, he took his comb out to fix tha' kiss curl of his. They all do tha', me Ma says; all them teddy boys are the same, just after one thing. They'd have yer knickers off in a flash if yeh let them.'

I felt like saying, *Fuck yeh and yer Ma with her gammy leg; she's just a jealous oul' cow, because she can't dance. Call me a fuckin' eejit, will yeh? I'll put the eyes crossways in yer head with a good punch one of these days. It won't be glasses yeh'll be needin'; it'll be a pair of binoculars by the time I'm finished with yeh. Bitch.* But of course I didn't say anything; I just bit my lip and ran off before she could say another word.

I had myself in a state by the time I got to the house. My face was roaring red with temper. As usual, the kids were all running up to me to see if I had a few sweets in my pocket. I sat on the steps playing with them for a few minutes, calming myself down. If Ma saw me all worked up, she'd be asking what had happened.

'Is tha' you, Kathleen?' Ma roared.

'Yeah, Ma, I'll be with yeh in a minute.'

'Wha' kept yeh?'

'I was talkin' to Breda Murphy.'

'She's a nice young wan, very well mannered, and her mother's a lovely woman, so she is.'

'I know, she's real nice.' I thought I was going to choke on the words.

'Kathleen, sit down there and eat yer bit of dinner. Sure it's nearly cold as it is. Well, yer Da said yeh can go to the pictures with tha' young fella – wha's his name again?'

'Alan.'

I was getting butterflies in my stomach just saying his name. That was it, I made up my mind there and then: *I'm goin' to meet him, so fuck tha' Molly wan.*

After dinner I went upstairs to get ready. It didn't take long to make up my mind what to wear – either the green suit with the brown polo neck or the beige pleated skirt with the brown polo neck, both hand-me-downs from my cousins. I wished for once I had something new to wear that was just mine. I was giving out to myself like hell at this stage and was getting in a right tizzy.

Carmel was sitting on the bed playing with her dolls, not doing a bit of harm to me or anyone around her. I lashed out and took my bad mood out on her.

'Are yeh ever goin' to grow up, Carmel? Every time I look at yeh, yeh're dressin' up or playin' with them bloody dolls.'

'Wha's wrong with yeh, Kathleen? Yeh never fight with any of us.'

'Ah, Carmel, I'm sorry. I didn't mean to loose me rag.' I put my arms around her. 'It's just, loads happened to me today. I don't know if I like bein' out there in the big world. Everyone keeps talkin' about things I don't know much about. It frightens me a bit tha's all. I'm afraid to ask Ma or Da about wha' they mean in case I shouldn't know, and then if I ask the girls in work they'd probably laugh at me because I should know. Ah, maybe yeh're better off in here with yer dolls, Carmel. Anyway, I didn't mean to give out to yeh.'

'Kathleen, Da brought home one of the parcels today. There was a nice yella cardigan in it. Ma gave it to me but yeh can have a lend of it if yeh like.'

'Ah, go on then, Carmel, give us a look. Jaysus, tha's lovely, tha'll go with the pleated skirt. Thanks, Carmel, yeh're a star.'

I went downstairs and got a pot of warm water to have a good wash. I was back up the stairs like a light before anybody else could get into the bathroom. As I was pouring the water into the sink, I looked down at the bath and thought to myself, *I'd love it to be filled up with hot water and loads of lovely fluffy bubbles. I could just slip in like yeh see in the films. But tha'll never happen, not for a long time anyway.*

Ma had always promised she'd try to get one of those new geysers that would heat the water, if she could ever get her gas bill straight. When we first got the house she used to fill a big pot with water and heat it on the gas cooker. Da would then carry the pot up and down the stairs a couple of times, but even then there'd be barely enough water to wet your arse, never mind have a good splash. As more babies came along, it became too much for him. That's when Ma came up with one of her bright ideas; it was a classic.

'Phil, we'll have to find some other way for washin' the kids. Somebody's goin' to get scalded goin' up and down them stairs with pots of boilin' water. I have meself a plan – we'll wash them in the machine.'

'*Wha*'? Yeh want to put the kids in the washin' machine?!

Are yeh gone stark ravin' mad altogether, Lil?'

'Jaysus, will yeh listen to me? We'll heat the water first, then take the plug out. I'll stand them in one by one and you'll dry them off. Right?'

Da thought to himself for minute. 'Now, Lil, I have to say, tha' deserves a pat on the back. A master brainwave if I ever heard one; only yerself would think of tha'.'

Da was delighted; the days of running up and down the stairs with boiling water were over. But as we all got older and our bits were starting to spring out, it was back to the bathroom sink with pots of warm water.

Ma would always tell us, 'Make sure yeh wash yer three bits where the smell comes from – yer feet, under yer arms and down below.'

For the boys, 'down below' was called the usual – 'willy' – but of course Phil and Noel had something to say about that.

'Ma, why can't we call ours "mickey" like all our pals.'

'There'll be no mickey talk in this house and if I hear any of it, yiz'll get the back of me hand.'

Us girls had to call ours 'Mary'.

'Why "Mary"?' I asked.

'Well, Kathleen, most women call theirs "fanny", but we can't do tha', because yer granny Kitty's donkey is called Fanny. Sure I wouldn't know if yeh were talkin' about yerself or the donkey; so "Mary" it'll be.'

And to the present day we still call 'down below' 'Mary' in our family.

I had just started washing myself and was bending down to put on clean knickers when the door was nearly kicked in on top of me.

'Who's in there?' Noel shouted.

'It's me – Kathleen. Go 'way, I'm gettin' ready.'

The door got another kick. 'Let me in before I piss on meself!'

'Go away, Noel,' I said. 'I'm not finished yet.'

'Kathleen, Thomas is out here too and he's goin' to shite all over himself.'

'Let me in, quick, me gick's comin' out,' roared five-year-old Thomas.

I opened the door slightly and peeped out, at the same time trying to cover myself. I had one leg in my knickers, with my arse still wringing wet.

'I'm not lookin' at yeh, Kathleen,' Noel mumbled. 'Will yeh let us in?'

'Yeh better not, I'm warnin' yeh.' I wrapped the towel around myself.

Just then Thomas pushed his way past me with his trousers around his ankles, 'Quick, Kathleen, it's nearly out!' I grabbed him and put him sitting on the pot.

'Jaysus, am I ever goin' to get peace in this mad house?'

I turned around and there was Noel, getting ready to piss in the bath.

'Noel, wha' the hell are yeh doin', yeh dirty little bastard?'

'I can't hold it any longer, Kathleen, let me go. Ma will kill me if I piss in me trousers – they're the only pair I have.'

'*I'll* kill yeh if yeh piss in the bath, never mind Ma.'

'Anyway, they all do it, Kathleen.'

'*Wha' de yeh mean "all"?*'

'Whoever doesn't make it to the pot has a piss in the bath.'

'Oh my God, who started all this?'

'Phil – but don't tell him I said; he'll kill me. I was havin' a shit one day when he pushed the door in and roared at me. "Right, Noel, get off the toilet pot, I can't wait any longer."

'"But, Phil, I'm halfway there – wait, it's nearly out."

'He walked up and down for a minute. I was turnin' purple in the face, tryin' to finish as quick as I could, but because he was standing there lookin' at me, everythin' stopped. It wouldn't move. "Tha's it," he said, "I can't hold it", and he went and pissed in the bath. He gave me a box in the head and told me he'd batter me if I told Ma or Da, but I told all the others. We only do it when somebody's havin' a shit and they're takin' ages. It's only piss, Kathleen; yeh turn the taps on and it washes away like the pot.'

'Well, now, Noel, seein's tha' yeh think it's okay, yeh won't mind if I tell Ma then, will yeh?'

'Ah, Jaysus, Kathleen, don't tell her. There'll be blue murder; yeh know wha' she's like. She'll batter me.'

'Right, then, I'll see Phil later.'

Noel started balling his eyes out.

'Tha's it, Kathleen, I'm dead. He said he'd kill me if I told on him.'

'Don't be such a fuckin' whinger, Noel, will yeh? He won't touch yeh because I'll tell him tha' if he goes near yeh, I'll tell Ma and Da he started it. Now get down them stairs and tell the others I want to see them.'

Noel gave them all the gypsy's whisper before they came up the stairs to me. They were all blaming one another, shoving and pushing at the same time. 'Kathleen, it wasn't me it was her'; 'She did it first, then I did it'; 'Noel said it was okay.'

In the middle of all this bedlam, Thomas, who was still sitting on the pot, called out, 'Kathleen, Kathleen, Kathleen.'

I turned around. '*Wha*'? Wha's wrong with yeh?'

'Will yeh wipe me arse, Kathleen?' I couldn't keep my face straight and started laughing and of course everybody else chimed in.

That's when Da came to the end of the stairs. 'Wha's goin' on up there, Kathleen? Yiz are makin' a fierce racket.'

'It's okay, Da, they're just helpin' me get ready for me date.'

I told them, 'I'm warnin' yiz, I'll be watchin' out for yella stains in the bath. And if I see the tiniest bit of rust – I don't care, yiz can all blame one another – every one of yiz will get it from me and Ma. I didn't wait all these years to have me bubble bath, when Ma is finally ready to get the hot water, only to find out I can't sit down because it's rusted to fuck from yiz pissin' in it.'

Clare always had to get her penny's worth in. She was as

cheeky as hell. 'Wha'll we do if there's a few of us waitin' to go? We can't wet our knickers now, can we, Kathleen?'

'Tha's right,' Marion joined in, 'I won't be able to hold it.'

'Then there's Jacinta and Patricia,' Carmel said. 'It won't be long before they're on the queue with the rest of us.'

Noel came up with what he thought was a good plan. 'Wha' about the shore in the back yard? It's not too close to the house. Now, I'm only sayin', only if yeh're really stuck, we could piss in tha'. Wha' de yeh say, Kathleen?'

'Tha's not a bad idea and it has an open grille, too. Ma could pour a drop of bleach and hot water to make sure it doesn't smell. Right then, off yiz go, I'll talk to Ma and Da about it.' They all finally left me in peace. 'Jaysus, look at the time! It's nearly seven o'clock. I'll be lucky if I make me date with all this goin' on.'

On with the pleated skirt – *Oh, thank God, this cardigan buttons right up to the neck. I won't have to worry about wearin' anything underneath. Oh shit, wha' about me diddies? I'll just put a bit of toilet paper in me bra; tha' Breda wan must have put half a roll in last night. I must have looked a right eejit. I better not be thinkin' about her or I'll just get all worked up again.*

'Ma, will yeh send one of the kids in next door and ask Mrs Kennedy will she lend me her umbrella? It's lashin' out; I don't want me hair goin' all flat, I have it just right. And can I put some lipstick on?'

'Yeh can put on a little bit, but yeh're not to put tha' black stuff on yer eyes. I got a fright last night when I opened the door; I thought somebody was after beatin' yeh up.'

'Yeh know wha' else I need, Ma? A bit of talcum powder – I can feel under me arms sweatin' already.'

'For Christ's sake, Kathleen, will yeh stop gettin' yerself all worked up? Yeh're an awful young wan for worryin'.'

Worked up? If she only knew what was goin' on a few minutes ago, we'd see who'd be worked up.

'Anyway, Kathleen, yeh're better off bein' a few minutes late. Yeh don't want him thinkin' yeh're too anxious.'

'Okay, Ma, yeh're right, I will.'

Clare handed me the umbrella before I left.

'Mrs Kennedy said yeh've to bring it straight back when yeh come home.'

'I will, I will. Right then, how do I look?'

Da smiled at me. 'Yeh look great.'

'Yeh're grand, Kathleen,' said Ma. 'Yeh've plenty of time; the picture doesn't start until eight o'clock. Off yeh go then and mind yerself crossin' tha' main road. And don't be late – make sure yeh're in here at a proper hour.'

* * *

I took my time walking up Kildare Road so I wouldn't have a red face when I got there. I looked across at the Candy Corner Shop. There was nobody there. *Tha's great*, I thought, *gives me a chance to fix me hair and lipstick.*

The rain was bucketing down that night and I could feel the cardboard inside my shoes starting to crumble. I seemed to be standing there for ages. I hadn't got a watch, so I went in and asked the women behind the counter the time.

'It's eight o'clock, luv. De yeh want to stand inside the door? Yeh're gettin' soaked out there.'

'I'm grand, thanks.'

I was afraid I'd miss Alan if I stood in the shop. *He must have missed the bus, tha's wha' happened, and he's walkin' down. Tha's it, I'm sure of it.*

I waited for another half hour, blue in the face with the cold, before I finally got the message. He wasn't coming. I cried all the way home, thinking to myself, *I'm such a gobshite, standin' there all tha' time, makin' a fool of meself. He was probably laughin' at me all the time; and I thought he liked me.*

By the time I got home, the side gate was locked, so I had to knock on the front door. Da opened it.

'I thought yeh were goin' to the pictures, Kathleen.'

'I changed me mind, Da. I was up talkin' to Breda.'

'Women! I'll never understand yiz, always changin' yer mind at a blink of an eye.' He shook his head as he made his way back to the telly.

I held my head down and passed him by. He had a sup on him, so he didn't notice that I was soaked to the skin and my eyes were swollen from crying. But Ma did. She handed me a towel.

'Dry yerself off there, Kathleen, and I'll make a cup of tea.'

The young kids were in bed asleep, the other half were looking at the telly, not minding me. I followed Ma into the kitchen.

'Well, wha' happened?'

I looked at Ma, trying to hide my red eyes and I thought for a minute about what she always taught us: *Never tell me lies, any of yiz, I'd trust a robber first before I'd trust a liar.*

'He never turned up, Ma.'

'Yeh mean yeh've been standin' out in tha' rain all this time? Jaysus, Kathleen, I thought yeh had a bit of sense. Could yeh not see after a few minutes he wasn't comin'?'

'I know, I know, Ma. He was so nice. I didn't think he'd do tha' on me.'

'Well, Kathleen, yeh have an awful lot to learn about men and life.'

I started balling my eyes out again. Ma put her arm around me.

'Come on now, stop tha' cryin', Kathleen. Yeh'll wake the kids up, and if tha' brother of yours Phil gets a whisper of this – and yeh know wha' he's like with his messin' – yeh'll never hear the end of it.'

Ma wasn't one for showing her feelings. I suppose she was always too busy looking after us to think that we might need a hug or a kiss now and again. But that night it felt good with her arm around me.

'Right then, Kathleen, get them wet stockin's and shoes off. Take a lend of Carmel's shoes and her raincoat. We're goin' out.' She roared into Da, 'Phil, as soon as tha' film is over, put the rest of them kids to bed. I won't be long.'

'Lil, where are yeh off to at this hour of the night?'

'I'm just goin' out for an hour with Kathleen.' She turned to me. 'Come on, yeh got ready to go to the pictures and tha's where we're goin', I have a few bob put by off the gas heater. We'll use some of tha'. If we hurry up we'll make the second film and we might have enough to get a single of chips on the way home.'

'Are yeh sure, Ma?'

'Just get tha' coat on. We're goin' and tha's tha'.'

We had a chat on the way up the road. I told her about the kids getting stuck waiting to use the toilet and nearly wetting themselves and the idea about the shore – 'Now, only if they're really stuck, Ma, tha's all.' I never mentioned the bath.

'We'll see, just enjoy tonight. We'll worry about tha' tomorrow.'

I suppose that's how she got by – there we were with a twenty-six-inch telly on tick, and not a drop of hot water in the house and barely enough food to go around. But does Ma worry about it? *No.* She would always say, 'Yeh deal with each thing as it happens; take each day as it comes.' That's what I was going to do from then on.

* * *

The next morning Rosie sat down beside me on the bus as usual. She was itching to know how I'd got on. She nearly died when I told her.

'Tha's not like Alan McGrath. Somethin' must have happened.'

Just then I heard giggling up the front of the bus.

'Did yeh hear tha', Rosie? They know.'

'No, they don't, Kathleen, how could they?'

'Look at them, they're all laughin' and lookin' down at us.'

'Tha's her, Kathleen.' Rosie whispered, pointing out this wan to me. 'Tha's Molly.'

She looked straight down, laughing at me; I stared right back. *Bitch*.

I learned the truth as the day went by, with Rosie slipping over to me every chance she got, filling me in on everything. It seemed Molly had sent a note to Alan telling him she was still mad about him and wanted to see him. Little did he know that while he went to meet her, she was standing across the road from the Candy Corner Shop, watching me. She thought it was great fun, telling everybody how long I'd been standing there and how she had made a fool out of the two of us.

'I'll bash her brains in, I swear I will, Rosie. The bitch, to do something like tha'.'

'She's not worth it, Kathleen. Just ignore her, I think she's sick in the head and hasn't got a brain anyway. Wait until I see Alan McGrath; I'll tell him wha's been goin' on.'

'Rosie, leave it, don't say anythin'.'

I just wanted to run out of the factory, but I didn't. That skinny little two-faced fuck Molly would have loved that.

I thought the day would never end; all I wanted was to go home and hide.

When the buzzer went off at six o'clock, I rushed to get my coat, trying to get ahead of everybody. Rosie caught up with me.

'Are yeh okay, Kathleen?'

'I just want to get out of here, Rosie.'

Just before we got to the main gate, I thought I was seeing things. Alan was sitting there on his Honda 50. Talk about rubbing my nose in it. I held my head down, hoping he wouldn't see me. *I'll never live this down, him comin' up to pick tha' Molly wan up. They'll really have somethin' to laugh about tomorrow.*

Just as I walked out the side gate, he got off his bike and walked towards me. He had on a pair of skin-tight blue jeans, a black leather jacket and a pair of black 'Beatle' boots. *Jaysus, he's gorgeous,* I thought. My face got so red it could have lit up the whole road. Rosie was linking me and had one of her hands in my pocket. She squeezed one of my fingers so hard she nearly broke it.

Alan stopped right in front of me.

'Can I talk to yeh, Kathleen, please?'

I looked behind me and I could see all the young wans coming out the gate including, Molly. Then I looked at Rosie; she gave me a nod and a wink and left to get the bus. I thought to myself, *even if it's only to get up tha' Molly wan's back, I'll talk to him.*

'Okay, Alan, but not here.'

'Right, Kathleen. Hop on the back of the bike and I'll bring yeh home.'

I jumped on, gave Rosie a big wave and, to the rest of the bitches, the biggest smile you ever saw. The look on Molly's face was priceless.

Alan stopped down the road from my house. I got off the bike and faced him.

'Yeh never turned up last night. I waited for ages.'

'I'm sorry, Kathleen, let me explain.' He went on to tell me how he used to go with this girl. 'She works in the same factory as you. De yeh know her? She's called Molly.'

'Does she?' I pretended I knew nothing.

'Well, she sent me a note askin' me would I meet her, tha' it was real important, tha' she wanted to get back with me. We were goin' together for six months. I was all mixed up, I thought I still liked her, but when I was waitin' on her, I kept thinkin' about you. Tha's when I made me mind up; I was goin' to tell her it was over, but she didn't turn up. I knew it was too late to meet yeh, yeh'd be long gone. I had great crack the other night with yeh, I laughed more with you than I did with her in the last six months. Kathleen, will yeh give me another chance?'

He didn't have to ask me twice. The butterflies were doing somersaults in my stomach.

This was the fella for me.

20

Alan Meets Ma and Da

I was going out with Alan only a few weeks and was as happy as anything. He was spoiling me rotten. I wasn't used to getting all this attention, but I was loving every minute of it.

Until Da turned around one night and asked me: 'Kathleen, when are we goin' to meet this young fella of yours?'

Straight away, I looked across at Ma, who didn't say anything for a minute or two. She just stared over at me and then came out with the words I didn't want to hear.

'Your father is right, Kathleen. Bring him home. Let's have a look, see wha' he's like.'

'I told yeh, he's real nice, Ma.'

'It doesn't matter wha' *you* think; yeh're only a child, barely fourteen.'

For a split second I was back inside my head, thinking, *I'm only a child, am I? Well, how come I've been grown up all these years when it suits yiz all? All I ever wanted was to be a child like the rest of the kids, but I couldn't because youse wouldn't let me.*

'He could be a right bowsie, for all we know.'

'No, he's not, Ma.'

'Are yeh givin' me back lip now, Kathleen?'

'No, Ma. It's just tha' . . .'

'There's no just about it. Kathleen. Yeh bring him home to meet us, and tha's tha'.'

Da put his arm around me. 'Wha' are yeh worryin' about Kathleen? We won't bite him.'

You might not, Da, but I don't know about Ma. She'll still have it in her head over me standin' in the rain tha' night after Alan stood me up. I'll go mad if she says anythin' to him, I will, I don't care. Wha' am I going to do when he comes into this mad house: the little ones crying, the other kids running all over the place? He'll run a mile.

* * *

Alan didn't talk much about his family; everything seemed to be very quiet there. He had only one sister and a little brother.

'How come there's only three of yiz?' I asked him one night.

'Me Ma died when I was thirteen.'

'Oh my God! I'm sorry. I shouldn't have asked yeh.'

He could see I was getting all flustered and didn't know where to look.

'It's okay, Kathleen, it's all right. I can talk about it. Me Da worked away in England for a long time. We used to see him only a couple of times a year.'

'Did yeh not miss him?'

'Yeah, I did, but Ma wouldn't move over there.'

'And who looks after yiz now?'

'Da and Auntie Connie, me Ma's sister.'

He went on talking about her for ages. I thought, *she sounds real posh. I'll shit on myself if he asks me to meet her.* And I did meet her after a couple of months. Alan went out and bought me a lovely pink coat with a leopard-skin collar, new shoes, a handbag and a pair of white gloves. He thought I didn't cop on to what he was doing and I never said; he was dressing me up to impress his Auntie Connie. He wanted so much for her to like me. You'd swear I was going to meet the Queen; I was only short of getting a crown on my head. It was my first set of clothes that weren't hand-me-downs. I looked and felt great when I went to meet her.

I could tell straight away that she didn't take a shine to me, as she thought I was beneath her and wasn't good enough for Alan. I hadn't got much in the way of reading and writing but I was years ahead with the teaching from Ma about life and people. I was well able to read Alan's aunt to a T. She was a bitch to me, but not in front of Alan, and I was always one step ahead. I would smile and agree with everything she said and she didn't like that one bit. I made it my business to keep out of her way, so she couldn't make any trouble.

As for my lovely pink coat, I only got to wear it twice. Ma asked me, 'Would yeh mind if I pawned it, just until Friday, Kathleen? I have electric and gas bills well overdue. I'll get it back out as soon as I get me wages.' But that never happened. She couldn't make the payment, so it was sold on to somebody else.

The pawn office was part of a lot of people's lives back then. If you had any clothes that were halfway decent, they would be brushed, pressed and folded up neatly, and brought to the pawn office on the Monday. You would try to get as much as you could from the pawnbroker, having to pay some interest on your return, which would usually be on the Friday. Ma didn't have much to pawn, but when she did, that would the ritual. It was more like robbing Peter to pay Paul.

'Kathleen, yeh don't realise how lucky yeh are, comin' from such a big family. Always somebody around and plenty goin' on.'

'Yeh can say tha' again, Alan; there's never a dull moment in my house.'

Little did he know he would be meeting them in the next few days; that might change his mind about big families.

* * *

Alan got a fright when I told him Ma and Da wanted to meet him.

'Why do they want to see me?'

'To make sure yeh're not a slag or a bowsie, Alan.'

'But I'm not!'

'I know tha', but please, Alan, they won't let me go out with yeh again if yeh don't. They just want to see yeh. Go on, Alan, please, just for me.'

'Okay, Kathleen, I will. Yeh know I'd do anythin' for yeh.'

* * *

'Ma, I told Alan to come down on Saturday night. Is tha' alright?'

'Good, Kathleen, yeh won't be in work. It'll give yeh a chance to get the place tidied up.'

'Ma, promise me yeh won't curse or smoke yer pipe, please?'

'I won't be puttin' any airs or graces on for anybody, yeh should know tha' by now. I'll just be meself.'

Jaysus, tha's wha' I'm worried about.

'Kathleen, if I've no Woodbines, I'll be smokin' me pipe; and as for me sayin' "fuck", I only say tha' when I'm all riled up. So yeh better talk to yer brothers and sisters, make sure they behave themselves. And tell yer father not to come in this house full of drink. Then I won't get all fired up now, will I?'

'Jaysus, Ma, tha's like askin' for a miracle. Yeh know all tha' won't happen at the one time and all in the one night.'

'Ah, yeh worry too much, Kathleen. I keep tellin' yeh.'

I suppose I didn't want Alan to see how poor we were and how little we had.

* * *

I thought Saturday night would never come and go. I had myself up the walls with worry.

I warned all the kids that if they started messing and making a show of me, I wouldn't bring home any chocolate ever again.

'And you, Phil, don't come in here with yer smelly stockin's on, stinkin' us all out of it.'

He smiled and gave me a sly grin.

'Did yeh see tha', Ma? Did yeh see him?'

'See wha', Kathleen? Wha' are yeh goin' on about now?'

Phil's laughin' at me! Did yeh not see him? Tha' means he goin' to mess and make a show of me in front Alan. Talk to him, Ma.'

'Phil, will yeh stop getting up her back, for God's sake? Yeh know wha' she's like for worryin'.'

I was cleaning all day, trying to make the place look something, which was nearly impossible. There were the two armchairs beside the fireplace: they had more footprints of muck on them from the kids jumping up and down. *I know wha' I'll do: put two blankets on them, tha'll clean them up a bit. Then there's the blue tubular table and four chairs, which were all covered in rips. I'll make sure the kids are sitting down on them; tha' way Alan won't see how bad they really are. There's nothin' I can do about the push chairs they'll just have to stay where they are. Ma likes to have the little ones beside her at the fire. Anyway, if they cry she just has to rock them to keep them quiet. I hope.*

'Ma, I'm goin' to get ready now. Will yeh make sure the kids take off their mucky shoes? I'm after scrubbin' every one of them floors. Alan will be here in half an hour. I told him he could bring his bike in the front garden. Is tha' okay?'

'Yes, yes, Kathleen. Will yeh stop fussin', for God's sake. As I said before, he'll just have to take us as he sees us, and tha's tha'!'

Da came in just then. 'The place looks great, Kathleen.'

'Thanks, Da.' *Tha's grand,* I thought, *he only has a small sup on him. At least there won't be a digging match tonight.*

I was just about ready when Carmel, Clare and Marion burst in the door, with little Thomas trailing behind them.

'Alan's here, Kathleen.'

Phil and Noel went out to look at his bike.

'Has Phil got his shoes on? Please tell me he has his shoes on.'

'How would we know?' Clare answered. 'We weren't lookin' at his smelly feet.'

'Yeh're a cheeky little fuck, so yeh are. I'll sort you out later.'

I peeped out the window. *Good, he has his shoes on.*

'Quick, the three of yiz take Thomas, get down and sit on them chairs and stay there until we go. I'll get extra sweets on Friday for all of yiz. Tell the others to be good.'

I got to the door just as Alan was walking in. He gave me a big smile and Phil gave me one of his sneaky grins. I could see how nervous Alan was, twirling his motorbike helmet around in his hands. Da put his hand out and they both shook.

'So, yeh're Alan.'

'Tha's right, Mr Doyle.'

'Mr Doyle, me arse,' Phil mumbled.

I knew it, I knew it – he's goin' to try and make a holy show of me, I thought to myself. *He's a pig, tha's wha' he is, a pig.*

I looked at Da and gave him the eye and the nod. He knew full well what I meant.

'Phil, be quiet there.' He turned back to Alan. 'We've been hearin' a lot about yeh around here. It's all Alan does this and Alan says tha'.'

I went as red as a tomato; all the kids start giggling. *Jaysus! Wha' did Da have to say tha' for?* I was mortified.

That's when Ma stood up and walked over to Alan. You could see the blood draining from his face. I was shitting myself, never mind Alan. She turned around and looked over at Da. He gave her the nod. She stood there with not a smile on her face.

'Right then, Alan, de yeh smoke?'

Alan looked over at me, not knowing what to say. I had told

him how Ma was if any of us ever lied to her. He looked Ma straight in the eye.

'I do, Mrs Doyle.'

'Tha's good, then, because we've none. Now give us a few, I'm gaspin'!'

Alan was so relieved, he gave her the whole packet. That was it: he was in Ma's good books from then on.

Phil kept his shoes on and the kids sat on the chairs just like I asked them. The little ones didn't cry too much. Ma had a few smokes in her pocket so there was no fucking and blinding out of her. Da was sober. All went well. I was happy that night.

They all did me proud.

21

The Strongest Finger

My brother Phil was so funny at times – a bit of a lunatic, to say the least. You never knew what he was going to do or say.

Alan had been coming down to the house a good few months now and I was always trying to impress him; making sure the kids were on their best behaviour, promising them the sun, moon and stars to be good for me, if that was at all possible. But Phil always had to get up to something.

I was sitting there one night, chatting away to Alan. Ma was in the kitchen with the babies. Da was upstairs reading his paper. Phil was sitting on the chair across from me and the rest of the kids were sitting on the floor, watching the telly.

I looked over and I could see Phil giggling and laughing away to himself. *Tha's it,* I thought to myself, *he's up to something.* Sure enough, a few minutes later he came out with it.

'De yeh know somethin', Alan? I bet tha' I could lift you, Kathleen and every one of them kids up off yer arses with just one finger and all at the same time.'

'Don't be so stupid, Phil, would yeh?' I said. 'Nobody could do tha'.'

'I have to agree with Kathleen,' says Alan. 'I think yeh'll be losin' yer bet on this one, Phil.'

'No, I won't, Alan, because I have the strongest finger in the world, and I'll prove it.'

All the kids started butting in, 'And wha's yer bet? Come on, tell us, Phil.'

'I know I'm goin' to win this bet, but if for some reason I leave even one of yiz sittin', well then, I'll make the tea and a heap of fried bread for yiz all. But when I win – which I know I'm goin' to – every one of yiz has to kiss me hand and say, "Phil's the Champ".'

We were breaking our hearts laughing at the thought of Phil having to make the supper, which would be a first.

'Right then, Phil, yeh're on. Let's have it,' I said. 'Let's see this famous finger work.' I was showing off in front of Alan, thinking Phil was going to make a thick of himself. Little did I know I would be the one with egg all over my face by the time he was finished.

'There's just one more thing I have to say, Kathleen. Whoever doesn't kiss me hand – and I mean this – gets the finger stuck up their nose. Tha's the deal, so does everyone else agree?'

'Right, right,' says Noel. 'The bet's on, now will yeh come on and let's see wha' yeh're made of.'

'Remember those words in a couple of minutes, Noel, when yeh're kissin' me hand,' said Phil, a big dirty grin on his face.

That's when he stood up off the chair and started bending up and down, flexing his muscles, pretending he was warming up like a body-builder and laughing all the while. I couldn't believe what he did next and was as sorry as hell I'd taken up the bet. He bent down, got his finger and stuck it between the crack of his arse, breaking his heart laughing all the while.

'Right,' he said, standing up and pointing the finger in the air. 'Who's first for a sniff?' And he made a run at us.

Well, you'd want to see the scatter from all of us. We were up off the chairs and the floor in seconds, running around, trying to get away from him. Half the kids ran screaming into the kitchen and hid behind Ma's back, shouting out, 'Phil has a smelly finger. He had it up his arse, Ma!'

At this stage, Phil was standing in the middle of the room, the tears running down his face with the laughing. I was over at the front door with Alan, and the rest of the kids were getting ready to run if he started again, when Ma shouted out to him: 'Phil, are yeh up to yer antics again? Wha' did I tell yeh about chasin' them kids around? Yeh have them all roarin', makin' a holy show of me. Wha' will the neighbours think? Yeh bloody eejit. Now get in here and wash tha' finger or I'll give yeh a clip around the ear.' Of course, she'd never carry through that threat.

'Five more minutes, Ma, tha's all I need,' said Phil. 'Right then, I think I won the bet. Now it's payback time.' We all knew that if we didn't honour the bet, Phil would get us back one way or the other and that the finger would be stuck up our noses somewhere along the line. Knowing him, he'd wait until we were asleep, so it was easier to get it over with.

'Noel, I'll let you be the first to kiss me hand,' said Phil, holding the smelly finger to one side and the other hand in front of Noel. There was nothing else he could do but kiss the hand. He just gave Phil's hand a quick bang of his mouth, muttered 'Champ' and walked away. We each did likewise, with me murmuring under my breath, so Alan couldn't hear me, 'Yeh dirty bastard.'

There was no way Alan was kissing Phil's hand, so he made his way in to Ma, laughing and shaking his head at the one time, probably wondering to himself, 'Wha' a load of head-bangers I'm after gettin' involved with here.'

Phil sat there with the biggest smirk on his face, as the last of the kids went through the ritual.

'Well,' he said, making his way over to the sink to wash his hands, 'Didn't I tell yiz all I had the strongest finger in the world? And did yiz believe me? No – but yeh have to admit it, tha' was a classic.'

'Well, yeh certainly got all of us up off our arses, and tha's for sure,' said Alan.

'De yeh know somethin', else, Kathleen?'

'Wha' are yeh on about now, Phil?'

'I must remember to keep this little episode in mind for any bits and pieces I want doin' for meself around here.' He grinned as he looked over at Noel.

'Yeh can fuck off, Phil Doyle,' answered Noel, who was still sulking over losing the bet.

We all settled ourselves back down, me sitting with Alan and the rest of the kids spread out all around the floor, when Ma walked in with a plate full of fried bread.

'There yiz are, now,' she said. 'Get yer teeth into tha' and make sure yiz all learned somethin' from tha' mad brother of yers tonight. Don't put yer mouth out there unless yeh know where it's goin', because it'll always bounce back into yer face when yeh least expect it, and tha's wha' happened here tonight. Yiz didn't think it through.'

Off she went back to the kitchen, leaving all of us with our mouths open. Ma should have given Phil a good box for what he had just done, instead of giving us a lesson.

He really got one up on us this time. He was one cute hoor, and that's for sure.

22

The Pig and the Fight

I was sitting in the kitchen putting a few rollers in my hair when I heard a tapping on the window. It was Phil, giving me the nod to come out to the back garden.

'Wha' de yeh want?' I yelled.

'Come 'ere, will yeh?' He was whispering, so I knew he was up to something.

'Who's tha' out there with yeh?'

'It's Noel and Thomas. Will yeh keep yer voice down, for Jaysus' sake, Kathleen? Just open the door.'

'Right, I'm comin'.'

Well, when I saw what they had I couldn't keep my face straight. I burst out laughing. Standing up between them was a dead pig.

'Well, Kathleen, wha' de yeh think? We got this for Ma.' He stood there with a grin on his face from ear to ear.

'It's a pig.'

'We know it's a fuckin' pig.'

'Yiz are after robbin' tha'. I know yeh have. Wha' are yiz goin' to do with it?'

'We didn't rob it, like breakin' into the butcher's shop or anythin' like tha'. Go on, Noel. Tell 'er.'

'Wha' de yeh mean *me* tell? I'm sayin' nothin'.'

'Yeh'd better tell me before Ma comes out,' I threatened. I folded my arms and stood there looking over at Thomas, who was picking his nose as usual and wasn't minding what Phil was saying. He gave Thomas a right box in the head.

'Wha' did I tell yeh about pickin? If the snots is not hangin' out, yeh're always pickin' and flickin' them, yeh dirty little fuck,' he roared, hitting him again. Thomas started crying.

'Leave him alone, Phil,' I yelled. 'Yeh're always hittin' him.'

'Ah, for fuck's sake, Kathleen, he's turnin' me stomach; he's always at it.'

That's when Ma came out.

'Wha's goin' on here, Kathleen?' I stood there with my mouth open, not saying a word. 'Well, Holy Mother of Divine God! A pig. Where did tha' come from? Who gave it to yeh? Did yiz rob tha'?'

'No, Ma. We swear, don't we?' the three of them answered, looking and tipping one another. Ma stood there with the arms folded, the froth slowly building up in her mouth, her temper starting to rise. That's when Phil stepped in with a classic of a story.

'Now, Ma, before yeh get yerself in a state, we were just walkin' up the road when this pig came flyin' outta the back of a lorry at us. Isn't tha' right, Noel?' he added, giving him a kick in the ankle.

'Tha's right, Ma. It nearly landed on me head, so it did.'

'Get yerselves into tha' kitchen before any of the neighbours sees or hears yiz.' She stood looking at the three of them for a few seconds, twisting the wet teacloth in her hands. 'Now, wha' I want to know – and yiz had better think hard before yiz answer me – was this lorry stopped or movin' when the pig landed on yeh, Noel?' She twisted the cloth tighter and tighter. We all knew what that meant – stripes on somebody's legs if the wrong answer was given. Poor Noel. His face was turning purple as he looked over at Phil for help. Phil stepped in straight away.

'Movin', definitely movin' Ma. Flyin' it was.'

The penny finally dropped with the other two.

'Yeah, Ma, tha's right. He was goin' up on paths, hittin' gates and all, could have killed us all.'

Shut the fuck up, will yiz? I thought. *Yeh're overdoin' it now.*

'Are yeh sure tha's the way it happened?'

'Ma, I swear, not a word of a lie,' Phil answered, making the sign of the cross, knowing full well Ma would be pleased – the crafty little fucker bringing in a bit of religion just at the right time.

'Well, tha's all right then,' said Ma.

I couldn't believe what she came out with next.

'All the same, Kathleen, isn't it strange?'

'Wha's tha', Ma?'

'The way the Holy Mother works. I'm sittin' here worryin' meself sick as to how I'm goin' to get through the next few days, with not a penny in me pocket for a bit of food, and wha' does she go and do? Only makes sure tha' the three boys are standin' in the very spot where tha' pig landed. I'll be up first thing in the mornin' to the church and light a candle, thankin' herself.'

I thought I was hearing things. I was afraid to look at Phil; he'd only make me laugh. The relief on Noel and Thomas's faces. She knew full well the little bastards had robbed the pig, but this was her way of glossing things over – when it suited her, of course.

'Clear tha' table, Kathleen. You three, carry the pig in.'

They were only in the door when the back gate opened.

'Tha'll be yer father. He must have a sup on him. Quick, quick hide the pig.'

'Where?' says Phil.

'Anywhere. Just don't let him see it; yeh know wha' he's like.'

They grabbed the pig and ran upstairs, with a couple of the smaller kids running after them.

'This is mental, Ma. Where'll they put it?'

'Say nothin', Kathleen. Here he is.'

Da had a right sup on him that night and Ma didn't half lash him out of it.

'Full of drink again, I see, Phil Doyle, and me with not a shillin' in me pocket.'

'Now, now, Lil. Not a penny did it cost me – sure, didn't I only go and meet Jimmy tha' I used to work with on the docks. I haven't seen him in over ten years. I couldn't stop him buyin' the Guinness for me.'

'Is tha' right?' said Ma, making her way over to the cooker.

'Lil, yeh'd want to see the wad of notes he took out of his pocket. Makin' a fortune over there in England, so he is.'

Da staggered over to sit down on the chair.

'Well now, yeh know wha' yeh can do with yerself, Phil Doyle.'

'Wha's tha', Lil?'

'Fuck off back over there with him and give me a bit of peace. It's Jimmy this week, Paddy the week before and God only knows who next week, yeh lyin', connivin' bastard! A waster of a man so yeh are.'

Oh my God, all hell is goin' to break out here, I thought. I decided to move little Jacinta and Patricia, who were sitting together with their arms around one another, terrified with all the shouting going on. I put my arms around them. 'Everythin's fine, girls, don't cry. Come on, sit on me lap.'

'Kathleen, is Ma' goin' mad again?' Jacinta asked, sobbing as she held on tight to Patricia. I looked in at Ma, who was really worked up at this stage.

'It's just a mad temper she has, brought on by lots of things tha' yeh're too young to understand. Now, why don't I get yiz a slice of bread and drippin'. Don't move, I'll be right back.'

As I walked into the kitchen, Ma lifted the pot with Da's dinner in it. Da just about saw what was coming and went to run. She caught him on the shoulder. The stew went everywhere. Da slipped and fell. Ma stood over Da and was getting ready to belt him on the head. I jumped in front of her and screamed, '*Stop!* Please, stop! The kids are cryin'! Yeh're frightenin' the life out of them.'

'I can't help meself, Kathleen. When I hear the string of lies tha' comes out of tha' man's mouth, I want to fuckin' kill him. Look at the two little ones with not a pair of shoes between them. I can't let them out the front to play for fear the neighbours will see them. I still have me pride, Kathleen. And there's yer brothers – cardboard inside all their shoes, tryin' to hold them together. Does yer father see any of this? *NO!*'

'Ma, calm down, please. Just let me get Da up to bed. We'll have a chat and sort things out when I come back downstairs. Make a cup of tea and just sit down. Now, give us the pot, will yeh?' She wasn't budging, still holding on tight to the pot. 'Please, Ma.' I put my hands over hers and eased the pot out of her hand.

'All right, Kathleen. I don't know wha' I'd do without yerself and young Phil.'

'Phil, come down and help me with Da,' I roared up the stairs.

Da had fallen asleep on the floor in the middle of all this mayhem. As we were lifting him up, he slipped and slipped again. As Da was starting to come around, I saw Ma coming at him with the pot again. I started to scream, 'Ma, stop,' as I tried to get her back into the kitchen once more. 'Let us put him to bed, please, Ma.' She reluctantly went back in and sat down.

Some of the pig's blood had got on to Da's hands as he lay on the floor. When he woke up all he saw was this blood and he started screaming, 'Jaysus, I'm open. Yer mother's after openin' me head. Look at the blood.'

Phil was great; he could make a story up in seconds. 'Will yeh get away, Da. Tha's just a bit of jam one of the kids must have dropped early on.'

'Is tha' wha' it is?' He was so drunk he couldn't tell the difference.

On the way up the stairs, I whispered to Phil, 'Where's the pig?'

'In the wardrobe.'

'*Wha*'? Yeh stupid tick. Wha' did yeh put it in there for?'

'Well, I didn't get much time, did I? With all hell breakin' out downstairs, I couldn't put it in the other room now, could I? The kids were all startin' to scream. They were afraid of their shit of it. I was goin' to put it in the bath in the first place, but I thought tha' the oul' fella would be goin' in for a piss. Kathleen, there was nowhere else.'

'There'll be blood everywhere, Phil.'

'Ah, here, give us a bit of credit, will yeh, Kathleen? I wrapped an oul' blanket around the head. Come on, help me get Da into bed. He'll be out cold in a few minutes. We'll take the pig back down the stairs first chance we get. I'll stay up here on the landin'. You go back downstairs to Ma before she gets all fired up again and starts wreckin' the kip.'

Downstairs, the two little ones were still sitting on the chair, cuddled together and sobbing their eyes out. I'd forgotten all about them. 'I'm goin' to get yiz tha' nice piece of bread tha' I promised yeh. I'll be straight back.'

Ma was eating the Woodbines.

'Ma, this'll have to stop. I'm nervous enough meself when all this starts, never mind the rest of the kids. Look at the little ones, afraid of their lives to move. It's not righ', Ma. It's just not righ'.'

'I know, I know, Kathleen.'

She was crying really hard at this stage. I called in Jacinta and Patricia.

'Ma just has a bad pain in her head; she'll be okay tomorrow. Now, here's yer bread. Go up to Carmel and Clare. They'll look after yiz. Say goodnight to Ma.'

The two of them looked over, said nothing and ran.

'Only I stopped yeh there Ma, Da would've been dead or hurt really bad. Did yeh see the pot yeh had in yer hand? The heavy iron one. His brains would have been all over the place.'

'I don't care, Kathleen, I just don't care any more.'

The words were only out of her mouth when we heard Da screaming. 'Lil, Lil, quick! Come up, come up to me, quick!'

'See wha' I mean, Kathleen. This is me life. This is wha' I have to put up with. Tha' man makes me go crazy mad.'

'Lil, Lil!' Da roared down again, but there was no moving her.

* * *

At this stage, Da was out on the landing. 'Lil, there's a pig in the wardrobe.' He shouted at the top of his voice.

Ma was out of the chair and up the stairs before you could blink an eye, with me running behind her. Da was standing on the landing with Phil behind him. Phil gave Ma the eye and the nod, pointing in towards the bathroom at the same time. She knew straight away what Phil meant. I took a quick look and there was the pig lying stretched out the full length of the bath, with Noel standing beside it, pointing to himself, letting me know that it was him who had helped Phil to make the big move. Phil, as usual, had a grin on his face, his pearly white teeth showing from cheek to cheek as he whispered in my ear.

'As soon as Da had his back turned, I had it out in seconds. I'd say tha' should get us back in Ma's good books. Wha' de yeh think, Kathleen?'

'Ah, I don't know, Phil. Is there such a thing?'

Ma pushed past Da, nearly knocking him back down the stairs. She went straight over and opened the door of the wardrobe.

'Well, Phil Doyle, wha's all the roarin' and shoutin' about? The wardrobe is empty. I don't see anythin'.'

Da looked in, 'There *was* a pig in tha' wardrobe, as true as all the saints are up in Heaven. I know I saw it.'

'Are yeh sure it wasn't an elephant yeh saw? Isn't tha' wha' drunks see? Not tha' I would know, seein' as I'm not a drinker meself,' she added, starting to raise her voice again. We all started laughing. She looked out at us and gave us one of her dirtiest looks that would cut you in two. That soon put a stop to our laughing.

'Maybe now yeh'll start listenin' to me when I tell yeh yer brains is gettin' damaged from the drink. This is only the start of it, mark my word, Phil Doyle.' Out she stormed past us down the stairs, lying barefaced through her teeth. Only that we knew the truth, we would have believed every word she spoke.

'Right, Phil. I'll get the kids settled into bed. You go in and get Da sorted. And wha'ever yeh do, make sure he's asleep this time.'

'Okay, Kathleen, I will.'

I was only in the room two seconds when I got twenty questions thrown at me from all the kids.

'Kathleen, who owns it? Where did it come from? Is it alive? Can it bite?'

'Shush . . . keep yer voices down. Now, all yeh need to know is, don't mention this in front of Da or yeh'll have Ma to answer to. The good news is, there'll be a nice bit of food for the next couple of days. Now off to sleep, the lot of yiz. Oh, and another thing, not a word about this outside the house.'

I thought, *tha' will give them somethin' to talk about; keep them out of Ma's hair for the night.*

As I closed the door behind me I heard Da ask Phil to check the wardrobe again and again. 'I keep tellin' yeh, Da, a bad nightmare it was, tha's all.' It took a good half hour before Da finally went off to sleep, and we got the pig back downstairs and into the kitchen.

By this time Ma had calmed down. She had the table cleared, a knife in one hand and a hacksaw in the other.

'Right, the pair of yiz, put tha' pig on the table. Young Phil, go next door to Peter and ask him would he lend me tha' hatchet of his.'

'Ma, tha' pig is huge. How are yeh goin' to cut all this and where will yeh put it?'

'Let me worry about tha', Kathleen.'

'There can't be any of tha' pig here when Da wakes up, Ma. Yeh know wha' he'll do. The priest will be brought down. We'll be told tha' yeh're after lettin' the devil get into us. There'll be more trouble.'

'Don't you worry about yer Da, Kathleen. The only devil he has to worry about is me and the only sight tha' will be seen of this pig by the time I'm finished will be the lumps of juicy bacon fryin' in the pan first thing in the mornin'. Now get yer arse up to Mrs Kearney and ask her could I put a bit of meat in tha' fancy fridge of hers and there'll be a free parcel in it for herself. And Kathleen, while yeh're at it, knock on a few of the neighbours' doors and tell them there's some cheap meat goin'. They can pay me next week when they get their children's allowance. Oh, and another thing, make sure and tell them to say nothin' about where it came from and not a word to yer father when they see him.'

Not many people had fridges back then. There wasn't much point having one, not in our house anyway. What was bought on the day was eaten and not a crumb would be seen anywhere.

Nobody asked too many questions that night as I knocked on the doors. They were all glad to be getting something for half nothing. 'Tell yer Ma we'll see her tomorrow, Kathleen, mum's the word.'

Ma was well pleased when I told her. 'Tha's grand, Kathleen. The rest is easy; this is no different to any of the fish tha' I filleted over the years with me mother. It's just bigger. The skin and guts are all gone, so tha'll make it easier for me.'

Down came the hatchet, off came the head.

'Phil, out the back yard with tha'. Them dogs will think all their birthdays came in one. As for the rest, I'll just glide me knife slowly through. It'll be done before yeh know it.'

And sure enough it was. Mrs Kearney got her parcel and held onto a few for Ma. Myself and Phil dropped off the rest to the neighbours while the dogs chewed on the bones for the night.

* * *

When Da came down the next morning, the only trace of the pig, just as Ma had said, were the lumps of juicy bacon frying in the pan.

'They're grand rashers yeh have there, Lil,' said Da.

Ma turned around and looked over at us. 'Thanks to me family. Not tha' yeh would've noticed, Phil Doyle, yeh drunken bastard, with the carry on of yeh.'

Da just gave a little cough and sat down at the table. He went on to tell us about the nightmare he'd had and how real it seemed to be.

'I'll have to give up the drink; it's startin' to make me see things, Lil.'

She just gave him the look and carried on cooking. The little ones sat and listened to Da's story, the others laughing and nudging one another, not saying a word.

* * *

Ma made herself a few bob from that night and was able to clear some of her bills. How she kept a straight face the day we went into the butcher's shop, I'll never know.

'Yeh must have had a windfall, Lil, clearin' the whole bill in one go,' smiled Mr Hogg, the butcher.

'Let's just say somethin' fell me way. Yeh know me, always pay me bills when I'm able. Tha' way yeh can knock again.'

'Yeh never said a truer word, Lil.'

And on they went, chatting away about the goings-on in the world. By this time, Ma was convinced the pig had been sent to help her and I suppose it was in a way. There would always be something or someone, just when she would be on her last legs. That's how she survived.

That was Ma.

23

The Ghost

After little Mary died, I really thought Ma was finished having babies. I was shocked when she told me there was another one on the way and a couple of months later little Paul arrived.

I was seventeen and I still had half of the kids sleeping in the bed with me. I woke up one night to the screams of Clare, who was around eleven years old. She was climbing all over me.

'Jaysus Christ, wha's wrong with yeh, Clare? Yeh're after frightenin' the shite out of me.'

'There's a ghost in the room, Kathleen,' she screamed hysterically.

At this stage she was nearly on top of my face.

'For fuck's sake, Clare, will yeh get off me and calm yerself down.'

She got under the covers and held the blanket over her head, screaming, 'It's at the end of the bed.'

I sat up in the bed and looked down. 'There's nothin' there, Clare.'

'There is, Kathleen. I saw it, I swear.'

With all the commotion going on, all the kids woke up.

'Wha's goin' on in there, Kathleen?' Ma roared in from the other room.

'It's okay, Ma. Clare is just havin' a bad dream.'

'Tell her to shut up. She has the whole house awake.'

'It's not a dream,' Clare shouted from under the covers. 'It's real. I'm tellin' yeh, I saw him.'

When she said *him*, a cold shiver ran right through me. I could feel myself slowly slide down in the bed as I pulled the blanket right up to my face.

'Right then, Clare. Tell me, wha' did it look like?' I said, trying to calm her down.

She peeped her head out from under the covers. 'He was a big man with a long dark coat on and he wore a hat, but he had no face.'

'Wha' de yeh mean, he had no face?'

'Kathleen, it was just empty under the hat, and he was standin' there lookin' down at us.' She pointed to the end of the bed. She was starting to cry and getting really upset.

'It's okay, Clare. Don't be gettin' yerself in a state. Come on. Move in here beside me and I'll give yeh a hug.'

'Wha' about me, Kathleen?' Marion whispered. 'I'm afraid too. I don't want to stay down the end of the bed on me own.'

'Okay, get in and squeeze in beside Clare.'

The two of them wrapped their arms around one another. With that, Carmel and Jacinta jumped out of their bed. 'We're not stayin' over here on our own. Move over, Kathleen.'

'Ah, for Christ's sake. Yiz can't all fit in here beside me. Get down the end of the bed. Carmel, go with Jacinta.'

Carmel got her spoke in, which was unusual for her as she was always so quiet.

'Yeh want us to go down there, after Clare sayin' she saw a ghost standin' at the bed? Are yeh mad, Kathleen? There's no way, we're stayin' up here. Come on, move over.'

It didn't matter what I said; nobody was moving. We were like sardines in a tin. It seemed to take ages before they all finally dozed off. I lay there, unable to go back to sleep. Every now and then I'd have a little peep over the blankets and look down at the end of the bed. I could feel that shiver come over me again. I was lying there thinking to myself, *thank God it's the weekend and I've no work tomorrow. I can have a bit of a lie-in, seein' as how I'm awake most of the night.*

It was getting bright outside when I finally drifted off to sleep.

When I did eventually wake up, there wasn't a sound in the room. I looked around but everybody had gone. Normally there would be a couple of the kids running around messing and acting the eejit, as they always do. Just then, I got a quick flash of what Clare had said and how frightened she'd been. I wasn't long making my way down the stairs, taking the steps three at a time, looking over my shoulder as I went.

Ma was sitting by the fire feeding Paul. Da was in the kitchen with the rest of the gang making the porridge.

'Ma, it's after eleven. Why didn't yeh call me?'

'It's not very often yeh take a lie-in. I thought it best to leave yeh alone. If yeh stayed asleep, well yeh must have needed it.'

'I thought when I woke up I was in the wrong house. It was tha' quiet and peaceful.'

'Well, we all know the reason for tha', don't we? Last night, all tha' shoutin' and roarin' out of Clare.'

'She was just dreamin', tha's all it was, Ma.'

'Well, Kathleen, yeh must have really been dead to the world tha' yeh didn't hear the goin's-on around here this mornin'. Clare Doyle must have only opened her eyes when she started on about some man she saw standin' at the end of the bed with no face. Did yeh ever hear the likes of it? There's a ghost in the room. It's frightenin' the shit out of them all. I don't know how yeh didn't hear them. They nearly killed themselves tryin' to get out of the room and down the stairs. I'm sure Mrs Kennedy next door must think I reared a shower of lunatics. How tha' woman doesn't complain to me I'll never know. Kathleen, go in and talk to Clare. See if yeh can make some sense out of wha' she's rammagin' on about.'

As soon as I walked into the kitchen I got questions thrown at me from all sides. Of course, Phil and Noel had to get their spoke in straight away.

'Kathleen, did yeh hear wha' tha' tick Clare is sayin'? Tha' she saw a ghost last night. Bloody eejit.'

'I did too!' roared Clare. 'I'm not makin' it up!'

I sat down beside her, trying to calm her down. 'Shush, will yiz! Keep yer voices down.'

'And wha' was it doin'?' Noel sneered at Clare, with a smirk on his face. 'Was it flyin' around the room and goin' in and out of the walls?' he said, nudging Phil, the two of them having a right laugh at her.

'I told yiz wha' happened. Now fuck off and stop laughin' at me.'

'Come on, Clare. Don't take any notice of them.'

'They're just fuckin' ticks, tha's wha' they are, Kathleen.'

'Will yeh keep yer voice down and don't let Ma hear yeh.'

'Well, if the ghost comes back tonight, I hope it stands over them. I bet yeh they'll piss on themselves with the fright and we'll see who has the last laugh then.'

I sat there for ages trying to convince Clare that there were no such things as ghosts, but no matter what I said there was no way she was backing down on her story.

'I don't care if nobody believes me. I know wha' I saw and I'm tellin' yeh, it wasn't a dream.'

That night it took me all my time to get Clare up the stairs. Ma coaxed her by letting her sleep at the end of her bed. There was no way she would go back into our bedroom. After a good bit of an effort, and with a little bribe, she convinced Jacinta to sleep in the bed with her, promising her that she would give her tuppence as soon as she got paid from her turf round.

* * *

A few weeks went by and all was quiet for a while – until I woke up to the sound of Ma roaring, fucking and blinding out of her again. The whole house was in an uproar, with not only Clare, but Jacinta also screaming that she'd seen the ghost. 'It was standin' over Ma and Da.'

That was it. From that night on, Clare never slept upstairs again. She was so nervous after that night, and she had all the kids the same way listening to her go on and on about the ghost.

'Kathleen, wha' am I to do? I can't get Clare up them stairs for love or money. She's really convinced tha' she saw a man up in the bedroom.'

'I wonder *did* Clare see somethin', Ma? Wha' de yeh think? Do yeh believe in ghosts yerself?'

'I do believe tha' there could be spirits floatin' around out there tha's not ready to go over to the other side, for wha'ever reason. Only *they'd* know tha'.'

'But, Ma, wha' would a spirit be doin' here with us?'

'Well now, if Clare really saw somethin' – and she's adamant tha' she did – the only thing tha' I can come up with is this. Remember a few years back, tha' young man in the big lorry tha' crashed into the gates of the turf depot?'

'Tha's right, Ma. I remember now. Da and Mr Kearney carried him in here. They put him lyin' there on the kitchen floor. Wha's tha' got to do with all the commotion goin' on now?'

'Well, he died of a heart attack, there on the very spot where yeh're standin'.'

I jumped and moved away.

'Ma, yeh told us he was just a bit sick and he had to go to the hospital.'

'Of course I said tha'. Yeh hardly think I'd tell yeh the truth? Yeh were all too young at the time. Isn't tha' why I told yeh to get all the kids out of the way and up the stairs when he was being carried out of the house? Sure, the poor craythur was already dead when yer Da carried him in.'

'Jaysus, Ma, yeh don't think tha' could be him wanderin' around the house?'

'Could be, Kathleen, could be.'

'Oh, I wish yeh hadn't told me tha' now! I'm goin' to be shittin' on meself.'

'Sure wha' are yeh talkin' about, Kathleen? The dead won't harm yeh. It's the livin' yeh have to keep yer eyes on. Anyway, don't go tellin' any of the others about wha' I just told yeh. They're all nervous wrecks as it is without addin' fuel to the fire.'

* * *

My brother Phil was a swine. Every chance he got, with the help of Noel, he would be jumping out from behind doors, frightening the life out of us girls, until one time, in the early hours of the morning, it all backfired on Phil and Noel . . . well, you would want to have heard the roars and screams out of them.

'I saw it, I saw it! It's standin' there, just like Clare said,' Phil roared. 'Will yiz wake up, Ma, Da?'

Noel was screaming with terror. 'I saw it too, Ma. Are yeh awake?'

'Shut the fuck up, the pair of yiz! Yeh're screamin' like banshees,' said Ma. 'Yeh hardly think I'd be asleep with the noise outta yiz, yeh bloody gobshites. The whole house is awake now. Tha's it. I'm goin' downstairs to make a cup of tea and get meself a Woodbine before I go crazy mad and kill the lot of yiz. I'm sick to death listenin' to stuff about this bloody ghost.'

Ma was only down the stairs when all hell broke out. The roars of her again! I thought she had seen something as well.

'Holy Mother of Divine God! Wha' the fuck is after happenin' here? Phil Doyle, come down here. Kathleen, get yer arse down them stairs now!'

I fell down the stairs, with Da right behind me. When I walked into the kitchen, I couldn't believe what I was looking at.

The table and four chairs had been painted silver. All the jam jars that we drank our tea from, the plates and the only two cups that we had to our name, were all painted gold. Da looked at me; I looked at Ma, who was looking over at Clare, her two eyes nearly popping out of her head. Da quickly stood in front of Ma.

'Now, Lil, let's not get too worked up about this.' He gave me the eye and the nod to get over to Clare, who was standing at the side of the fire with the armchair pulled right up in front of her, hoping that Ma couldn't get at her. Ma was screaming, fucking and blinding out of her like I never saw before. It took Da all his strength to hold Ma back and, with a lot of effort, he got her to sit down on one of the silver chairs and smoke a Woodbine. Then he went through the presses, hoping to find a jam jar that Clare hadn't got her hands on so that he could make Ma a cup of tea to calm her down.

'Kathleen, she's goin' to kill me,' said Clare.

'Will yeh keep yer voice down? I'm goin' to have to get yeh out of here before Ma loses it altogether. Jaysus, Clare, yeh really did it this time. Wha' were yeh thinkin'? Yeh even painted the jam jars.'

'I don't know, Kathleen. I didn't mean to paint everythin'. I got carried away tryin' to keep meself awake.'

'Clare, yeh're goin' to have stop all this ghost business. There's no ghost. De yeh hear me?'

'There is, Kathleen, there is. I know wha' I saw. So did Phil and Noel, and I'm really glad about tha'.'

At this stage Ma was eating the Woodbines in the kitchen. I had Clare in the parlour, out of her way.

'Da, wha' are we goin' to do? Ma's really losin' the plot. She'll kill Clare if she gets her hands on her.'

Da shook his head. 'Kathleen can yeh blame her? I mean,

look at the state of the place.' He turned to Clare. 'Clare, yeh have me heart broke. Wha' am I goin' to do with yeh?'

'There *is* a ghost, Da. I saw it. I swear.'

'Be quiet, Clare, I'm not listenin' to any more of this nonsense. Kathleen, take her with yeh and ask Mrs Kearney can she stay with her for a couple of hours until I clean this mess up and try to calm yer mother down, if tha's at all possible. Oh, when yeh're up there, ask her if she has any empty jam jars lyin' around in her press. There's nothin' left to put a cup of tea in.'

It was starting to get bright out as I knocked on Mrs Kearney's door. She listened to me as I filled her in on the goings-on of the night.

'I don't know how your poor mother is still sane, Kathleen. You're a wild bunch. That's all I can say. Tell your father that's no problem. Clare can stay with me, but I think this will take more than a few hours to blow over. Come on in and sit down, the two of you. Kathleen, help me get these jam jars for your father. He knows I always save them up for your mother.'

Mrs Kearney had a soft spot for Clare and held on to her for a couple of days until Ma calmed down. There was no way the table and chairs could be cleaned, so they were chopped up for firewood. Da had got to know a couple of the shopkeepers beside Portobello Bridge from dropping in and out, selling bits of scrap to them over the years. He picked up a second-hand table and chairs, with the promise that he would take extra rubbish each week until the debt was paid. That way no money ever changed hands.

Ma was happy enough when she heard that. Things slowly got back to normal, if you could ever call it that in our house! Da got the priest down to bless the house, hoping it would settle Clare. It never did. She never, ever slept upstairs again, God love her! It cost her a lot of money, as all of the kids would charge her a couple of pennies to go upstairs with her whenever she had to use the bathroom.

* * *

On and off over the years there would be other sightings of the ghost, causing chaos every time. Everyone had the same story to tell – 'a man standing at the end of the bed, a man with no face'. I never did see the ghost myself, but was Clare's dream so real in her own head that she had convinced herself and everybody else that it was true? Could it have been the young man who died in the kitchen that day, his spirit unable to get to the other side, as Ma would put it? All I know is that the seed was planted that night, and the story still goes on to this very day among my family.

Is there really a ghost? I wonder.

24

The Engagement

It was Sunday morning and the sun was splitting the trees. I slipped out of the bedroom and made my way down to the kitchen. Ma was sitting there feeding Paul.

'It's really warm out, Ma. Will I open the back door and let a bit of fresh air in?'

'If yeh want, Kathleen.'

'Yeh must have been up very early. I see the porridge and all is made.'

'I didn't sleep very well last night.'

'Is Paul keepin' yeh awake then?'

'No, the child's fine. I've just a bit of a headache.'

'A nice cup of tea will sort tha' out, Ma. I got up early so's I could get all me work done around the house. Alan said he'd be down early. Maybe I'll go out to Portmarnock, seein's it's so nice out today. The beach is lovely there. We should try and bring the kids someday; they'd love it. Wha' de yeh think, Ma?'

'Wha'ever yeh say, Kathleen.'

I looked a bit more closely at her. 'Yeh're not even mindin' anythin' I'm sayin', Ma.'

'I've things on me mind, Kathleen. Now leave me be,' she snapped.

231

That was it – Ma was in bad form, so I knew to shut up. I kept out of her way for most of the morning, with a few of the kids helping me. We weren't long getting the cleaning done and the younger ones washed, while Da was out the back tidying around. He was doing everything and anything to try to please Ma, but she wasn't having any of it; even with him taking the pledge, it made no difference. I made my way out to him.

'Da, is there somethin' wrong with Ma? She's terrible snappy. She bit the head off me earlier. Did she say anythin' to yeh?'

'Best leave her be, Kathleen, she'll come around; she always does.'

'Okay, Da.'

Just then I heard Alan arriving. I ran back into the house. 'Ma, the place is sorted, and the young ones is washed and fed. I'll be off now – is tha' okay? I won't be late.'

'Right, Kathleen.' She didn't even lift her head as she spoke.

* * *

We finally got to Portmarnock and were walking along the beach holding hands. I loved the open space and the freedom was great.

'Come on over here, Kathleen, and we'll sit down. I want to talk to yeh about somethin'.'

'Yeh look real serious, Alan. Wha's wrong?'

'De yeh love me, Kathleen?'

'Don't yeh know I do.'

'It's just, yeh never say it.'

'Well, I get shy when it comes to all tha' stuff, Alan. I know I'm the happiest when I'm with yeh, and when yeh're not there, all I do is think about yeh. So I think tha' means . . . I love yeh. There, I said it.'

'Tha's all I wanted to hear, Kathleen.' He put his arms around me and gave me a big hug. 'I have somethin' for yeh.'

Alan always spoiled me rotten, buying me little presents, and I loved every minute of it. He handed me a little box and as I opened it he said the words . . .

'Will yeh marry me, Kathleen?'

I didn't have to think twice. 'I'd love to marry yeh, Alan!'

We kissed, not caring who saw us.

'Do yeh like the ring then?'

'I love it, Alan! Are yeh serious though – us gettin' married?'

'Yeah, of course I am.'

'Will I be able to have a long white dress and veil? Can everybody come? Oh, and the kids, I can't leave them out. They've to come before anybody else.'

I was so excited, he was laughing his head off at me. I ran around the sand dunes, jumping from one to the other like a child. When I think back now, that's all we were – two kids, so young.

Then I got a flash of Ma. I stopped in my tracks and screamed, 'Ma'll go crazy mad.'

'No, she won't. I get on real well with yer Ma and Da.'

'Da'll be okay, Alan, but Ma'll have a stroke. Yeh know she depends on me for everythin'. She won't let me, I know she won't.'

'Jaysus, Kathleen, I was alright until yeh said tha'. Now I'll be shitin' meself askin' them.'

'Leave it to me, Alan, I'll talk to them first.'

'No, I'm not havin' tha'. We'll do it together.'

'Okay, but not tonight. Ma is in the height of it. I don't know wha's wrong. She's snappin' at everybody the past few days.'

* * *

Alan dropped me off at the door and went on home. I went into the kitchen, Da was sitting at the fire reading the paper and Ma was making the lunches for the next day. A couple of the kids were looking at the telly.

'Yeh look tired, Ma. Will I take Paul in with me tonight? Give yeh a break. Let yeh get a good night's sleep.'

'Yeh've to get yerself up early for work tomorrow. He'll have yeh awake durin' the night lookin' for the diddy.'

'Why don't yeh squeeze some milk into the bottle? I'll look after him; I don't mind, Ma, honest.'

'Go about yer business, Kathleen, leave me be.'

Da gave me the eye and the nod to leave her alone. I said good night and went upstairs, not knowing what to think or what could be wrong.

I was standing in front of the bathroom mirror, squeezing a few blackheads out of my chin, when Phil tipped me on the shoulder.

'Jaysus, yeh're after frightenin' the life out of me.'

'Have yeh got a minute, Kathleen?' He sat on the side of the bath. 'I'm goin' away.'

'Stop messin', Phil, will yeh.'

'I'm serious. I'm off to Canada. I have me papers and all.'

'But yeh have no money. Yeh're not goin' away. Will yeh stop actin' the eejit.'

'The Canadian embassy pay yer fare and get yeh a job. Yeh don't have to start payin' them back until yeh're sorted. I'll get sixty pound for me Honda 50. Tha'll do me 'til I get meself goin'.'

'Does Ma know?'

'No, not yet, but Da does. He thinks it's great for me to get out there and see a bit of the world.

'I don't believe this – yeh're really goin' to leave us.'

'I got the word today. I'll be gone in about two weeks. There's no goin' back now; me mind's made up.'

My eyes started to fill up.

'Kathleen, I never thought I'd see the day tha' yeh'd be cryin' over me.'

'No, I'm not, yeh eejit, there's just somethin' in me eye.'

'Get away, yeh're only an oul' softie after all.' He put his arms around me. 'I thought yeh'd be glad to see the back of me.'

'Yeh drive me nuts most of the time, Phil, but I never wanted yeh to go away. Not tha' far anyway.' I pulled back and looked at him. 'I have a bit of news meself; Alan asked me to marry him tonight. Wha' de yeh think?'

'So wha' did yeh say, Kathleen?'

'I said yes. Look, he gave me the ring and all.'

'Alan's a skinny little fucker, but I like him. Yeh're doin' all right there. When's all this happenin'?'

'Not for about a year. It depends on how quick he gets the money together.'

'Good, I should've plenty of money made by then. The wages is great in Canada. So I'll be able to give yeh a few bob, help yeh get a few things.'

'Will yeh really, Phil?' I put my arm around and gave him a big hug. 'I'll miss yeh, so I will. Promise me one thing – yeh'll come home for me weddin'. I'll go mad if yeh're not there.'

'There's no way I'll be missin' tha'. Yeh don't have to worry there. But do me one big favour first; let me tell Ma me bit of news first, then yeh can drop yer bombshell.'

'Jaysus, Phil, wha'll Ma say when she hears the two of us is movin' out? I'm goin' to be shittin' meself tellin' her. She's goin' to lose the head altogether.'

'It'll be only for a day or two, and then she'll come around. Some of us has to start movin' out, for fuck's sake; we're like flies on shite – we're all on top of one another, and now there's Paul, another baby cryin', fartin' and shitin' through the night. You're alrigh', yeh have just one or two of them younger ones pissin' on yeh, but I'm in the same room with Ma and Da. He's gruntin' and snorin' like a pig when he has a sup on him, which is most of the time. Then yeh have Ma fuckin' and blindin' out of her about one thing or another. *And on top of all tha'*, I have Jap-eyes Noel sleepin' in the same bunk bed with me, his smelly feet stuck in me face all night. I wake up every mornin', gaspin' for breath thinkin', *Oh my God, one of them is after shitin' on me face* – the smell's tha' bad. No, I'm on me way, I don't care; there's no changin' me mind. So yeh'll say nothin', Kathleen?'

'Okay, I suppose I'll have to wait with me bit of news.'

* * *

Phil told Ma the next evening. We were all sitting around the table having our tea when he just came out with it.

'Ma, I'm goin' to work in Canada.'

Ma nearly fainted. Da had to run and get her a cup of water.

'Where in God's name is tha', Phil?'

'It's beside America.'

'*Wha*'? Tha's the other side of the world! I'll never see yeh again.'

'Yes yeh will, Ma, sure won't I be able to send yeh loads of money?'

Da wasn't saying a word; Ma looked over at him.

'Did yeh know about this, Phil Doyle?'

'I did, Lil.'

'And yeh never told me about it, yeh connivin' bastard.'

'Young Phil wanted to tell yeh himself.'

Ma broke down crying. Da put his arm around her.

'Now, Lil, don't be gettin' yerself upset. It'll do him good to see a bit of the world before he settles down.'

She just gave him one of her looks and pushed him away.

'Fuck yeh and fuck the world! I don't care, I don't want me son goin' away. I'll never see him again. Leave me be, now, leave me be.'

She was crying really hard, and the kids were getting upset, so I got them all to come upstairs with me.

'I want yiz all to stay up here and be quiet.'

'Kathleen, it's too early for us to go to bed.'

'I know, I know – play a game or somethin', just don't come down. Ma's in the height of it.'

Phil and Da were on their way out when I got to the end of the stairs.

'Where are yiz goin'? Da, don't leave me with Ma in this state.'

'There's no talkin' to her, Kathleen. Best tha' I keep out of the way. Phil's goin' up to the boxin' club to do a bit of trainin'. I'll tag along with him.' Phil was a great boxer; he had become All-Ireland Middleweight Champion and had represented Ireland at international level.

And off they went, leaving me to try to sort things out. I made my way into the kitchen.

'Will yeh have a cup of tea, Ma? Are yeh alright? Are yeh sick? Will yeh talk to me?'

She just rocked backwards and forward in the chair. She had her face covered with one of the baby's towel nappies. I had only seen Ma this upset before when her mother and Maisie died.

'Yeh're not just cryin' over Phil leavin', are yeh, Ma? Will yeh tell me, please?'

She took the nappy away from her face; her eyes were red from crying.

'I'm tha' way again, Kathleen.'

'Wha' de yeh mean, Ma, wha' way?'

'Jaysus, Kathleen, yeh know wha' I mean.'

'I *don't* know. Wha' are yeh talkin' about, Ma?'

'De yeh not understand wha' I'm tryin' to say? *I'm havin' another child.*'

I couldn't get my head around what she had just said. Then the penny finally dropped. 'But yeh just had a baby! Paul's only four months old. Jaysus Christ, Ma, I don't believe this! Yeh're nearly forty-five. This is madness; yeh can't keep havin' babies like this.'

'De yeh not think I know tha', Kathleen? I'm goin' out of me mind with the worry of everythin'.'

Paul started crying. I picked him up and walked him up and

down, frantic, screaming inside my head. *Christ, wha' am I goin' to do. I'm never goin' to be able to leave! It's not fair, it's just not fair. I'm leavin', I don't care – I'm not mindin' any more babies. It's not my fault.* Paul was screaming at this stage.

'Kathleen, give me the child. He's lookin' for the diddy.'

I didn't hear her. I was still walking up and down, trying to take it all in.

'Kathleen!' Ma shouted. 'Give 'im to me, before he takes a fit with the hunger.'

'Sorry, Ma, here, here.'

I sat down while Ma settled Paul for his feed. *This is it, I'm sayin' it. I don't care, it's now or never.*

'Ma . . . I want to say somethin' . . . eh . . . eh . . .'

'Hold on a minute there, Kathleen, 'til I fix Paul.' She stuck the diddy in the baby's mouth. 'Now, wha' is it?'

'I . . . I . . . eh . . . Alan asked me to marry him today, and I said yes.' *Tha's it – I've said it.*

Ma went into shock and went silent for a few seconds. I didn't know what would come next.

Then all hell broke loose.

'*Holy Mother of Divine Jaysus!* Are yiz all tryin' to kill me around here with worry? Just when I'm startin' to make ends meet, yeh're all lookin' to leave me. I'm not havin' it! Anyway, yeh're too young, Kathleen. Yeh're only a child. De yeh want to end up like me, Kathleen, never a shillin' in yer pocket? Maybe young Phil is right. Get out there and enjoy himself before he settles down, and you do the same yerself when the time is right.'

'But when will tha' be, Ma? I'm not bein' cheeky, but if I stay here tha' won't happen. As far back as I can remember, all I do is mind kids and clean the house for yeh. I was never a child, *never*. I want to start doin' things for meself for a change.'

By this time I was balling my eyes out. It was my first time ever to speak out and say a little of how I was feeling. I would say plenty inside my head, but never out loud. Ma sat there looking at me, tapping her foot up and down. I didn't know if it was temper or nerves. Either way, I was easing myself up off the chair, and taking a step back, getting ready to run, just in case.

'Sit yerself back down there, I'm not goin' to kill yeh. And wipe the snots off yer face. Yeh had a lot bottled up there in tha' head of yers, so yeh had.'

God, if she only knew! Tha' was only the tip of the iceberg.

'I know. I'm sorry, Ma.'

'Yeh should have said how yeh were feelin'.'

'But Ma, yeh had nobody else to help yeh, and I was too afraid to say anythin'.'

'Am I tha' hard, Kathleen?'

'Yes, yeh are, Ma.'

'Well, I don't mean to be, but if I don't keep things right around here, yer father certainly won't. Anyway, when yeh've things on yer mind, it's best to get them out in the open; otherwise they only seed inside, eat away at yeh, so they do. Tha's wha' I've been doin' the past couple of weeks. I've nobody to turn to, since Mrs Kearney moved to her posh new house out there in Dun Laoghaire; visited me only once, after all them years of us bein' neighbours. People don't be long forgettin' yeh, Kathleen. If only Maisie was here; she got me through so many bad patches in me life, always saw the funny side of everythin'. She's probably up there in heaven laughin' down at me, callin' me all the gobshites under the sun for gettin' meself into this state.'

'*I'm* here, Ma; yeh can always talk to me, and then there's Da.'

'Don't mention tha' man to me. I want to fuckin' kill him, so I do. The things I wanted to say and give out about yer father over the years weren't for yer ears, Kathleen. Anyway, there's just some things yeh don't say to yer child, no matter how old yeh are. Now, tha's enough said on tha' matter, but

I'm glad yeh know wha's been wrong with me and it's out in the open. But how will I ever manage without yeh? Yeh're the only one tha' looks after the place and keeps them young ones in hand when I'm not here.'

'Yeh'll be here yerself all the time now, Ma. Yeh won't be goin' back to work, not with another baby comin' along. It's time yeh stopped anyway. I don't know how yeh lasted this long.'

'Yeh're right there, Kathleen. I'm very tired and not able for them late nights anymore.'

'There's a couple of the others kids comin' up soon for work. Tha'll bring a few shillin's in for yeh and I promise I'll hand me pay packet up until the day I get married. It's not as if I'm goin' far away, like Phil.'

'Don't mention tha' to me or yeh'll start me off cryin' again.'

'I'll be callin' into the house all the time. Yeh'll see, Ma.'

'Does yer father know about this?'

'No, no, we were goin' to tell the two of yiz together.'

'Are yeh sure he wasn't keepin' this to himself as well? Bastard of a man.'

'I swear, Ma, it's just the way everythin' went tonight. Alan will go mad, he wanted to ask yiz himself.'

'Hmm, I see . . . He seems to be a good young fella, not afraid to put his hand in his pocket if he sees yeh're stuck for a smoke, and looks yeh straight in the eye when yeh talk to him. Are yeh sure about this, Kathleen? Is it wha' yeh really want?'

'It is, Ma, I really love Alan.'

'Right then, once yeh're sure, yeh have me blessin'.'

The words were only out of her mouth when there was a big cheer from all the kids. They'd been listening all the time. I didn't care; I wrapped my arms around Ma, hugging and kissing her.

'Jaysus, Kathleen, yeh're after knockin' the diddy out of Paul's mouth. The milk's after goin' into his eye. Will yeh calm

yerself down and hand me tha' dry nappy there? For God's
sake, wha' the hell's got into yeh?'

'I'm sorry, Ma, it's just yeh've made me so happy.'

'Right, right. I'll talk to yer father.'

'No, Ma, let Alan ask the two of yiz together, please.'

'Okay then, we'll say nothin'.'

* * *

We got all the kids ready and up to bed. I tidied the place and
we sat there, just Ma and I, talking and working things out. Da
was late coming home with Phil. I suppose he was half hoping
everything was okay. It was, but Ma didn't let him know that,
not for a while anyway. She gave him one of her looks and that
was enough for him.

'I'll say goodnight then, Lil. I'm off to bed.'

She grunted under her breath.

As Da went upstairs, I followed him, telling him I knew why
Ma was so upset.

'Thank God, she told yeh, Kathleen.'

'Just go along with her, Da. She'll come around, yeh'll see.'

'Good, good. Thanks for lookin' after things for me. I don't
know wha' we'd do without yeh.'

I went back downstairs. Phil was in the kitchen.

'Yeh knew all along wha' was wrong with Ma, didn't yeh,
yeh swine?'

He swore on everything that was holy that he knew
nothing.

'I don't believe yeh! Yeh're a sly fucker, Phil Doyle.'

He was laughing his head off. 'Will yeh stop gettin' yerself
all worked up, for Jaysus' sake; Da only told me on the way up
to the club. Wha' beats me is, how are they managin' to do it
with all of us sleepin' in the same fuckin' room?'

'Oh my God, Phil, will yeh keep yer voice down? Imagine
even thinkin' about Ma and Da doin' things like tha'.'

'Yeh know somethin', in between all tha' snorin', the sly bastard must've been doin' it all the time and I never copped on. He has to be one fast man. I can tell yeh tha' for nothin'. In and out like a light.'

'Yeh know wha' you are, Phil? Just a filth, I mean it, yeh are.'

'Would yeh get away with yeh, Kathleen, actin' all high and mighty! Don't tell me tha' Alan never felt more than the top of yer leg or yer arse for tha' matter. He's not bringin' yeh out to Portmarnock every chance he gets for nothin'.'

'Will yeh stop, Alan's not like tha'.'

'Would yeh give it over. He'd have yer knickers off like a flash of lightnin' the first chance he got, which he probably already has.'

'Yeh can get tha' dirty grin off yer face, Phil, because he hasn't. I don't do things like tha'.'

'Yeh mean yeh're still a virgin after all this time with Alan?'

'Wha' are yeh talkin' about? I'm not a virgin, right – I missed Mass twice last month and I only said me rosary once this week, because I was tired. Now, wha' de yeh say to tha', smart arse?!'

At this stage Phil was rolling around the floor screaming, he was laughing so much.

'Stop, Kathleen, stop. I'm gettin' pains in me chest here. Are yeh for fuckin' real or wha'?'

'I don't know wha' yeh think is so funny, Phil.'

'I don't believe this – yeh're still so innocent, Kathleen. Ma!' he shouted. 'Ma, come out here and talk to this wan, will yeh? Before she's the laughin' stock of Crumlin.'

That's when Ma came in.

'Wha's goin' on with the pair of yiz, shoutin' at this hour of the night? Yeh'll have the whole house awake.'

'Don't mind him, Ma, it's nothin'. He's messin' as usual.'

'For Jaysus' sake, Ma, will yeh ever sit her down and tell her a few things. Yeh know, about men and women stuff – yeh know wha' I'm talkin' about, Ma. She knows fuck-all.'

'Mind yer lip there, Phil. Yeh're not too big to get the back of me hand.'

'Ah, I'm sorry, Ma, I can't help it.' He shook his head, still laughing as he went upstairs.

'Kathleen, wha' has Phil been sayin'?'

'He said tha' I'm still a virgin – the cheek of him. Well, I put him straight and told him I wasn't.'

She nearly choked on her cup of tea. *'Yeh wha'?!'*

'Phil thinks I'm a real Holy Mary because I go to Mass and say me prayers every night. He's always makin' a laugh of me.'

'Didn't I tell yeh, Kathleen, I don't know how many times, not to be lettin' Phil wind yeh up? Now, wha's this – are yeh tellin' me straight to me face tha' yeh've done the other with Alan?'

'Wha' are yeh talkin' about, Ma, wha' other? Wha' de yeh mean?'

'You know . . . yeh're not tha' fuckin' stupid, Kathleen. Men and women, together – doin' the other!'

The penny finally dropped with me. 'Yeh mean tha'? Oh my God! No, I haven't! Who said tha'?'

'*You* did. Yeh just said yeh weren't a virgin. Tha's wha' tha' means.'

'Good fuck! I didn't know tha', nobody told me. Ma, why didn't yeh say somethin'? I thought bein' a virgin meant bein' like the Virgin Mary herself.' I was off again, tears and snots everywhere. 'I'm such a gobshite, Ma, I know nothin'. No wonder Phil was laughin' at me.'

'Sshh now, Kathleen, yeh're no different than the rest of us women. These are things tha' nobody talks about. Yeh're just supposed to pick them up as yeh go along. It's my fault, I should've talked to yeh – not tha' I know tha' much meself, yeh know wha' I mean.' She got herself a bit flustered. 'But there's one thing I know for sure, and tha's how to have babies.'

'Yeh can say tha' again, Ma.'

I got a half-grin off her. I wasn't sure if I should laugh or stay serious, so I said nothing more.

'Just make sure yeh keep yerself to yerself, Kathleen, and don't be lettin' anybody interfere with yeh down below. A heart attack yeh nearly gave me, sayin' yeh're not a virgin and all! It's bad enough me bringin' too many babies into this God-forsaken world, without you startin'.'

I went to bed that night still mixed up, but a little bit wiser.

The next morning I had a hundred and one questions for Phil. 'Seein's yeh know so much, yeh better fill me in on a few things.'

'So the penny has finally dropped, huh, Kathleen?'

Phil wasn't long putting me straight on the facts of life.

'How de yeh know all this, Phil?'

'There was a few oul' fellas on the site when I started work. They don't be long tellin' yeh wha's for wha', and where it goes. Then I just picked meself up a mot here and there and, Bob's yer uncle, I was away in a hack.'

* * *

Every night for about a week, Alan tried to get Ma and Da on their own to ask them about us getting married, but with one thing or another – the kids fighting, Ma in the height of it, Da having a sup on him – no time was the right time.

Saturday night came and Alan was down early.

'This is it, Kathleen. I'm sayin' it tonight. I don't give a damn wha's goin' on or who's here. They can all listen. I don't care.'

'Right, then. We'll say it together.'

Ma and Da were sitting each side of the fireplace. Phil and Noel were lying head to toe on the old couch; the rest of the kids were sitting on the floor looking at the telly.

I nudged Alan and whispered, 'John Wayne's on, so none of the kids will move. They all love the cowboy films.'

'I don't care, let them.' Alan gave a little cough, trying to get Da's attention. 'Excuse me, Phil, can I have a word with yerself and Lil?'

'Ah, there yeh are, come in, come in. Move up there, Noel, and let Alan sit down.'

'Yeh're all right, Noel. I'll stand.'

We stood there, side by side, hand in hand. Alan stood tall, looking directly at Ma and Da and came right out with it. 'We'd like to get married, if it's okay with yiz.'

I squeezed his hand and thought, *he's so grown-up compared to me.* Ma just sat there and didn't bat an eyelid. I thought that she might have softened the blow a bit and helped him out; but no, she made him run the gauntlet all the way. The questions came left, right and centre, but Alan was well able for them. He had all the answers. I was so proud of him.

'Hmm . . .' said Ma, 'Yeh seem to have it all worked out then, Alan.'

Just then, Phil jumped up off the chair and switched the telly off. The kids all started giving out. 'Wha' did yeh do tha' for Phil? Put the telly back on.'

'Shut the fuck up, this is better than any John Wayne film.'

Alan gave a little cough again and answered.

'Yes, I think so, Lil.'

'Well now, Phil Doyle, wha' have you got to say about all this?'

There wasn't a sound. You could hear a pin drop. Da was surprised, but not shocked like Ma had been.

'It's comin' a bit earlier than I expected, but yeh're a good young fella, Alan, and I know yeh'll do well by Kathleen. Isn't tha' all any father wants for his daughter? Yeh're sure now it's wha' yiz want?'

Both of us answered at the one time. 'We do, we do.'

'Okay, but there's just one thing wrong, Alan.'

That soon took the smile off both our faces. 'Wha's tha', Phil?'

'We haven't got a shillin' to our name to help yeh out. Yeh'll have to carry the load yerselves, if it's a big weddin' yeh want and all.'

'Tha's fine, Phil. I'll look after everythin', yeh can be sure of tha'.'

'Right then, yeh seem to have yer minds made up. I'm happy for yiz. Wha' de yeh say, Lil?'

Ma had made her way over to the kitchen table. She was standing there with a large sliced pan in her hand, getting the supper ready. She buttered every slice without a word.

'For God's sake, Lil, will yeh answer Alan? Say somethin'!' Da roared.

'I will when I'm ready.'

She walked over and stood right in front of the two of us.

'Have yeh any smokes on yeh, Alan?'

'I have, Lil. I got yerself and Phil a packet each on the way down.'

She looked him straight in the face.

'Yeh're a smart young fella, Alan, so yeh are.' Then she looked at me. 'I won't say tha' I'm happy about yeh leavin', Kathleen. Ah go on then, yeh have me blessin'.'

Da jumped up and shook Alan's hand.

'It's about bloody time, Lil. I never saw anythin' to be dragged on so much.'

The words were only out of Ma's mouth when I had the ring out of the box, and on my finger. The girls were over in seconds, trying it on and asking if the diamonds were real and how many there were. Phil put his arm around the two of us.

'Yeh know somethin', Alan?'

'Wha's tha', Phil?'

'Yeh're one cute whore, so yeh are. Tha' was like lookin' at a boxin' match in the stadium. Yeh went every round, and didn't get knocked down once, but when yeh took them smokes out, I knew yeh had it won. Fair play to yeh, tha's all I can say.'

Alan gave Noel and Clare a few pound and sent them down for fish and chips and a few bottles of lemonade for everybody. We sat there for hours, the whole family, the younger ones sitting on the floor back looking at the telly, the rest laughing, joking and planning what they were going to wear and who would be doing what at the wedding. I looked over at Ma. She was smiling and talking to Da.

I thought to myself, *Good, she's comin' around at last.*

The table was full of food for a change; there was a full packet of smokes in Ma's pocket, thanks to Alan; Da was sober – and all in one night. *This is good; this is the way it should always be.*

It was a happy house that night.

25

Departures and Arrivals

The next two weeks went by so fast. It was the night before
Phil was due to go to Canada. We were all in bed; most of the
younger ones were asleep. Ma and Da were downstairs and
Phil and I were in our beds, talking to one another across the
landing. The rest of the kids were messing and acting the eejit.
Then Phil went really quiet. I thought he had gone asleep. All
of a sudden I heard this voice.

It was Phil singing.

'Shush, stay quiet, will yiz?'

I had no idea he could sing like that. I said nothing, just
listened. It was one of Roy Orbison's greatest hits:

'*I hear the sound of distant drums*
Far away, far away . . .'

He sang every word of that song, right down to the last
verse. There was complete silence when he finished. Nobody
said a word. They all let on they were asleep, but you could
hear the sobs under the blankets, including mine.

* * *

Phil was up bright and early the next morning. He filled a small haversack with his painter's overalls, a couple of scrapers, a few paintbrushes, and a few bits of clothes, heading off to make his fortune.

'Tha's me packed and ready to go, Ma.'

She sat there in silence.

His flight was early, so there wasn't much time to sit around. He knew full well how upset the whole family was; I think he planned it that way – and there was no way he would let any of us go to the airport with him.

'How will I know yeh're safe and well, Phil?' Ma asked.

'Don't worry, Ma, I won't be long gettin' friendly with somebody. I'll get them to scribble a few lines to let yeh know how I'm gettin' on.'

I stood back and watched him. One by one, he hugged and kissed every one of the kids. You could see he was choking, trying to keep the tears in. He tried to make a bit of a joke with Noel and Thomas, giving them each a clatter on the back of the head.

'You two keep yerselves in yer place. I'll be back.' He put his arms around both of them.

'Well now, Kathleen, it's yer turn. Come over here and give yer big brother an oul' squeeze and don't be puttin' any tears and snots on me good shirt. It's the only one I have.'

I hugged him as hard as I could. 'You come back now, Phil, de yeh hear me?'

'Didn't I swear I would?' I couldn't breathe, he was holding onto me so tight. He whispered in my ear. 'Cock yer ear up there, Kathleen. I want to ask yeh somethin' without the others listenin'.'

'Wha's tha', Phil?'

'Kathleen, are yeh still a virgin?'

He laughed his head off; all I could see were those pearly white teeth of his. Right to the very last minute, he was still trying to wind me up; but I wouldn't be wound up that day. I just gave him back a smile as big as his.

He went over and shook Da's hand; they looked into one another's eyes. There were no words. There didn't have to be; that special look was enough.

As he made his way over to Ma, there wasn't a murmur. Phil had been doing well up to that, putting on a big front. Now, his lip started to tremble. He gave her such a big hug. Ma held onto him and wouldn't let go. Her legs were nearly going from under her as she cried out.

'Don't go, Phil, please don't go.'

He was choking as the tears fell from his cheeks. Da made his way over.

'Come on now, Lil, I know it's hard.'

He eased Ma from the clutches of Phil's arms. She fell to her knees as Da tried to console her.

Phil picked his haversack up, stood back and looked at us all for a second, not saying a word. Then off he went, running down the road without looking back.

I cried my eyes out, watching him fade away in the distance, with little more than the clothes on his back and the sixty pounds that he got for his Honda 50, heading off to Canada to make his millions. *He'll do well*, I thought, *I know he will. With tha' big smile, how could he not?*

There was doom and gloom over the next few days. The house was very quiet for a change. Phil was such a messer. You'd always be looking over your shoulder, waiting on him to pounce out on you. If he wasn't doing that, he'd be sticking chewing gum inside your bra or putting balls of muck in the only pair of clean knickers that you had to your name. *I'll miss him, so I will.*

* * *

Over the next few weeks, every chance we got, Alan and myself were out pricing anything to do with the wedding. Alan sat down one evening for hours doing his sums.

'Right, Kathleen, if it's the Victor Hotel yeh want, with the prices they're lookin' for – and I can tell yeh, it's not cheap – the most tha' can come to the weddin' is fifty, no more.'

'Is tha' countin' all the kids, Alan?'

'It is; and if I put me mind down to it and save every penny, we can get married for Christmas.'

'I don't believe yeh! Jaysus, tha's very quick, Alan. But where will we live?'

'I have it all worked out, Kathleen. Me Granda said we could stay with him for as long as we want.'

'Oh Alan, I don't know about tha'. I don't want to live with anybody. Ma said it's best to have our own place.'

'Well then, we could forget about the big weddin' and wait until I have enough money for a deposit on our own house and just get married on the quiet – but tha'll take me about two years.'

'I don't want to wait tha' long, de you?'

'Yeh know I don't, Kathleen. I'll tell yeh wha' – I'll bring yeh down to see me Granda's house, see wha' yeh think. It's not far from yer Ma's house, just ten minutes' walk. It's still early; come on, we'll go down now.'

'Hold on, Alan, 'til I get me coat. Ma, de yeh need anythin' in the shops? I'm goin' out for an hour.'

'Tha's grand, Kathleen, yeh can pick me up five Woodbines and a couple of loaves of bread on yer way home. Have yeh got half a crown to spare, Alan? I'll pay yeh back on Friday as soon as Phil gives me the wages. There should be a couple of pennies left – see if yeh can get me one or two ice pops. Yeh know, the orange ones. Me mouth's waterin' here just thinkin' of them; I have a longin' yeh'd never believe.'

'Right, Lil, we'll pick them up for yeh and we won't be long.'

We were standing outside Alan's Granda's house before I knew it.

'Wha' did I tell yeh, Kathleen? Only minutes away.'

I took one look and wanted to run.

'It's in bits, Alan. Could we not get a flat or somethin'?'

'De yeh not realise how much a flat would cost, Kathleen? The rent's only five shillin's a week to stay with me Granda. We could kill two birds with one stone: yeh could have the weddin' yeh always dreamed about and save for a house while we stay here on the cheap. It would be just for a while; with the two of us workin', we'd have the money together in no time. Wha' de yeh say?' He put his arm around me and gave me a big squeeze. 'A drop of fresh paint and a bit of elbow grease, and I'll have this place spick and span by the time we move in. Come on, Kathleen. Me Granda is a quiet man; yeh'd hardly know he was around.'

'Okay then, once it's only for a short time – promise me, Alan.'

It was late when we got back so Alan went on home. The kids were all in bed.

'Here's the ice pops, Ma; sorry, they're nearly melted.'

I started to tell them all about the wedding.

'Hold on there for a second, Kathleen. Hand me one of them jam jars. These ice pops are breakin' up in me hand. I'll have to eat them with a spoon. Go on, wha' were yeh sayin' there?'

I launched into the ins and outs of what was going to happen and where we were going to live.

As soon as Ma heard I was going to live with Alan's Granda, she went mad. The jam jar was smashed down so hard on the table, it nearly broke in half. Lumps of ice pop splashed all over her dress. 'Kathleen! Look wha' yeh made me do!'

'Ma, will yeh just listen?'

'No, you listen to me and take good heed of wha' I'm sayin'. Don't move onto anybody else's floor; it never works out. Mark my words, I know wha' I'm talkin' about. Even if it's only one room with just floorboards and an orange box to sit on, yeh have to answer to nobody only yerself – isn't tha' right, Phil Doyle?' She gave Da the look.

He just rolled his eyes in the air and shook his head. 'I'll leave yiz to it. I'm off to bed. Goodnight.'

'I'll see yeh in the mornin', Da.'

Ma was still rammaging on; she was on a roll.

'People get set in their ways and don't like change, Kathleen, and tha's when the trouble starts. Yeh don't have to splash all tha' money on a weddin', not for us. Wait a bit and get yer own place. Listen to me, I know wha' I'm talkin' about.'

But no, I wasn't having any of it. I wanted to be a princess for a day.

'It'll only be for a while, Ma. I'll still get me house.'

'I can see yeh're takin' no heed to wha' I'm sayin', so I'll say no more on the matter, and tha's tha'.'

'Ma, don't get all annoyed with me. I just want to have me big day.'

'Big day me arse, Kathleen. It's the hard way yeh'll be learnin', mark my word.'

Everything went quiet for a minute.

'Ma, will I make yeh a cup of tea?' I said, trying to soften the subject. 'Oh, by the way, when is the baby due?'

'And why would yeh be askin' me tha'?'

'It's just yeh have to give the hotel and church plenty of notice. The weddin' is goin' to be around Christmas time, Ma.'

'Hmm, tha' quick now, is it? Well, the child is expected around the end of November, all goin' well, with the Holy Mother of God watchin' over me.' She blessed herself three times.

I put my arms around her. 'Yeh'll be grand, Ma. Don't worry. I'll make sure we wait until the baby is born and Christmas is over.'

'And tha's supposed to make me feel better, is it, Kathleen?'

'Come on now, Ma. Yeh gave me yer blessin' and all.'

'It's just tha' it's bad enough bein' down two wages and on top of all tha' yeh won't be here to give me a hand. How will I ever manage?'

'Ma, didn't I tell yeh, I'd look after everythin', and I will, I promise.'

* * *

We booked the wedding for the 27th of December 1967. I got my way: St Agnes' Church, Crumlin, and Hotel Victor, Dun Laoghaire. Not a week went by that I wasn't in town or up in Meath Street looking for bargains, trying to dress all the kids for the big day. The months went by so fast.

There were a couple of letters from Phil in the meantime; always a few lines scribbled down on one page, just to say that he was safe and working away, with a few dollars tucked inside the page. 'It's not much, Ma. I hope it helps.' He always signed the end: 'Love, young Phil.' That made Ma happy. She knew he wrote that bit himself.

In one of his letters, Phil told Alan to go ahead and ask Noel to be best man, as he wouldn't be getting home until the last minute and there would be no time to get measured for a suit. Noel was only fourteen, but he had grown so much in the past few months, he looked more like a man than a boy. All his puppy fat was gone. He wasn't far off six foot in height, with his black curly hair and tiny moustache.

'Tha's my Errol Flynn,' Ma would say. 'He should be in the films, so he should. He's tha' good lookin'.'

Carmel was to be my bridesmaid. That kept her happy.

* * *

Before I knew it, it was November. Ma was so big she could hardly walk.

'Yeh don't look the best, Ma; are yeh alright?'

'I don't feel well at all, Kathleen.'

'Have yeh started? Are yeh in labour?'

'No, but there's somethin' wrong. The child's after movin''

crossways in me. I can feel it. I better get meself down to the hospital. There's a brown bag under me bed with a few bits in it. Go up and tell yer father I want him; he's not to make a fuss. Just leave the bag at the end of the stairs. I'll get it on the way out.'

'Jesus, Lil, is it tha' time already? Will I get the ambulance?'

'De yeh want to put the heart crossways in them younger ones, lookin' at me goin' off in an ambulance? For fuck's sake, Phil, would yeh ever use yer head for once, and not be leavin' everythin' to me?'

I looked over at Da and gave him the nod to say nothing. Thank God Alan had just arrived; a few weeks earlier he had traded his bike in for a black Austin Eight Forty – not a big car by any means but it got us around and that was all that mattered.

'You look after the kids, Da. We'll take Ma down to the hospital.'

It must have taken us the guts of ten minutes to try and get Ma into the car. As we were pulling away I looked back and there were little Jacinta and Patricia balling their eyes out.

'Are the kids okay, Kathleen?'

'There's not a bother on them, Ma, they're fine – none the wiser.'

Ma was right. We were only in the door of the hospital when she was rushed off in a wheelchair. I couldn't get anybody to tell me what was happening. Every time I asked, they just kept saying, 'There will be somebody with you shortly.' We seemed to be sitting there for ever. Then, finally I saw a nurse walking over to me. I jumped up off the seat, not knowing what to expect.

'Can I see me Ma? Is she okay?'

'Mother and baby are fine. We had to do an emergency section. Everything went well.'

That night my brother Mano was born, Ma's twelfth and last baby.

* * *

It was late by the time Alan dropped me home. Da was walking the floor with Paul. When he saw me, he stopped in his tracks, white in the face with worry.

'Ma is fine, Da. A big baby boy, eight and a half pound!'

'Is yer mother okay, then?'

'I didn't see her, Da; she had to be sectioned.' I explained everything the nurse had told me. 'Here, Da, give me Paul, I'll try an' settle him'. Paul was a little over a year old and all he wanted was his Ma.

'He's cryin' since yeh left, Kathleen. I can't get any good of him at all.'

'He's frettin' for Ma, Da. Ah, look, his little eyes are all swollen. I'll put him in the bed between me and Patricia.'

'Sure she's as bad; herself and Jacinta are after cryin' themselves asleep, waitin' on yer mother to come home. I didn't know wha' to be tellin' them. Yer mother always looks after these things.'

Patricia and Jacinta were wrapped in Ma's coat, asleep on the chair. The rest of the kids were asleep on the floor in front of the fire.

I shook Jacinta and Patricia. 'Wake up, girls.'

'Kathleen, where's me Ma?' Patricia asked, her little voice trembling. I put her on my lap, my arm around Jacinta, the rest of them waiting to hear what I had to say.

'Ma's fine, she's just very tired and needs a rest for a few days.'

Paul was still screaming.

'Now, if yeh're all good and there's no more cryin', I'll bring home a big bag of chocolate sweets on Friday. Come on, give us a smile – let me see them dimples, Jacinta.'

A little grin, that's all I got. I was too tired to make up a story about the new baby. *I'll leave tha' one for Ma. See wha' she comes up with.*

'Right, up to bed with yiz.'

I finally got them settled and myself into the bed. Paul was still crying. There was no way I could settle him, even after a bottle. I was falling out of my standing for the want of sleep. He kept pushing his little head under my arm and into my chest.

'Kathleen, can yeh not keep him quiet?' Da shouted in. 'He's at it since this mornin'. The neighbours will think we're killin' him.'

'I'm tryin', Da. It's Ma he wants, not me.'

A voice came from under the blankets. 'It's her diddy, yeh mean.' said Clare, sticking her head out. 'Why don't yeh give him *yers*?'

'Clare, I'll give yeh such a kick up the hole if yeh say another word – I'm warnin' yeh!'

'Go on, Kathleen,' the rest of them said. 'He's drivin' us mad with all tha' cryin'.'

'I can't do tha'; anyway, I'm as flat as a pancake. I haven't got any.'

'Yeh can say tha' again,' Noel shouts in, laughing his head off.

'Don't you speak to yer sister like tha'. I've had a bad enough day without listenin' to the likes of tha' talk.' Da was really annoyed and tha' soon shut Noel up.

That's when I came up with what Da afterwards called a masterplan.

'Right, Clare, since you started all this, run downstairs and get me one of them tits tha's in the bowl of water in the kitchen.'

'De yeh want a bottle as well, Kathleen?'

'No, just the tit – and make sure it's one of the old ones. Marion, get me a bit of brown paper.'

'For wha', Kathleen? I'm tired.'

'To wipe her arse with, yeh gobshite, Marion,' Thomas shouts in.

'Tha's it,' Da said. I could hear him jumping out of the bed. 'It's the belt the two of yeh will be gettin', if there's one more word. Don't think just because yer mother's not here tha' yeh'll be carryin' on like bowsies.'

He was banging his belt off the end of the bed, trying to put the fear of God in them. Everything went quiet for a few seconds – except for Paul, who was still screaming. Then the giggling started. We all knew Da inside out; he never put a finger on any of us. He was just a big softy.

I stuffed the teat with the brown paper to make sure Paul wouldn't suck any wind in.

'Right, Carmel, hold him for a second till I take me jumper off. Turn around, the rest of yiz, and don't be lookin' at me.'

I put an old t-shirt on, leaving one arm out.

'Now, give me Paul.'

I got the rubber teat between my two fingers and placed it over the front of my own nipple (if you could call it that; it was more like a jelly tot). I stuck the teat in Paul's mouth. It took him a couple of minutes to get settled, and that was it. The crying stopped; he was asleep in no time.

'Not a word out of any of yiz outside the house about this, de yeh hear me?'

'We all swear, don't we?' said Clare.

I got the nod off all of them; they were just glad the crying had stopped and they could go to sleep. It took me a couple of nights, but I slowly got Paul off the teat and onto his own soother before Ma came home from the hospital. Thank God! The thoughts of her sitting there with two babies, one sucking off each diddy, didn't bear thinking about.

* * *

Ma was in hospital for over two weeks; with only a week to go to the wedding, my nerves were gone. I was running around like a lunatic, flying down to the hospital to see Ma for a few minutes each night, then on over to the dressmaker's, up to the church, out to the hotel, back to the kids. Alan was great and so was Da.

Da promised me the day Mano was born, 'I'll have a sup tonight, Kathleen, to wet the baby's head. I'll give yeh me word tha' not a drop of Guinness will pass me lips 'til the day of yer weddin'.'

And he was true to his word. He was there day and night with me, even when Ma came home.

I'll never forget the look on Jacinta's and Patricia's faces. Their eyes nearly popped out of their head when Ma walked in with Mano.

'Who's tha'?' Jacinta asked.

'Tha's yer new baby brother, love.'

'Where did yeh get him from, Ma?' little Patricia asked. The older ones started giggling and tipping one another.

'Hold on there till I get meself settled. Carmel, hold the baby for me. Kathleen, give Paul over here 'til I give him a cuddle.' He was only in her arms two seconds and he was asleep. 'It's grand to be back on me own floor again. Right, gather around and sit down beside me. Now, have yiz heard of Michael the Archangel?' One or two said 'Yeah'; the rest of them stood there with their mouths open, not having a clue what Ma was on about. 'For Jaysus' sake, are they teachin' yiz nothin' up there in tha' bloody school? Yeh should be gettin' told all about the angels in yer acadiacism class.' She stopped to light a Woodbine. 'Now, wha' was I sayin' before I interrupted meself? Oh yeah. Isn't Michael only one of the top guardian angels up there in heaven? Wha' does he only go and do?'

I thought to myself, *this should be a good one.*

'Wha', Ma, tell us, wha'?'

'He landed on me bed in the middle of the night in the hospital. Such a fright I got. He said he was lookin' for a home for a little baby. "Wha' baby?" says I. Tha's when his wings opened and there little Mano was. Sure, how could I say no?'

The older ones started to drift to the back yard one by one, knowing full well it was one of Ma's yarns. The rest wanted to know how big his wings were.

'The width of the room, so they were.'

I went into the kitchen to help Da with the dinner. Ma sat there chatting away about the Holy Mother, heaven and the angels.

'Kathleen, where does she get the stories from?' Da said. 'Would yeh have a look at them young ones' faces. They're gobsmacked. I tell yeh somethin' for nothin', tha' woman could nearly be a poet, if she put her mind down to it.'

I just looked at him. 'Are yeh for real, Da?'

He just laughed. 'Had yeh goin' there for a minute all the same, Kathleen.'

'I don't think so Da. Will yeh do me a favour?'

'And wha' would tha' be, Kathleen? If it's in me power, don't yeh know, I will.'

'I've to pick me weddin' dresses up on Thursday. I need yeh to stick a few nails in the wall up in the bedroom, so's I'll have somewhere to hang them. And yeh better put a few in yer own room for the fellas' suits.'

He was peeling the potatoes. I was going on about all the things I had to do before the week was out, and didn't notice how quiet Da had gone. I tipped him on the shoulder.

'Da, are yeh listenin' to me?'

When he turned around, I could see the tears were ready to drop.

'Jaysus, Da, wha's wrong with yeh? Are yeh alright?'

'Yeh know, it's only hittin' me now, Kathleen, tha' yeh're not goin' to be here all the time. I'm goin' to miss yeh. It's always been the two of us lookin' after things when yer mother's not here.'

I thought, *When Da? When was tha'? When were you here and not in the pub?* Even so, I got such a lump in my throat when he said that to me.

'I'll still be here, Da. I won't let a day go by tha' I won't drop in.'

'I know yeh'll be here, but yeh won't, if yeh know wha' I mean. Who's goin' to stop yer mother from bashin' me brains in when I have a sup on me? Yeh know tha' temper of hers.'

I put my arm around him.

'Come on now, Da. Don't get upset. Just make sure when yeh go for a pint tha' yeh don't forget to come home. My wages won't be there anymore, so yeh'll have to give an extra few bob. Ma's not gettin' any younger, and with two more babies to feed it's not goin' to be easy for her. Yeh can't blame her gettin' all fired up. Just look how hard the last few weeks were with her not bein' here. Just think about it, Da.'

He stood there thinking his own thoughts for a minute.

'Kathleen, yiz were always ahead of yer years, yerself and Phil. I suppose yeh had to be with the likes of me not facin' up to me responsibilities, shuttin' everythin' out with the drink. The coward's way out, tha's wha' it is.'

I wanted to agree with him but I hadn't got the heart to. 'Don't be too hard on yerself, Da. It's never too late to change.'

'And tha's wha' I'll be doin'. I really mean it this time, Kathleen. I'll take a sup at yer weddin' and then it's the pledge for me once and for all. Now, will yeh carry on with the rest of the dinner, so's I can sort them nails out for yeh?'

'Tha's grand, Da, thanks.'

Off he went believing to the very depths of his soul that he meant what he said, but I knew he didn't.

26

The Wedding

The next few days went by so fast. It was Thursday, two days before the wedding, and Phil was on his way home from Canada. You could see Ma's heart starting to lift. Her blue-eyed boy was coming home.

The look on Ma's and Da's faces was priceless when he walked in. The whole room lit up with that smile of his. You could have handed them the world, and it wouldn't have meant as much.

Between the kids and Da, he had a hundred and one questions thrown at him. Ma just sat by the fire with the two babies in her arms, as happy as anything. I slipped out of the room with Alan. We sat on the end of the stairs, chatting and going over the last few things that had to be done.

'Yeh've been so good over the past few weeks, Alan. Yeh've the patience of a saint. I've barely had time to talk to yeh, I mean, I know we talked and all, about the weddin' and stuff.' I was rammaging on and on. He sat there looking at me, not saying a word. 'Wha's wrong, Alan?'

I started to have one of my super blushes.

'Will yeh stay quiet for one minute and give us a kiss, Kathleen.'

I just about got a kiss when Phil jumped on top of the two of us.

'Caught yiz! I see yeh're still tryin' to get into her knickers, Alan.'

'The big city hasn't changed yeh anyway, Phil,' Alan answered. 'Nice to have yeh back.'

'Come over here, sis, and plant one right there,' said Phil, pointing to the side of his face.

I bent over to kiss him on the cheek. What does he only go and do: picks me up in the air, throws me over his shoulders, runs all over the house, lashing the arse off me. The kids thought this was great. I even caught Ma laughing.

'Put me down, yeh bloody eejit!' I screamed. And he did – right on top of Alan. 'Yeh didn't grow up at all, Phil Doyle. I thought yeh might have come back with some brains in tha' head of yers, but yeh're as mad as ever.'

'Fuck the grown-up stuff. I'll be doin' tha' for long enough. Come 'ere and give me a big hug, the pair of yiz.'

We were like two little kids underneath his big broad shoulders. It felt good. He had kept his promise, like I knew he would. I was so happy he was home.

We sat there for a while talking, Phil telling us all sorts of yarns; he was probably making up half of them, if the truth be known. I went in to Ma and left the two of them chatting away on the stairs. Half of the kids were asleep on the floor as usual. Da started carrying them upstairs one by one. Phil and Alan came in.

'Kathleen, I'll drop in tomorrow for an hour; we've to go out to the hotel. I'm off now so I'll say goodnight to yiz all.'

'See yeh tomorrow so.' I gave him a little smile as he left.

Phil looked around at all the kids. 'I see nothin's changed, Ma.'

'Would yeh give yer father a hand there, Phil?'

Phil bent down, put one on each shoulder, and had them all up in minutes where poor Da would have been huffing and puffing for the best part of half an hour. Some nights the kids would slip back down so that they would get a second jockey-back, as they called it. Da always knew but pretended he didn't, until Ma would let a roar. Then they'd nearly shit on themselves with the fright and wouldn't be long running back up to bed.

When everybody was gone to bed I sat there talking to Phil.

'I won't be stayin', Kathleen.'

'I know, Phil; I can see it in yer face.'

'I'll be gone as soon as I get a few bob behind me. I used up every penny to get meself home for the weddin'.'

I put my arm around him and rested my head against his. 'I knew yeh wouldn't let me down, Phil.'

'Kathleen, it was so hard out there in Canada, and I'm not talkin' about the work. I can do tha' standin' on me head. I was so lonely and missed everybody so much. I could have filled Niagara Falls up with the tears I shed.'

'Niagara Falls? Wha' the hell is tha', Phil?'

'Yeh never saw the likes of it, Kathleen, the most amazin' sight yeh ever saw. Mountains and mountains of water, never stops. Unbelievable, I swear. I know I'll make meself a good life out there. Would yeh not think about goin'? Yerself and Alan would do well with the two of yiz workin'. Yeh'd have a mansion in no time. Yeh'd want to see the size of the houses. First, they have half a house under the ground. Don't ask me why. They call tha' the basement. Then, wha' do they only go and do – build a full house on top of it again. There's tha' many rooms, sure yeh wouldn't know where to be sittin'. Wha's wrong with yeh, Kathleen? Why are yeh lookin' at me like tha'?'

'Alan already asked me to go to Canada. He got the forms and all, Phil.'

'Did he send them away?'

'Yeah, but I told him I don't think I'd go. He sent them, anyway. He's hopin' I'll change me mind.'

265

'For fuck's sake, Kathleen, there's half the battle won, him wantin' to go and all.'

'I wouldn't last a month, Phil. I'd die if I didn't see the kids. And wha' about Ma? I promised I'd always be here for her. And then there's Da. Wha' about when he hits the bottle? Who'd be here to help sort things out with Ma?'

'There's plenty of the other kids to do tha'.'

'They're all too young, Phil. Anyway, the thing is, you really want to go back to Canada, tha's yer dream. Alan would like to go, but I don't, and tha's the difference.'

We sat there until the early hours of the morning talking, Phil doing everything in his power to try to convince me to go back to Canada with him. Eventually we fell asleep there on the couch, my head on Phil's shoulder.

* * *

The next morning I was woken up by Patricia and Jacinta diving on top of us, hugging and kissing Phil, knocking me to the floor. That was the start of a hectic day.

'I see yeh're awake then, Kathleen,' said Ma.

'I am now, Ma. Wha' time is it?'

'After nine. There's some porridge in the end of the pot. Add a drop of milk and water, tha'll do yerself and Phil. When yeh're finished eatin', Kathleen, grab a couple of them older ones to give yeh a hand. The house needs a good goin' over. Yeh'll have a couple of the neighbours droppin' in in the mornin' to have a look at yeh, and don't yeh know they'll be glancin' around the place. I mightn't have much, but wha's here I want spick and span.'

'Right then – Carmel, Clare, Noel, we'll start upstairs. Marion, stay here and give Ma a hand.'

Once we were out of Ma's sight, the messing started. I had to do more shouting to get them to help me. My head was pounding. I was so tired and I could feel a sore throat coming on. I sat down on the side of the bed. Out of the blue, there were tears and snots everywhere. I couldn't help myself.

'Jaysus, Kathleen, wha' are yeh gettin' all whingey for?' Noel asked. 'We're only havin' a bit of laugh.'

'Leave her alone,' Clare chimed in. 'Can't yeh see tha' her nerves is at 'er and all? Yeh big eejit.'

'Don't call me an eejit. Yeh little fuck.'

Before I could open my mouth, the two of them were on the floor killing one another, each trying to outdo the other with the name calling: 'No brains!' 'Fat arse!' 'Gobshite!' 'Smelly knickers!' 'Rotten feet!'

'Will yeh stop, the pair of yiz. I don't feel well.'

They jumped up. 'Jaysus, Kathleen, wha's wrong with yeh? Yeh're real cranky.'

'I'm crippled here with a pain in me side, me throat feels like sandpaper, and yeh're not helpin' with the carry-on of yiz.'

'Kathleen, I can fix tha' pain in yer side,' Clare said. 'I know wha' it is. Tell 'er, Carmel, don't I know loads?'

I looked over at Carmel, who didn't see or hear what was going on. She was on another planet, as usual; too busy looking at herself in the mirror, trying on the hairpiece she'd got for the wedding. Carmel never gave two shites what was going on around her.

Clare carried on. 'Will I tell yeh, Kathleen?'

'Go on then. I'm listenin'.'

'It's a big fart tha's caught in yer belly, tha's wha' it is. Yeh have to get it out real quick or it goes all over yer stomach. De yeh want me to show yeh how to get it out?'

Before I could say anything, she was on the floor.

'Are yeh watchin'? Turn yer head, Noel Doyle. You don't look.'

'I'm not lookin' at yeh, righ'?'

'For God's sake. Don't start again, the pair of yiz.'

'Yeh just get yer two legs together and pull them right back over yer head, like this; rock back and forward for a minute or two.'

It took me all my strength not to laugh. There was muck all over her knickers, and they were all caught to one side.

'When yeh have tha' done, give a big grunt, and there'll be farts flyin' everywhere.' She sat up. 'Wha' de yeh think?

I burst out laughing. *How on earth could I leave them?*

'Yeh're laughin' at me, Kathleen.'

'No, I'm not, Clare. It's just . . .'

I didn't get time to finish. Noel was off again. 'Skid marks, skid marks! Clare has skid marks!'

She was on top of him like a light. 'Yeh fuckin' bastard. Wha' about yer rotten feet, huh, *Jap-eyes*?'

They were off again, punching and kicking one another. I just didn't have the energy, so I left them to it and went back downstairs to Ma.

'Wha's wrong with yeh, Kathleen? Yeh're like death warmed up, the colour of yeh.'

'I don't feel the best, Ma.'

'Would yeh listen to yerself? Yeh'd think there was a frog caught in yer throat, Yeh're tha' hoarse. I'll soon fix tha'.'

'Oh no, Ma, please, not the salt! It goes everywhere; I'll have a rash walkin' up the aisle. It does be in me skin for days.'

'And wha' does tha' matter, once it makes yeh better?'

'But it doesn't, Ma!'

'Don't talk nonsense, Kathleen. Haven't I been curin' yiz all for years with me remedies?'

There was no talking to her and at this stage I was just too tired to argue.

'Come 'ere, Marion, there's an oul' pair of tights in tha' bottom drawer, bring them here to me and tha' drum of salt from the press. Hurry yerself up there – and bring a knife in with yeh as well.'

Poor Marion, she'd get all flustered when Ma would shout at her. She was so quiet.

Ma cut one of the legs off the tights, poured the salt in, tied a knot at each end, rolled it until it looked like a long sausage and then put it against the fire until it got hot. She then wrapped it around my neck.

'There yeh are now, Kathleen! Doesn't tha' feel better already? Tha'll take all the badness away. Yeh'll be bran' new tomorrow.'

It never worked.

I looked over at Phil, who was still lying on the couch. He had one of Da's ties wrapped around his neck with his tongue sticking out to one side, pretending to be hanging himself. Sick or not, I still had to get on with tidying the house and that's all I did for the next few hours.

Alan arrived around tea time.

'Jaysus, Kathleen, yeh look terrible.'

'Me throat's just a bit sore.'

'Yer Ma's not still doin' tha' salt thing? Yeh know it doesn't work. Yeh'll have to go to the doctor.'

'Sssh, Alan, Ma will hear yeh. Anyway, I haven't got time for all tha'. Just pick me up a packet of Disprin. I'll gargle me throat a few times. Tha'll fix it.'

'Kathleen, we need to head over to the hotel. I have the cake out in the car. Are yeh right?'

'I can't. I still have a hundred and one things to do. Phil, will yeh go with him?'

'Thanks be to Jaysus, I thought yeh'd never ask! Get me out of this madhouse for an hour or two.'

You could see Phil had got used to living on his own and wasn't able for all the noise.

'See yeh then in the mornin'. Are yeh sure yeh're okay, Kathleen?'

'I'm grand, Alan. Don't forget the tablets. Give them to Phil when yeh're droppin' him off.'

I walked him out to the hall. He put his arms around me and gave me a big squeeze. 'Love yeh; can't wait for tomorrow.'

'Me too, Alan.'

Phil was out in the car, beeping the horn.

'Hurry up, Alan, for Jaysus' sake, will yeh? I'm freezin' to death out here.'

'I'd better go before the neigbours start givin' out. Don't keep me waitin' at tha' altar!' I got another little kiss.

It was non-stop from then. Between more cleaning, the shouting and the crying, trying to get the young ones washed and the older ones to wash themselves, it was bedlam all the way. It was well past two o'clock in the morning before silence fell over the house. There was just Ma and myself in the kitchen, and Phil asleep on the couch beside the fire.

'There's a drop of tea for yeh, Kathleen. By God, yeh got some work done here today. I haven't seen the place look this tidy in years.'

'For a while anyway, Ma. Once it's okay for tomorrow. Isn't tha' wha' matters at the minute, anyway?'

'Each day at a time, Kathleen, each day at a time. Hand Mano over here to me till I give him a few sucks of the diddy. Tha'll keep him goin' 'til the mornin'. Now, you get yerself up to bed. Yeh have a long day ahead of yeh.'

'I can't keep me eyes open, Ma. De yeh mind?'

I bent down to give her a kiss. As usual, there was no response, nothing back. She didn't lift her head.

'I'll go on up then, Ma.'

'I'll be awake with this fella before six, so I'll give yeh a shout, Kathleen.'

Just as I got to the hall, I turned and looked back at Ma, and thought, *I could do with a hug right now. I want yeh to tell me things, tell me everything's goin' to be fine.* But as usual, it was all inside my head, never out loud.

When I got to the top of the stairs, I peeped in on Da, half hoping he would be awake. He was dead to the world, along with Noel and Thomas. I went on into the girls' room. I stood and looked around. There wasn't much; just the two double beds, the press in the wall and about half a dozen black plastic bags that held everybody's clothes, in place of a wardrobe.

Clare and Marion were at the bottom of my bed, little Paul at the top. Carmel, Jacinta and Patricia were across in the other bed. I went around each of them, brushing the hair out of their eyes, fixing the blankets, sobbing as I bent down to give them a kiss, knowing that this would be my last night to ever share a bed with them again.

Jaysus, wha's wrong with me, gettin' meself into a state like this? I'm only goin' to be livin' ten minutes down the road. I stripped and slipped in beside Paul. He put his little arms around me, cuddling himself into me. I put my two feet up between the girls. They were better than any water bottle, especially on a cold winter's night.

I'll miss them all so much. Then I thought, *Sure all I have to do is bring a couple of them home at night with me. Alan won't mind. I know he won't. Just 'til I get meself settled.*

I finally managed to doze off a little bit happier with that thought in my mind.

* * *

I felt like I'd only closed my eyes for a few seconds when the alarm went off. There wasn't a stir out of any of them. Paul was lying across my chest. I checked his nappy – not too wet, thank God! He opened his eyes and gave me a little smile. 'Aren't yeh a great little fella?' Before I moved, I checked the sheets; they were dry. *Good, nobody pissed on me last night; tha's a good start, anyway.* I got up, put Paul over my shoulder and went around pulling the blankets off the others.

'Come on, wake up! Up, up, the lot of yiz!'

They were all giving out. 'Jaysus, Kathleen, it's still the middle of the night. Wha's wrong with yeh?'

Just then Da woke. 'Wha's goin' on? Who's cryin'? Where's yer mother?'

'It's nothin', Da. Come on, yeh'll have to get up, start helpin' me. Ma must be downstairs with Mano. Make them get up, will yeh?

'Right, Kathleen, I'm up.'

I went down to the kitchen; my brother Phil was sitting there with Ma.

'Ma, did yeh get to bed at all?'

'I dozed off for an hour or two on the chair, Kathleen. It wasn't worth me while goin' up. I knew yeh'd be up at the crack of dawn. Anyway, never mind all tha'; where's yer father?'

'He's gettin' them all up.'

'Right then. We better get movin'.'

They all started to dribble in one by one, as Ma dished out the orders.

'Carmel, fill tha' big kettle up to the brim. Clare, hand me the pan, I've a couple o' pound of sausages here and a few eggs; tha'll do yiz, with a bit of bread. Marion, get yerself over here and start butterin' the bread.'

I was sitting there giving Paul his bottle when Ma chimed in.

'All the same, Kathleen, I won't know meself, me sittin' there, bein' waited on hand and foot, gettin' tha' fancy dinner of yours handed up to me. Sure me body's nearly goin' into shock just thinkin' about it.'

'Yeh're in great form, Lil,' Da said as he walked in.

'Hmm . . . is tha' right?'

'Holy Mother of God, Lil, just for one day, and the day bein' in it, could yeh not be a bit civil? Not for me, of course, tha' would be too much to ask, but for Kathleen. She's put a lot into the weddin', so let's not spoil it on her.'

He stood there, right in front of Ma. You could hear a pin drop. Nobody said a word.

Da would usually just take his cup of tea and walk out of the room or go upstairs, but not today. He stood firm. 'Well, Lil?' He was starting to raise his voice.

Holy Jaysus, I thought, *there's goin' to be blue murder here. Of all days Da has to pick to stand up to Ma. I don't believe this.*

'Ah, sit yerself down and stop actin' the big fella, would yeh? With yer fancy words. Move over there and make room for yer father. Start dishin' them sausages out; these eggs are nearly ready. Marion, did I not tell yeh to do tha' bread?'

And on she went without blinking an eyelid. All the kids dived on the food; that's all they cared about at the minute. Da looked over at Phil and me. He had his two fists clenched. He never hit Ma – she did enough of that for the two of them – but that morning I really thought he was going to give her one.

'Sit down here, Da, and calm yerself down,' said Phil.

'Tha' woman, I swear, she'd bring the devil out of any man.'

'Wha's tha' yeh said, Phil Doyle?'

'Nothin', Ma, he said nothin',' I answered. I lowered my voice then. 'Please, Da, don't say anythin', will yeh. She'll only get all fired up and we all know wha' tha' means.'

'I'll stay quiet, seein's the day tha's in it, Kathleen, just for you.'

That was the start of my fairytale wedding.

'Noel, are yeh finished yer breakfast?'

'Yeah, Kathleen.'

'Well, will yeh get yerself dressed and up to Alan as quick as yeh can. He'll be waitin' on yeh. Mick said he'd be up there from early. Hurry!'

'I'm goin', Kathleen, stop shoutin' at me.'

Mick was Carmel's boyfriend. Alan and he became friends over the months and he asked him if he would like to do best man with Noel. That way he could keep an eye on Noel, who was only fourteen. I was like a sergeant out of the army, giving orders all over the place. I told Ma just to look after herself and Mano, and to leave the rest to me.

When all the kids were finally ready, I lined them up in the kitchen, making sure everyone was gleaming. Just then there was a knock on the door. It was one of the neighbours, coming to collect Mano, as she was going to mind him for the day.

'Ah, it's yerself Mrs Swan. Come in, come in, Lil's in the

kitchen, go on through,' Da said as he went upstairs to get himself ready.

Mrs Swan smiled over at the kids. 'Well, all I can say, Lil, is they're a credit to yiz.'

Ma was fixing Mano in his pram. She lifted her head up and looked across at us. 'They are, aren't they?' She didn't say anything else, but you could see she was well pleased, and so was I.

Ma carried on talking to Mrs Swan, telling her how she had squeezed enough milk into a couple of bottles to see the baby through the day, and rammaging on and on about I don't know what.

By this stage I was pacing the kitchen floor waiting on them to stop talking. Eventually I had to butt in, 'Ma, yeh know it's quarter past nine and I've still to do yer hair yet. The car's outside. Phil's takin' a couple of the kids with him on the first run. Then he'll be straight back for you and the rest of them.'

'Is it tha' time already? I'd better make a move, Mrs Swan.'

'Go on then, Lil, don't worry about the baby. I'll take care of him. Enjoy yerself.' Off she went with Mano in the pram.

I was so worked up I had my fist in my mouth, trying to stop myself from screaming. Just as well I had myself ready and only had to slip into my dress.

'Da, are yeh ready?'

'I'm dressed and practisin' me speech, Kathleen.'

'Tha' should be good,' Ma said, as she came into the bedroom. 'I see yeh have yerself all worked up as usual, Kathleen.'

'De yeh blame me, Ma? The mornin' tha's in it.'

'I'll have meself ready in two minutes. I had a good wash last night when yiz were all sleepin'. All I need now is a bit of lipstick and you just run the comb through me hair and help me clip me hat on. Carmel, me coat and dress is hangin' on the back of the door. Go get it for me.' That was it; Ma was ready. She stood there, puffing her Woodbine. 'Wha' did I tell yeh,

Kathleen? Two minutes. Look at yeh, gettin' yerself all excited for nothin'.'

Just then the driver started beeping. 'Yiz have to go, Ma.'

'Kathleen, slip into yer dress and let me have a look at yeh there.'

'There's no time, Ma, yeh have to go now.'

'I'm not movin' until I see yeh in yer dress.'

'Right! Carmel, help me, quick!'

I got the dress on. Ma stood there and looked at me for a few seconds. 'Well, Ma, wha' de yeh think?'

'Yeh did well, Kathleen.'

Not a hug, not a kiss; off she went to the church with not another word spoken.

Da called up to me, 'Are yeh right, Kathleen? They're all gone up to the church. The cameraman is here. He wants to take a few pictures before yeh leave the house. It's five to ten – hurry yerself up, will yeh?'

When I walked into the kitchen, the smile on Da's face said everything. 'Tha's a grand frock yeh got yerself, Kathleen. Yeh look smashin'.'

'Ah, thanks, Da.' It felt good to hear him say that.

There were a few pictures taken in the parlour alongside Ma's new china cabinet. Before I knew it, I was making my way out to the front garden, bursting with excitement, dying to show off, thinking all the neighbours would be outside to wish me good luck. To my surprise and disappointment, not a neighbour was to be seen, not even on my special day.

I was outside the church in no time. Carmel was fixing my veil when Phil came over to me.

'Kathleen, Kathleen, there's no music in the church for yeh.'

'Wha' de yeh mean? Course there is – I booked it ages ago. Now don't start yer messin' today, I mean it, Phil.'

'Jaysus, will yeh just listen to wha' I'm sayin, Kathleen? Alan's in there gettin' blood pressure and on top of all tha' the clerk hasn't turned up either. He can't be found anywhere.'

'*Wha*'! I'm not goin' in unless I have music, I don't care, Phil. I'll look stupid walkin' up the aisle with not a sound.'

'Yeh'll have to. Yer woman tha' plays the organ sent over word; her stomach's in a right oul' mess, and there's nobody else. Too short notice, the priest said.'

Da said in a low voice, 'More like the drink from the night before.'

He didn't think I heard him.

'I swear, Da, if tha' oul fuck is sick from the drink, I hope she gets the shites for a month. Lettin' me down like this on me big day.'

'Jaysus, Kathleen, will yeh watch yer mouth? Outside the house of God – if anybody heard yeh!' I wasn't moving. The tears flowed down my face and I couldn't stop them.

'Kathleen, yeh'd want to make up yer mind,' said Da. 'I'm freezin' to death standin' here, and if yeh don't make a move soon, I'll bring meself over to Mooney's pub. If I get settled with a pint in me hand and a bit of heat, yeh won't move me for love nor money, weddin' or no weddin'.'

'Would yeh really do tha to me, Da?'

'I'm tellin' yeh, if yeh don't move now, I'm goin'.'

Phil stepped in, trying to calm the situation.

'Come on, Kathleen, the kids are all gettin' fidgety. There's nothin' yeh can do now.' He put his arm around me. 'Come on, it's only a bit of music. I'll whistle a tune if yeh want.' He gave me a big smile, showing off his pearly whites. Phil would always try to see the funny side of things, but I wasn't laughing.

'Go away, yeh big eejit.'

I peeped inside the church. I could see Alan; he looked lost on his own. I made my mind up; nobody was going to ruin my big day.

'Right, Da, I'm ready.'

I could hardly breathe with the lump in my throat as I walked up the aisle, smiling and nodding, feeling like a fool, in complete silence. When I got to the altar, Alan took my hand

and gave it a tight squeeze. That helped, but only a bit.

When I looked and saw the priest, I nearly fainted. *Tha's not the priest tha' we spoke to. They gave me Blinkey! I don't believe this.* He was as blind as a bat; his glasses were like milk bottles. He needed the clerk big time to help him. I just stood there and thought: *This is goin' to be a right shambles.* As sure as hell I was right. Everybody stood when they should have been sitting, kneeling when they should have been standing and praying.

In the middle of the ceremony, a shower of water hit me in the face. I stood there for a second with my mouth open, turned and looked at Alan; the water was dripping down his face. He didn't blink an eyelid. The mascara started to roll down my face. Alan slipped a hanky in my hand. *I don't believe this! The blind fucker is after drownin' us with the holy water.* I could hear the giggling going on behind me. I didn't blame them one bit; it was like a funny farm up there.

We finally got through the Mass, then it was outside for a few quick flashes of the camera. The heavens were open, the rain was belting down, so off we headed for the hotel.

Alan always said the right things at the right time and knew how to calm me down, for a little while anyway. *God,* I thought, *wha' more could go wrong?* Little did I know what was ahead of me.

* * *

Everybody was there when we arrived. The Victor Hotel didn't know what had hit them. The kids were running around like lunatics, sliding down the stairs, swinging out of the curtains and screaming. You'd want to have seen the look on Alan's aunties' faces. *Stuck up bitches,* I thought. *Who do they think they are?* Anyway, I had promised I wouldn't fight with the kids that day. 'They are just excited,' I found myself saying as I walked by everybody smiling.

I went around and gathered the kids up.

'Right, are yiz listenin' to me? I want yiz to calm down. They're all watchin' yiz. Give them nothin' to talk about, right?'

'Okay, Kathleen,' they all mumbled.

'The dinner will be ready in a few minutes. Don't let me catch any of yiz eatin' with yer hands. Use the knife and fork like I told yeh.'

'De we have to use the two of them at the same time?' they asked.

'I went through this I don't know how many times over the past week. Just cut the food up and then use the fork the way I showed yeh, right?'

Clare was just about to butt in as usual, but she shut up. It was probably the grinding of my teeth that stopped her.

'Jaysus, wha's tha' smell?' I whispered.

'It's Paul, Kathleen,' Jacinta answered. 'He done a dirty big shite when yeh were in the church.'

My breathing nearly stopped as I looked over my shoulder to see if anyone was listening. 'Did yeh have to say it like tha', did yeh? Could yeh not just say his nappy was dirty? Makin' a holy show of me!'

'Sorry, Kathleen, I forgot.'

'Marion, take Paul over to Ma. She has a couple of nappies in her bag. She'll look after him. When yeh have tha' done, follow the rest of them over to Alan. He'll get yiz all some lemonade. Off yiz go. Don't let me down, now.'

'We won't Kathleen,' said Clare. 'We swear, don't we?' She laughed, with a dirty big grin on her face.

'Laugh, will yeh, Clare? Now, for bein' such a smart arse, yeh're goin' to get the job of watchin' Thomas for the day. Make sure he doesn't pick his nose at the dinner or any time through the day; and if I catch him even once, *you'll* get the box off me, not him. Now run along.' They all gave me the nod as they made their way over to Alan.

I made my way around, trying to mingle with everybody. It took every bit of energy I had. I could barely swallow the spit in my mouth, and the pain in my side was getting worse.

After a while Alan made his way over to me. 'Jaysus, Kathleen, the colour of yeh! Yeh're waxy in the face!'

'I'll be grand, Alan. Help me gather everybody up; the dinner's ready.'

'Will yeh go in and sit yerself down before yeh faint. Phil, come over here and give us a hand.' Sure enough, they had everybody sitting in their seats in minutes.

Da didn't spend too long on his speech, just a few quick words. Little did he know he was supposed to wait until everybody had finished their dinner. He was so nervous and just wanted to get it out of the way. We all let him get on with it and said nothing.

He cleared his throat. 'Thanks to yeh all for turnin' up. Alan, yeh're a good young fella and I know yeh'll do Kathleen well.' And down he sat.

I was mortified as the place erupted with the laughter. Da didn't realise the meaning everyone was taking – 'to do well' meant doing the other.

The kids did me proud. I couldn't help but laugh every time the waitress asked, 'Would you like more?' They all put their plates up, not only once, but two or three times. I caught a couple of them out of the corner of my eye, when they thought I wasn't minding, lifting the plate up and giving it a good lick. I looked over quickly to see if Alan's aunties were looking, and then I thought, *Fuck them, snobs, the kids are enjoyin' themselves and tha's all tha' matters.*

I couldn't eat a thing myself and was glad when the dinner was over. All the men made their way over to the bar and the women settled themselves around the room as the waitress cleared the tables. I was on my way over to Ma when I copped Noel, standing with a pint of Guinness in his hand, and him only fourteen.

'Jaysus Christ, Noel Doyle, wha' de yeh think yeh're doin'?'

'There yeh are, Kathleen.' He put his arm on my shoulder.

'Yeh're drunk. Who bought tha' for yeh?'

'Now, now, sis, don't be worryin'.' He picked me up in the air and threw me over his shoulder, twirling me all over the place.

'Put me down, yeh gobshite.' I was trying to whisper. 'If Ma finds out tha' yeh've drink on yeh, there'll be blue murder, never mind Da.'

'And who de yeh think bought me the last couple of pints? Only the oul' fella himself.'

I thought, *Good God! Da must be really plastered himself.*

He finally put me down. I was left sitting on my arse in the middle of the floor in the bar, the headdress lop-sided on my head. All the men were laughing as I struggled to get up. Noel was bent over from laughing. Finally, one of Da's friends came over and gave me a hand.

'Don't be gettin' yerself all annoyed, Kathleen. The lad's only havin' a bit of fun.'

I gave him a polite little smile as I tried to fix myself, when all I really wanted to do was scream from the top of my voice – what was left of it – *'Fuck off, everybody!'*

Alan came over and took me by the hand.

'Kathleen, before yeh say anythin', I tried to stop Noel, but every time I turned me back he had a pint in his hand, him bein' the best man and all. Tha's wha' happened. They all think he's older with the size of him.'

'Where's me Da?'

'There's no point sayin' anythin' to him, Kathleen. He's well on his way.'

'Alan, just tell me where he is.' My temper was starting to rise like a volcano.

'He's in the hall with Mr Daly. They're tryin' to get a sing-song goin'.'

'Don't let them start all tha', Alan. Get the music goin'.

Tha'll put a stop to it.'

'Tha's wha' I wanted to talk to yeh about, Kathleen. The band never showed up.'

'Oh my God, oh my God. I don't believe all this is happenin'. Wha' are we goin' to do?'

'Me uncle Joe is over there with the manager, they're tryin' to see if they can get some sort of music for us.'

I sat on the end of the stairs and cried. The whole day had been a big joke from start to finish. I just wanted to run out of there.

'Come on, Kathleen, please don't get upset. It's taken me all me time to keep on top of things. Wha' de yeh say, love?' He lifted my chin and gave me a tender kiss. 'Yeh know, I'd take on the world if I thought it would make yeh happy. I'll get up and do a jig meself to get things goin'. So come on and dry them eyes. Let's go talk to this manager fella, see if he's sorted somethin' out.'

And sure enough he did. It wasn't a band or anything like one – just one man on his own. Paddy was his name; he played the mouth organ and the accordion. I was so happy to get somebody at such a late hour. I wouldn't have cared if he'd just sat there banging two spoons together. By the time he got to the hotel everybody was well full of drink. While he was setting up, I asked if he knew any rock and roll. I knew that would get everybody going.

'You just name it, love, I can play it.'

He nearly had the mouth organ talking. Bill Haley's 'Rock Around the Clock', you name it; he had all the songs of to a T. The place was hopping. Even Ma and Da got up to dance. I couldn't believe it.

'Alan, would yeh have a look at this? Ma and Da!'

'Say nothin', Kathleen. I slipped her a few brandies through the day.'

'Good, help her forget all her troubles, for a few hours anyway.'

As myself and Alan danced around the floor, everybody was saying, 'Kathleen, it's a right oul' hooley yiz put on there.' I was well pleased when I heard that.

* * *

Everything turned out right in the end. The next few hours went by so quickly – talking to everybody, checking on the kids, trying to be so grown-up. I was so tired.

Phil came over to us. 'Why don't yeh take yerselves off, the pair of yiz. Meself and Carmel will look after things. Sure, the night's nearly over, anyway.'

'Phil, where's Noel?'

'Look at yeh worryin' again, Kathleen. Forget about him.'

'I said, where is he?'

'He's out cold in the bar on one of the sofas; he's green in the face. Don't worry, I'll sort him out. A couple of fingers rammed down his throat won't be long gettin' half of the drink out of him. I tell yeh, he won't do it again in a hurry by the time I'm finished.'

'Don't mind all tha',' Carmel said. 'Go and get changed. I'll tell them all yeh're leavin' soon.'

Alan took me by the hand and we made our way up to the room. I could feel myself getting all nervous inside.

'Are yeh alright, Kathleen? Yeh're all shaky.'

'No I'm not.'

As soon as we got into the room I started to take my clothes out of the case.

'Would yeh look at yeh, all fidgety. Come over here and sit down beside me. Come on!'

I sat down on the side of the bed. Alan had me lying down before I knew it. I was all right having a wear, but as soon as Alan's hands started to roam, that was it. I was up like a light.

'We better hurry, they're all waitin' downstairs.'

I had the wedding dress and veil off and I had changed in seconds.

'Jaysus, Kathleen, tha' was quick.'

'I know, I know. I can hear them all; they're waitin' on us, we have to go.' I was out the door before he could say another word. Poor Alan; the look on his face.

I stood outside the door, shaking; my heart was thumping. I felt so stupid. *Jaysus Christ, wha's after happenin' to me in there? I thought when this time came I'd be okay. Wha' am I goin' to do? I have to take me knickers off tonight and I don't want to.*

All those years saying, 'No, Alan, it's a sin, it's a sin.' Da had it drilled into my head: the church, the church. That's all you got, day or night, sober or drunk: 'If yeh bring a child into this world outside marriage, yeh'll be looked down on by everybody. No priest would let yeh set foot inside the holy grounds, ever. Not a man on this earth – I don't care who he is or where he comes from – would have any time for an easy woman. Mark my word, Kathleen, tha's the God's honest truth.'

Then there was Ma on the other side: 'Men, they're all bastards. They only care about one thing – satisfyin' their own selfish needs, nothin' else matters. Pigs, so they are.'

Then there were the girls in work – not that I mixed much with any of them; I was always a loner. But I'd always pick up bits here and there in the cloakroom or toilet. I overheard two of them talking one day, one telling the other how she would never forget as long as she lived the first time she'd had sex with her fella.

'Yeh want to see the size of his mickey – an elephant's trunk hadn't got a patch on it. I couldn't walk right for a month afterwards.'

I nearly fell down the toilet with the fright.

Is it any wonder my head was a mess with all that I was listening to? If all that wasn't enough to put me off sex and men for life, I don't know what would.

I could hear Alan moving around, so I made my way downstairs. Everybody started cheering and throwing confetti. Alan came down behind me with the suitcase in one hand and my coat in the other. I turned away so that I wouldn't have to look him in the eye.

I looked around the room. All the little ones were asleep on chairs. Noel was standing, leaning on Phil's shoulder, still green in the face. There were hugs and kisses from everybody. Da had one arm around Alan, while he held on tight to his pint of Guinness with the other.

'It's a man yeh are now, Alan, and I'll be keepin' an eye on yeh, makin' sure tha' yeh take care of my Kathleen.' Alan just smiled.

Ma waited until the last minute, until I was about to get into the car. She didn't kiss or hug me, but I thought she might have, given the day that was in it. She looked at me, held my hand for a split second, then turned and walked away. I wanted so much to talk to her, to say how I was feeling, how nervous and frightened I was. But it wasn't to be; she'd let herself get so hard over the years, she just wasn't able to show her feelings, ever.

Phil must have been watching. I swear, sometimes I think he could read my mind. He would always say or do some little thing that would be just right at the time, when I needed it most. He stuck his head in the window, gave me a kiss on the cheek and Alan a pat on the back.

'Away with yiz and have the time of yer life, de yeh hear me, Kathleen?' he said, banging the top of the car as we drove away. I turned and watched Phil waving and smiling as he faded into the distance.

I didn't have a clue where we were going. I had left all that to Alan. He broke the silence after a while.

'I got us a lovely place, Kathleen, just as yeh pull into Brittas Bay – Rochford House it's called. Uncle Joe phoned ahead. I booked us a table. We'll have a nice meal; yeh haven't eaten a thing all day. Wha' de yeh say, love?'

'Tha'll be nice, Alan.'

'I know yeh're not feelin' the best, with yer throat and all.

But is there's somethin' else wrong?'

'The day was hectic, Alan; I'm just a bit tired. I'll be fine.'

'Yeh're sure then, Kathleen?'

'Keep yer eyes on the road, Alan. The rain is gettin' very heavy.'

I sat in silence for the rest of the journey, watching the rain pelt against the windscreen, sick with worry, not knowing how I was going to cope with what was ahead for me.

27

The Honeymoon

It wasn't too long before we saw the sign for Rochford House. The plan was to stay there one night and then to head off and see a bit of Ireland.

'This is it, in to the left. Tha' took just over an hour. Looks good. Wha' de yeh think, Kathleen?'

'I can't see out Alan, the rain is so heavy.'

'I'll drive straight up to the door, you just jump out there while I park the car.'

'I'm not goin' in on me own.'

'Don't be silly, Kathleen, yeh'll be drowned walkin' from the car. Just stand inside the door. I'll be back in two minutes with the cases.'

'Right then, don't be long.'

I made my way inside. There was a woman standing beside a big blazing fire. She had the back of her skirt pulled up, giving her arse a good roasting. I just about had time to give the place a quick look over. I'd never seen the likes of it before. The walls were painted snow white and the lighting was dim. I could feel my feet sink down into the thick red carpet. Two large brown sofas sat beside the fire.

The woman got herself a bit flustered, fixing her skirt as she made her way over to me. 'You have to excuse me, love. I was out getting a few logs for the fire; I wanted to have the place nice and cozy for when you arrived. The cold must have gone straight through me. I just can't get the heat into me.'

'It's okay, sure me Ma does tha' all the time when she's cold.'

'You must be the young couple down from Dublin, Mr and Mrs McGrath. I'm Sheila, I'm pleased to meet you.' She put her hand out to shake mine.

Alan walked in just then. 'This is Alan,' I mumbled, 'my . . . oh, em . . . my husband.' Alan was well pleased when he heard that.

'Look at you, Mr McGrath, you're soaked! Let me get you a towel from the kitchen; I'll be back in a jiffy.'

'It looks very posh, Alan,' I whispered.

'It's supposed to be – we're on our honeymoon.' He put his arm around me and gave me a kiss.

The woman came in and caught us. I didn't half blush. She smiled as she handed Alan a towel.

'Would you like me to show you to your room now?'

When she said that I took the shakes inside. *Oh God, wha' am I goin' to do? This is it now; I'm so scared.*

So I jumped in quickly: 'No, no, tha's fine, we'll stay here for a while, if tha's okay with yeh.'

'Here's a menu, then, you can have a look while your sittin' there.'

'Before yeh go, Miss, could I have a cup of tea, please?'

'I'll get it right now. You just relax there.'

'Yeh're gas, Kathleen. Yeh should be orderin' Babycham or somethin' like tha', not tea. We're supposed to be celebratin'.'

'We are, we will, it's just, it's just . . .'

'Wha' is it, Kathleen? *Wha's wrong with yeh?*'

Before I could answer him the woman was back with the tea.

'There you are. Now, have you decided what you would like to eat?'

'I don't mind, Alan; just get me wha'ever yeh're havin'.'

'Right then, two nice juicy steaks and wha'ever goes with it – all the trimmin's. Oh, em . . . can I have a beer and a Babycham with the meal as well, please?'

'That will take me a little while to prepare; is that okay?'

'Tha's grand,' Alan answered, 'we're not rushin' anywhere.'

'I don't know why yeh got tha' drink for me, Alan; yeh know I hate the stuff. I won't touch it.'

'I know, I know, I suppose I'm just showin' off. Just let on yeh're drinkin' it, in case anybody's lookin'.'

'I don't think yeh have to worry there. It looks like we're the only ones here; there's not a sinner in the place.'

'Suppose it bein' Christmas time, they wouldn't be gettin' many visitors. Anyway, never mind all tha'. Yeh're not yerself at all today. I usually can't get a word in edgeways. Why are yeh so quiet? Oh, and another thing – wha' was all tha' about back there at the hotel? Yeh were out of tha' room before I could say a word, never mind get a wear.'

'Sorry Alan, I'm not feelin' great and now yeh're gettin' all worked up, givin' out to me.' The tears started rolling down my face.

'Don't cry, Kathleen. I'm not givin' out to yeh. I'm worried, tha's all. Come on, if tha' woman comes in and sees yeh like this she'll think I'm a right bowsie.'

'No she won't, Alan, nobody would think tha' about yeh.'

I just about got myself calmed down enough to get through the meal – not that I was able to eat much of it. I didn't know if I was feeling so sick from my throat, the pains in my side, or the pain in my head with the worry about going to bed. I never saw Alan talk so much – not that I minded; it was good for a change. I sat there, half-listening. Maybe he was just as nervous as me, and he wasn't saying anything either.

We finally made our way to our room; I couldn't stall any longer. It was lovely – really fancy, with a huge bathroom. You could have fit me and half of the kids in at the one time. My mind start drifting: *They'd love this. One of these days, when I've the money, I'm goin' to bring the lot of them to a nice place like this and spoil them rotten. There I go again; I'll have to stop thinkin' about the kids. Jaysus, I miss them already.*

'Kathleen,' I could hear Alan saying, 'yeh're miles away there.'

'Sorry, I was thinkin' . . . All the same, Alan, it must be great to have loads of money. Just look at this place.'

'We'll have all this some day, Kathleen, just you wait and see. I'll work every hour tha's goin' to give yeh all the nice things yeh ever wanted.'

'And I'll be right beside yeh, Alan'.

'Ah, come on, enough of all the serious talk, Kathleen. I'll hang the clothes in the wardrobe; you go get tha' famous bubble bath ready. Yeh know, the one tha' yeh're always talkin' about for years.'

'Shite! I forgot to get the bubbles.'

'Well, I didn't.' And out came a bottle of bubble bath from his case.

'I don't believe yeh remembered, with all the goin's-on!' I gave him a big hug.

'Go on, then, run the water. I'll be there in a minute. Make sure yeh don't fill it up too much. Yeh don't want the water flowin' all over the place with the two of us in it.'

The panic set in once more.

'Wha' de yeh mean the two of us? Yeh can't get in the bath with me.'

'Why not, Kathleen?'

'Because yeh can't, yeh just can't, Alan. I'm not lettin' yeh!'

'It's okay. We're married now; yeh're not doin' any harm.'

'I don't care, I don't care.'

He could see how nervous I was getting.

'It's okay, Kathleen, calm yerself down. You just go and have yer bath; soak yerself for a while. Anyway, I've to go lock the car up for the night. It went out of me head, rushin' in with the cases earlier. I'll be back in a while.'

The look on his face as he left the room; he was in shock.

I had myself so worked up, I shook the whole bottle of bubble bath in the water. The bubbles were halfway up the wall, flowing over onto the floor. I didn't care at this stage; I just wanted to slip into the warm water, relax and try get my head together.

I lay there thinking: *It'd be nice if Alan was in here with me. But then if I call him in, he wouldn't just sit there; he'd be thinkin' of me under all them bubbles with no knickers on. He's rarin' to go. Jaysus, can I blame him after five years holdin' him back? I better not. I'd probably drown meself in the panic tryin' to get out if he starts.*

I drifted off to sleep. It must have been quite some time before I woke; the water was cold and I could hear Alan knocking on the door, asking me if I was okay.

'I fell asleep.'

'I know yeh did. I kept checkin' to make sure yeh wouldn't go under and drown yerself.'

'Sorry I took so long. I'll just dry meself off.'

I stalled and stalled, sitting on the side of the bath, nightdress and dressing gown on, buttoned right up to my neck, with not a sight of flesh showing anywhere. I was only short of putting a veil over my head.

Alan called again. I said nothing.

'Kathleen, did yeh hear me?'

'I'm not comin' out, Alan.'

'Wha' de yeh mean yeh're not comin' out? Wha' the hell is wrong with yeh? Don't be silly; yeh can't stay in there.'

My voice trembled. 'I don't care, Alan. I don't want to do tha' – I don't want to do the other.' *There: I said it; it's outside my head at last.*

Alan went quiet for a minute or two. I sat there crying, not knowing what to do next. Alan, being the gentleman he is, called out: 'Come on, love, just come out and get in beside me; yeh don't have to do anythin' yeh're not ready for.'

I slowly opened the door and peeped out. Alan was stripped and under the covers.

'Yeh promise, Alan?'

'I promise. Now, will yeh come out and let me in the bathroom before I piss on meself?'

As I walked out, Alan jumped out of the bed. I stole a glance at him, checking to see if he had anything on. He had, thank God! I jumped under the covers, housecoat and all. It wasn't long before Alan was back in beside me.

'Now, Kathleen, wha's this all about? Gettin' yerself in such a state like tha'. Yeh know yeh can talk to me about anythin'.'

'I know. I didn't think I was goin' to be like this tonight. It was supposed to be special. I'm a gobshite, tha's wha' I am. I've ruined everythin'.'

'No, yeh haven't. Wha' have I told yeh before, Kathleen? Sex is not the be all and end all of a relationship. It's nice to have and yeh know I'm only goin' mad to get into yer knickers – me mouth's waterin' just at the thought of it – but I'll wait 'til yeh're ready. Wha's special here tonight is you bein' here beside me. It'll happen in time.' Then, with a big smile on his face, he added: 'But will yeh make sure yeh don't take too long?'

I finally got around to taking the dressing gown off. We kissed and cuddled and that was all. I lay there in Alan's arms as he slept, and thought: *How did he get so wise and grown-up for someone so young?*

* * *

I woke to the sound of banging on the door. It frightened the life out of me. I didn't know where I was for a second.

'Alan, get up, get up, quick!' He was in noddy land. I couldn't wake him for love nor money.

I jumped out of the bed, barely opening the door. Standing in the narrow corridor was the woman of the house with a big smile on her face and a tray in her hands.

I could feel myself blush.

'Himself said that you would be having breakfast in bed. I hope I'm not too early.'

'No, no, it's okay. I woke up ages ago. I was asleep all night – the whole night, I really was.' I was getting more embarrassed by the minute. I don't know what I was shiting out of me, but she just smiled again.

'If I could step inside there, love, and put this tray down; it's a heavy old thing.'

'Yes, yes. Come in, come in, sorry.'

'It's a nice Irish breakfast and homemade bread. Get it into you while it's nice and hot.'

I didn't know what to say. I'd never had a big breakfast like this in my life, never mind in bed as well. I just about got 'thank you' out of my mouth as she left the room.

I sat at the edge of the bed. Alan was starting to come around.

'Would yeh have a look at this, Alan. I never saw so much food for two people. This would feed us and all the kids.'

'I knew yeh'd be surprised, Kathleen. Come on, let's get tucked into it. I'm starvin'.'

Alan ate his and the best part of mine.

'Are yeh goin' to eat nothin', Kathleen?'

'It's me throat, Alan. I can't swallow.'

'Bend yer head back there and open yer mouth, let me have a look. Good Jaysus, Kathleen, yeh've blisters the size of grapes hangin' out of yer tonsils. I'll have to get yeh to a doctor quick.'

'It's okay, I have a few Disprin here in me bag. I'll gargle me throat a couple of times. It'll go away; tha's wha' I always do. Now, will yeh stop fussin'. We'll find a chemist in the town and I'll get a few more.'

'Right, then. I'll give it one more day and if yeh're still not better, yeh either go to a doctor down here or I'm drivin' back to Dublin. Yeh've hardly eaten a scrap in three days. There'll be nothin' left of yeh if yeh keep this up.'

'Okay, I promise yeh, Alan. Now, help me pack these few things. We'll get ready and go pay the bill. All the same that woman was real nice to us – de yeh think we should give her somethin' for herself? Yeh know, sixpence or somethin'?'

'If we're goin' to give her somethin', it'll have to be at least two shillin's.'

'Right then; I'll leave it to yeh, Alan.'

You could see he was as proud as punch paying the bill.

'There's a little somethin' for yerself. Have a drink on us.'

She smiled and wished us all the happiness in the world.

* * *

It wasn't long before we were pulling into White's Hotel in Wexford, right in the heart of the town. I took a shine to the place straight away.

'This looks like a nice town, Alan.'

We made our way around and found the chemist.

'Alan, will we come back out later and see wha's happenin'?'

'Okay but now let's go back and get ourselves a room.'

At the hotel, Alan wasn't long telling them we were just married. They made a right fuss over us and, as usual, I made an arse of myself. Alan was talking to the woman behind the desk when a fella came over and took our two bags and walked away with them.

'Hey you! Come 'ere, where de yeh think yeh're goin'? Put them bags back!' I shouted at him.

He looked over at the woman, who looked at Alan, who turned around to find me struggling, trying to get the bags off your man.

'Kathleen, wha' are yeh doin'? The man works here. He's the porter.'

'And wha's tha', Alan?'

'His job is to carry the bags up to the rooms for people stayin' in the hotel. I got us a room. He was bringin' them up there.'

Alan gave me the eye and the nod to let go of the bags, then he took me by the hand back to the desk. I felt such a fool.

'I'm sorry,' I told the woman. 'It's just it looked like . . .'

Alan tipped me on the arm to let me know to stop talking and not to make the situation any worse. She smiled and handed the key to Alan, who at this stage was red with embarrassment.

The two of us walked behind the porter, with not a word spoken.

'Here we are now, sir, the best suite in the place.'

'Sorry about tha' bit of hassle,' Alan said, handing the porter the price of a pint.

'Not at all, sir.' He gave me a wink on the way out, which made me feel a bit better.

'I'm such a gobshite, Alan, lettin' us down like tha'. I really thought he was robbin' the bags.'

'Would yeh stop worryin'? I wouldn't have known meself, only the woman on the desk had just told me. Come on, leave the bags there and let's go for a walk, see wha's happenin' in the town. There might be some music goin' on later on. We'll have an oul' dance, maybe a bit of a jive – of course, tha's if yeh're up to it.'

'Let me gargle me throat a couple of times before we go out. I should be feelin' okay by tonight.'

'Wha' did yeh say there, Kathleen?' He winked at me.

I knew what he meant and I should, right there and then, have dived on him and kissed the face off him – what any young newly-weds would be doing. But no, I just stood there with the glass in my hand, looking straight into his face, not moving, saying nothing. He put his arm around me. 'Yeh know how much I love yeh, Kathleen.'

'I know, me too, Alan.'

'Will yeh hurry yerself up there. The day will be over before we know it.' Once again he glossed things over.

We walked around the shops for a while, in and out of a

couple of pubs, me drinking a cup of tea, Alan having a shandy. As we walked back to the hotel, I could feel the pain in my side getting worse. Alan was going on about dancing the night away and having the craic. 'Yeh might even have a Babycham, Kathleen. Wha' de yeh say?'

'Maybe I will then, Alan.'

'Tha's the spirit; tha's my girl.'

When we got back to the room, I went straight to the bathroom to gargle my throat, trying to get rid of the 'grapes', as Alan mildly put it. How romantic I must have looked; my head hanging back, making all sorts of noises. How Alan didn't run a mile from me, I'll never know. He had the patience of a saint.

Suddenly, I felt a really sharp pain in my side. My head started spinning and I could feel my legs go from under me. I don't remember much after that; when I came around, I was lying on the bed with a wet towel across my head. Alan was talking to someone and I could hear the panic in his voice as I tried to sit up.

'Alan, wha' happened?' I asked.

'Jaysus, yeh've come around, Kathleen! Yeh put the heart crossways in me.'

Then I heard a woman's voice calling my name.

'Mrs McGrath, my name is Mary. I'm one of the staff from the hotel. The doctor's on his way. A right fright you just gave that husband of yours. The roars of him on the phone! I was half afraid to come into the room. I thought you were after dropping dead.'

Just then there was a knock on the door. 'That will be the local doctor.' She opened the door and this small man came in, with a head of snow-white hair and a high-pitched voice. 'So you're the patient?' He sat down beside me and picked my hand up, feeling for a pulse. 'What's this I hear – honeymooners?'

I lay there, too sick to answer.

Alan went on to explain what had happened and how I'd been feeling over the past few days. The doctor gave me a right going over, checking all my bits, from top to bottom.

'Now, young lady,' he said, taking the scope out of his ears. 'I'm afraid it's the hospital for you. Your temperature is sky high, your throat is in a right state, and on top of that, your appendix is grumbling like mad; sure, is it any wonder you fainted?'

I was struggling to get the words out. 'But doctor, I can't go into hospital. I'm on me honeymoon and all.'

'There's no buts about it. I'm phoning for an ambulance straight away.'

I looked at Alan. The shock on his face! He didn't know if he was coming or going. The doctor pulled him to one side. They stood talking for a minute and in no time at all I was being carried to the ambulance.

'Alan, I don't believe this.' I was off crying again.

'Yeh have to go, Kathleen. The doctor said yeh're real sick and tha' he wouldn't be responsible. They'll fix yeh up, yeh'll be as right as rain in a day or two. We'll be able to go off and have a great time. Wha' de say, love? Come on, don't cry.'

'Tha's all I seem to be doin' the past two days. Everythin's goin' wrong. It's not fair, it's just not fair.'

The hospital was just outside the town, so we were there in no time. The ambulance man left me in the hands of a lovely friendly little nurse, who relaxed me straight away. She chatted away to Alan as she read over the letter from the doctor.

'We'll have to get you seen to straight away to get that temperature down – that's first on the list. I'll put you into this cubicle and get this fan going to cool you down while the doctor checks you out. I'm afraid you'll have to leave, sir.'

'Please don't put him out, Nurse.'

'Can't I stay for a little while?' Alan asked. 'Just 'til she gets herself settled?'

'I'm sorry, sir, it's not me; Sister makes the rules and no one dare break them. Visiting time is over and no one is allowed in the hospital after that. Here's comes the doctor; I'm sorry, you'll have to leave, sir.'

I got a quick kiss on the cheek and a whisper in the ear: 'I'll be here when yeh wake up in the mornin'.' And that was it. He was gone. I couldn't believe it was all happening so quickly.

The doctor gave me the once-over and handed me a few tablets to take. He told me the head man himself would see me first thing in the morning. The nurse brought me to a ward and tried hard to make me see it was all for the best. I wanted to be grown-up and not let them see me cry. I was so frightened. It was the first time in my life that I'd ever been on my own, without Alan or the family. I didn't get much sleep that night. The nurses were in and out all night sponging me down, with a fan going to keep my temperature down.

Bright and early the next morning, in walked the head sister herself. I could see why the nurse wasn't taking any chances letting Alan stay. You'd want to see the serious puss on her face as she stood at the end of the bed.

'Hmm . . .' she said, looking over the top of her glasses and checking the folder in her hand, 'they tell me you're married.' I turned my head and said nothing. *Bitch,* I thought to myself, *Alan could've stayed only for you.*

'Mrs McGrath, the doctors will be around soon, so any jewellery you have on, I want it taken off now. We have to have you ready in case they decide to operate.'

I nearly fainted when she said that. Reluctantly I handed her my engagement ring and the chain on my neck.

'And the wedding ring also, if you please.' She stood there with her hand stretched out into my face. I looked down at my hand, holding on tight to my wedding ring.

'Come on, child, I haven't got all day.'

'No! Yeh're not gettin' it.'

'What did you say?'

You could see she wasn't used to anybody back-answering her.

'I said, *No!* I'm not takin' it off. I only got it yesterday and it's stayin' on me finger always.'

'Now, stop this nonsense, child!' She bent over, trying to get the ring off me. I pushed her back, shouting, 'I'm all grown-up, I'm not a child.' I could feel the temper rising in me. I was sick and tired of being told I was a child when it suits everyone.

'I want to see Alan. Where is he?' I was getting more frightened by the minute.

'And who might that be, Mrs McGrath?' she said, a smart tone in her voice.

'He's me husband. He was to be here real early this mornin'. He promised me.'

'Oh, that's right. There was a Mr McGrath here at the crack of dawn this morning. I sent him on his way. Nobody gets into my hospital unless it's visiting hour, which is not until seven o'clock tonight.' She had a big sly grin on her face.

Now I was really mad. Just then, Ma popped into my head. She always taught us to have respect for our elders and never to be cheeky – but on the other hand she'd say, 'Sometimes there's special occasions when you have to fend for yerself and not be walked on.' This was definitely a special occasion.

'Yeh could have let Alan in for a few minutes. Yeh were just bein' bad – yeh're only a bitch.'

She put her hand out once more, 'I said, the ring.'

The blood rushed through me; my temper exploded. I don't know where the words or the nerve came from; it just flowed out of me.

I screamed, 'Yeh know wha' yeh can do with yerself? Yeh can go and . . .' Then, I stopped and thought: *No! I won't let meself down in front of this wan.* 'I want me clothes. I'm not stayin' here. Who de yeh think yeh are? There's no need for yeh to treat me like this.'

She glared at me once more, saying nothing, turning as red in the face as I was. She probably would have bashed me on the head with the folder if she'd had her way. She scribbled a few things down on the folder, got herself together and stormed out.

The nurse was biting her lip, trying to be really serious. I was shaking inside. I couldn't believe I'd said all that. I didn't want to be cheeky, but there was no need for her to carry on like that; she could have been a bit nicer. The nurse bent over me, pretending to be fixing the pillows.

'My, my, my, am I glad my shift's finished in a few minutes! Sister will be on the rampage for the day.'

'Will yeh get me clothes, nurse? Please, I wanna go. I'm leavin'.'

'Just wait until the doctor checks you out. Come on now, love, don't be too hasty; you're not well.'

I had no choice but to stay, since I had nothing to wear. I lay there watching the clock on the wall, every second ticking by, wondering what Alan was doing and if he was okay. Then Ma popped into my head again. I wasn't sure if she would have been proud of me for standing up for myself, or boxed the head off me for answering back. Not that I was feeling proud or anything like it myself. I was just scared and upset.

The doctors finally came around after about an hour – a big tall man and a small Chinese fella. They examined me from head to toe. Between the Chinese doctor's broken English and the strong country accent, I couldn't make out a word they were saying. It would have been all double Dutch to me, anyway.

After a while the Chinese doctor stood beside me. 'Appendix must come out,' he said in a low voice. I understood that bit alright.

'No!' I said. 'I'm goin' home, doctor, I'm not stayin' here.'

'What she mean?' he asked, trying to understand the thick Dublin accent. The other doctor came over and stood in front of me.

'Sister tells me she was in with you.' He didn't lift his head from reading the chart. I was sure she'd been giving him a right mouthful about me. Doctor Wang was still rammaging on but at this stage it was all going over my head anyway; all I wanted to do was get the hell out of there.

'You know, young lady, my colleague is right. Your appendix is very inflamed and has to come out.'

The tears started flowing again; I wasn't listening to anybody.

'I wanna go home, Doctor, I just wanna go home.'

'Young lady, you have yourself very stressed out and that's not good.'

I'd never heard that word before and didn't know what he was talking about. Not that I gave a shite; this wasn't the time or the place to be brushing up on my education.

He walked away and stood to one side as he spoke to the Chinese doctor. When they eventually came back over to me, the country doctor spoke.

'We have decided to send you back to Dublin. Your temperature is down now. It was very high last night and we don't want it going up again, but if you keep getting yourself stressed and upset like this, it's going to go back up and we won't be able to operate, anyway.'

In the middle of all this mayhem, my brain clicked in to what the new word, 'stress', meant. It was just a fancy word for being upset and worried. *They could've said tha' in the first place, with their fancy words confusin' me altogether.*

'I'm going to give you an injection for the pain. That should keep you going until you get to your doctor. Pick these tablets up in the chemist for your throat.' He handed me a piece of paper. 'I'll leave a letter at reception for you to pick up on your way out. And I mean this, young lady, you must go straight to your doctor. He will make arrangements with the hospital to get you in straight away.' He raised his voice a little and was getting worked up himself – not that I could blame him with my carry-on.

'Thanks, doctor. I will, I promise.' I would have said anything to be on my way.

KATHLEEN DOYLE

The two of them walked off, mumbling to one another, the Chinese doctor with his hands up in the air, still insisting that I should get the knife there and then. It wasn't long before the nurse was in to give me the injection.

'I see your name is Kathleen,' she said as she gave me a jab in the arse.

'Nurse, if I give yeh the name of the hotel I was staying in, would yeh give them a ring and ask would they tell Alan McGrath – tha's me husband – to collect me?'

'A bride of only two days, I hear. Is it any wonder you're upset?'

'Yeh don't think I'm bein' stupid carryin' on like a kid, cryin'?'

'Not at all. Anyone would have themselves in a state, if they were as sick as you've been and on their honeymoon as well, you poor thing.'

'Thanks, nurse. Tha' makes me feel a bit better.'

'It will be at least two hours before you can leave – doctor's orders – so you just lie there and get yourself nice and calm, keep that temperature down. He won't let you leave unless it's right.'

'Okay, I will. Before yeh go, nurse, could yeh get me ring and chain when yeh're pickin' me clothes up? I don't want to see tha' sister.'

She smiled. 'I think that might be best. I'll go and make that phone call for you. Now, remember what I said, Kathleen.'

The two hours went by quickly. The nurse was in and out checking me and chatting, asking all about the wedding. She couldn't believe how many brothers and sisters I had, and how young they all were. That was it – once I started talking about the kids, I was happy.

'My, that father of yours was a busy man,' she giggled.

I didn't know how to answer that one, so I said nothing.

'And your mother, she must be some woman. How on earth does she cope?'

302

Without batting an eyelid I found myself saying, 'Because she's great, nurse, tha's how.'

'Now, isn't that a nice thing to say? I'm sure she'd be very pleased to hear that.'

I thought to myself, *Yeh never know with Ma, she'd probably tell me to stop being so sloppy, carryin' on like an eejit. Then again, maybe tha's wha's wrong with her a lot of the time; she thinks none of us care about her. I'll talk to Phil when I get home, see wha' he thinks.*

'Kathleen, would this be himself walking down the corridor?'

My heart skipped a beat when she said that. I jumped down to the end of the bed. 'Tha's him, nurse.'

'Look at you. You're glowing all over. That's one handsome lad you have there, I'd be keeping a tight rope on him, if he was mine.'

'I know, nurse, I will.' Then I blushed from head to toe. 'Ah, yeh know wha' I mean, nurse.'

Alan and I were hugging and kissing before I knew it. We forgot the nurse was standing there. She gave a little cough. 'Everything seems to be fine now, Kathleen. You can go ahead and get dressed. Your clothes are in the locker beside you.'

'Yeh mean they were there all the time?'

'Yes, but we weren't going to tell you that, now, were we?' She handed my ring and chain to me.

'I'll go and make sure the doctor left that letter out for you.'

The nurse met us on the way out and handed me the letter. She winked and said, 'Herself is in the office, so we'll say no more.'

Alan looked puzzled. 'She means the Sister. I'll tell yeh when we get in the car.'

'Make sure you do what the doctor said and the best of luck to you both.' She held an umbrella over me while I got in the car.

As soon as we on our way, I told Alan all about the Sister

pulling off my ring. 'And then there was this Chinese doctor – he wanted to give me the knife there and then, and yeh wanna see the height of the other doctor, he was real posh but nice.'

'Yeh're feelin' better then, Kathleen?'

'Now tha' yeh're here, Alan, I am.'

'Yeh haven't stopped talkin' for the past couple of minutes, so I know yeh're on the mend.'

'Will yeh stop yer messin'. Yeh're always teasin' me.'

I cuddled into him.

* * *

In no time at all Alan had us back at the hotel and checked out. We got plenty of waves and goodbyes as we pulled away. It wasn't long before we came to the main road: Dublin one way, Cork the other. The thought struck me: *I don't want to go back yet. I want to try and fix things; I have to make it right between us.*

'Stop the car, Alan.'

'Wha' de yeh mean? Wha's wrong?'

'Just stop – come on, let's go to Cork.'

'But, Kathleen, the doctor said . . .'

'I know, I know. I feel a bit better. Come on, Alan, I'll be okay. We didn't get a chance to talk or enjoy ourselves – yeh know wha' I mean.'

That was it; you could see the gleam in his eyes straight away. I didn't have to say another word. He revved the car so much there was smoke coming out of the wheels as he took the road to Cork.

It was a long drive. We talked and talked, planning out our future, the great adventures we were going to have. Two kids, with not a worry in the world at that moment in time, anyway, but for one thing – I only hoped I could get it into my head that loving was not dirty or bad. I was lost in my thoughts again.

'Kathleen, are yeh asleep or wha'? I'm talkin' away here and

I don't know if yeh're listenin' to me.'

'I was just restin' me eyes for a couple of minutes, Alan. Go on, wha' were yeh sayin'?'

'We haven't got far to go now. I was thinkin' we could get ourselves a room in the city. Tha' way we can have a mosey around, maybe find somewhere with a bit of music, have tha' oul' dance we were supposed to have the other night. I don't mean jivin' or anythin' like tha'; yeh know: a nice lurch. Or would yeh prefer just to go for somethin' to eat?'

'I don't mind, Alan. You can pick.'

'Right then, tha's settled; we'll have music and fish 'n' chips walkin' back to the hotel.'

This was no problem, as it turned out we were right next door to a pub that was blasting out some rock and roll. It was great to hear after being stuck in the hospital. We booked into the hotel, dropped the bags and headed for the pub. The place was hopping, everybody was singing along with the band and there were a few dancing over in the corner.

This is more like it, I thought. *The way it's supposed to be.*

But that was all soon to change. As the night went on, the pain came back with a bang. The injection was starting to wear off. I just about managed to get through the night without fainting. Alan knew that I wasn't feeling great when I didn't want to get up to dance. I was usually the first on the floor.

'Let's head back, Kathleen. Try an' get a few hours' sleep. Yeh look tired. We'll make our way back to Dublin tomorrow.'

I didn't argue. He was right.

* * *

We got up at the crack of dawn. By this time I was bent over with the pain. Alan was starting to panic once again.

'I shouldn't have listened to yeh, Kathleen. We should have made our way back to Dublin yesterday. Wha' was I thinkin'?'

'Will yeh stop gettin' yerself in a state, Alan. I'll lie down in the back of the car. It's not as bad when I do tha'. We'll be home in no time. Come on, I'll be okay.' I was trying not to let him know how bad I was really feeling.

He calmed himself down, paid the bill and we were on the road in no time.

Some honeymoon!

28

Marital Bliss . . .

Alan talked all the way up to Dublin. I don't know what he was going on about half of the time. I agreed with everything he said. He was going so fast he was taking lumps out of the road.

'If we keep goin' at this rate, Kathleen, I'll have yeh back in time for Dr Johnson's surgery. If anyone can get yeh into hospital quick, he will.'

And he did. I was only in the door when he saw to me immediately. I handed him the letter the other doctor had given me. He glanced at it and looked at me with a frown.

'Kathleen, you should have been here yesterday.'

'I know, doctor, but I was startin' to feel a bit better.'

'There's no "buts" about it. Alan, you should have had more sense. I'm not even going to examine you, Kathleen. I only have to look at your colour . . .' He scribbled out a few lines on a bit of paper. 'Take this and go down to the Adelaide Hospital straight away. I'll phone and let them know you're on your way. They'll see to you right away.'

And sure enough, as soon as we got to the hospital I was taken to see a doctor. He didn't pull any punches either. He nearly pressed my stomach up into my mouth; the whole hospital must have heard the roars of me. 'Right, young lady, it's the theatre for you; the appendix has to come out now, and I mean *now*!'

'But, Doctor, me Ma doesn't even know I'm here.'

'And how old are you?'

'I'm nearly nineteen.'

'You're too young. Nurse,' he called out, 'we have to get a consent form signed.'

'Alan's outside. Will he do? He's me husband, doctor.'

'Send him in to me on your way out. Nurse, take this young lady and prepare her for theatre. There's no time to delay.'

As I brushed past Alan, I just about had time to tell him to sign the form for me. At this stage my legs were starting to go from under me with the pain. The nurse quickly got me into a wheelchair and stuck a bowl in my hand: 'Just in case, love.' And she was so right; I was only halfway down the corridor when there were noises coming from both ends, between the farting and spluttering at one end and the throwing up at the other. I was all over the place. Not that I cared; I wanted the pain to go away. They could have done anything to me at that stage.

The nurse wasn't long getting me ready and before I knew it, I was on a trolley getting wheeled down to get the knife. Just as we got to the door of the operating room – the theatre, as the doctor called it – the nurse let out a gasp: 'Christ, your nail polish is still on! It slipped me mind rushing about getting you ready.' She called to one of the other nurses, 'Quick! Help me get this off before doctor gets here. He'll have a blue fit if you're not ready when he comes in.'

He was having a fit anyway. Alan was too young to sign the form; you had to be twenty-one and he was only twenty.

The doctor came over to me as he glanced at the chart: 'Now, Kathleen, has your family got a phone?'

'No, Doctor.'

'Has anyone near your home got one?'

'The corner shop down the road from me Ma's has one.'

'And the name of that is . . .?' I could see he was getting himself all worked up; he was red in the face and grinding his teeth together.

'It's called the Windmill, Doctor.'

My bottom lip was starting to tremble. He knew he was making me nervous.

'Everything's going to be fine, Kathleen.' It was like he was trying to calm himself down as well as me. 'I have to operate very soon or you're going to be in serious trouble. Do you understand me? There's no time to waste.' Out he went, his hands flying in the air, mumbling and giving out to himself, frustrated as hell.

What did he only go and do? He got onto Crumlin garda station straight away and informed them of the situation. A garda was sent down to the house in no time. They brought Da down to the phone, and his consent was given. The doctor was back before I knew it.

I got a jab in the arse. 'Right, Kathleen, I want you to count to ten for me.'

'One, two . . .' wasn't even out of my mouth and I was gone.

* * *

When I came around I was so sick! Alan had to hold my head with one hand and a bowl under my chin with the other. Every time I tried to tell him I was sorry, up it kept coming. I looked a right mess, I'm sure.

That's when the nurse came in: 'I think it's best if you go, sir. She'll be like this for a couple of hours. If you leave it until tomorrow evening, there will be a big difference in her, I promise.'

And the nurse was so right. I was sitting up – still green in the face, mind you – but a lot better, when Alan walked in with Ma and Phil. Ma settled herself down on one side of the bed, Alan on the other.

'Kathleen Doyle!' Ma got her spoke in straight away. 'Yeh put the heart crossways in me and yer Da. De yeh know tha'? The police comin' to me door! Wha'll the neighbours think?'

'Sorry, Ma, I didn't send them – it was the doctor.'

'I thought it was one of them kids after gettin' into trouble, but when they said yer name and the hospital, I thought yeh were dead. I mean, who sends the police to yer door when somebody's only sick? Did yeh ever hear the likes of it?'

I looked across at Phil, who was standing behind Ma. He had a grin on his face from ear to ear. He was making all sorts of faces at me. Alan wouldn't look at him. I kept trying to move myself around, letting on to cough so that I didn't laugh. Sick or not, if Ma thought you were making fun of her, she wouldn't care; she'd still give you a right box.

After all that giving out and rammaging on and on about neighbours and what have you, she finally turned around and asked me: 'Anyway, Kathleen, how are yeh? Yeh're like death warmed up with the colour of yeh, with yer waxy face. How long are yeh goin' to be in this place for? I miss yeh terrible helpin' with the kids and the bit of cleanin'.' *Jaysus, Ma, I thought, put yer arms around me, tell me how happy yeh are tha' I'm okay.* But no.

'I have to stay in for ten days, Ma.'

'For God's sake, Kathleen. I'd be after havin' two babies and home in less time than tha'.'

'The doctor said it was very serious, Ma. Only Alan got me here when he did, I could have been a goner.'

'Hmm . . . is tha' so? Are yeh sure yeh took him up right, Kathleen? Yeh could have died, like. Was it tha' serious then?'

'Yeah, Ma!' I was pushing it a bit, hoping that she might soften. 'All this poison stuff leaks all around yer insides; the nurse told me all about it. If they don't get to yeh quick, yeh're finished. I mean, dead. Tha's why the police went to the house to get Da to give the go-ahead, because me and Alan were under-age.'

'Well then, when yeh put it like tha', I suppose it makes sense yeh not droppin' off at the house to let me know wha' was happenin'. Yeh were wise, Alan, to bring her straight here. I want to thank yeh for tha'.' I was well pleased when she said that, and so was Alan. 'Now tha' I see yeh're alright, I'll be on me way.'

'Wait, Lil. Just give me a few minutes with Kathleen. I'll drop yerself and Phil off.'

'Yeh're okay, Alan. I'm in this far now; I might as well make me way up to Meath Street. Come on, Phil. Yeh needn't think I'm leavin' yeh here with yer messin'. De yeh think I don't know wha' yeh do be doin' behind me back. I didn't come up on the last load, yeh know!'

'Ah, go on, Ma, don't be givin' out.' With that Phil grabbed her and lifted her up, squeezing her to bits – and he was able to. A fine big fella he turned out to be. The muscles on him! And by God, you'd need them to lift Ma; she was small but had plenty of meat on her. *Jaysus,* I thought, *she'll kill him when they get outside.*

'Put me down, yeh bloody gobshite.' She swung her bag and hit him on the head. But at the same time, she was trying to keep a straight face; I could see a little grin on the corner of her mouth. She was enjoying it, I could tell. 'This eejit's gone mad, Kathleen. Will yeh talk to him? I don't know wha's got into him since he came back from tha' Canada place.

'Ah, would yeh get away with yerself; yeh love havin' me home, Ma, don't yeh?' He kept tipping her on the arm, laughing his head off, watching her getting all riled up.

'See wha' I mean, Kathleen? I'll go before he gets us thrown outta the hospital. Yer father will be up tonight. I'll get him to bring a couple of the older kids. They're all dyin' to see yeh. I'll do me best to get up in a day or two and maybe bring a few of the little ones; I'll check if they'll let them in. Come on, Phil. Let them have a bit of time together. Yeh're okay then, Kathleen?'

'Thanks, Ma, I'm fine.'

On the way out Phil turned back towards us, laughing and making all sorts of signs with his hands.

'Wha's he doin', Alan?'

'Don't mind him, Kathleen. He's messin' as usual. I mean, yeh saw him with yer Ma; anythin' for a laugh. Anyway, never mind Phil. The visitin' time is nearly over. How are yeh feelin' now?'

'I'm just a bit sore, tha's all. I'm sorry, Alan. Nothin' seems to be goin' right for us.'

'It's just a bit of a blip, tha's all, Kathleen. Yeh'll be back on yer feet in no time. We'll put this all behind us. Just yeh wait and see.'

The nurse came in ringing the bell.

'I better go, Kathleen.' He gave me a hug and a kiss. 'I'll try and get up during the day on me own. Look! There she goes ringin' the bell again. It's really loud this time. I better run.'

* * *

Alan's Da had no problem letting him off work for an hour to come up and visit me. Phil made his way up one of the days and got there a bit early, before Alan.

'I see yeh're startin' to look a bit normal again, Kathleen. Yeh looked a bit ropey there for a while.'

'I'm okay now, Phil. Listen, I want to ask yeh somethin' before Alan comes up. Wha' were yeh on about the other evenin'? Yeh know, when yeh came into the hospital first. Yeh were makin' these signs with yer hands. Wha' did it mean?'

'Ah, tha'! I was just havin' a bit of craic with Alan. Yeh know him, yeh can say anythin', he never gets annoyed.'

'Well, yeh thought it was very funny and I could do with a good laugh. So go on, tell me.'

'No. Yeh'll only go and get all hyper on me.'

'I won't, Phil,' I promised.

312

'Okay. Yeh asked. I told Alan tha' he must have a right whopper in his trousers, tha' he ended up puttin' yeh in hospital.'

'Jaysus Christ, Phil, yeh didn't!'

'See wha' I mean? I told yeh, yeh're gettin' yerself all worked up. Blokes talk like tha' all the time to one another. It means nothin'. It's just a bit of craic.'

'Yeh don't understand, Phil. Yeh don't realise wha's goin' on with me and Alan.' And before I knew it, I was pouring my heart out, telling him everything. He sat and listened. And there was no messing.

'Wha' am I goin' to do, Phil?'

'Holy Jaysus, I don't know, Kathleen. Poor Alan. He must feel like shite; not sayin' tha' you don't, but this kind of thing, it's real big with blokes. When yeh get yer first score, tha's it. Yeh're up there in the clouds. Yeh're a man and all tha' stuff. This is real serious. Yeh're goin' to have to get yer head around this.'

'De yeh not think I know tha', Phil?'

'Kathleen, yeh're married and grown-up now. Yeh shouldn't be thinkin' about wha' Ma and Da used to preach. They were just afraid of yeh gettin' yerself up the stick. And don't get me started on about the church and priests – them fuckers, messin' with people's heads: this is a sin, tha's a sin, yeh can't do this, and yeh can't do tha'.'

'Jaysus, Phil, would yeh stop talkin' like tha'? If anybody hears yeh!'

'I don't give two shites who hears me. I've learned a few things in the nine months bein' away, and it makes me blood boil when I think of the way they try and rule people with their ways. They wouldn't tell me wha' to do. I can tell yeh tha' for nothin'.'

'Wha'ever yeh do, Phil, don't let Ma or Da hear yeh talk like tha'. There'll be killin's in the house, I'm tellin' yeh.'

'Just listen to yerself, Kathleen. We're not kids anymore.

We're grown-ups and should be able to say wha' we think.'

'Phil, de yeh always say wha's inside yer head?'

'If it's worth sayin', I do. Why?'

'Ah, it's nothin', I was just wonderin', tha's all.'

'Come on, Kathleen, seein's yeh're on a roll, spit it out.'

'Right then; there is one more thing but yeh're not to laugh.'

'Go on, I'm listenin'.'

'De yeh ever tell Ma tha' yeh love her, Phil? I want to know; it's important to me.'

'For Jaysus' sake, wha' are yeh on about, Kathleen? She knows we all love her.'

'Maybe she doesn't, Phil. Tha's probably wha' does be wrong with her half the time. She thinks we don't care and tha's why she's so serious all the time.'

'Will yeh stop, for fuck's sake, Kathleen. Imagine standin' there and sayin' to Ma, "Yeh know I love yeh, Ma." I know wha' she'd say: "Fuck off and give over yer messin'." I'm tellin' yeh, she would. Anyway, I think yeh have more to be worryin' about at the minute than to be thinkin' about wha's goin' on inside Ma's head. Yeh'll have to sort this out yerself. Nobody else can do it for yeh.'

'Promise me, Phil, yeh won't tell anybody about this.'

'Yeh won't have to worry there. I'm not a gobshite altogether. Look! I can see Alan walkin' up the corridor. I'll head off now. Give yeh a bit of time to yerselves.'

'Thanks for listenin', Phil. I feel a little better now tha' I told yeh. Say nothin', de yeh hear me?'

'Didn't I say I wouldn't?'

Alan walked in just then. 'Say nothin' about wha'? You two look very serious. Wha's up?'

I looked at Phil, not knowing what to say.

'I was just sayin' to Kathleen I might stay on for a while, if I get meself some work. I don't want her sayin' anythin' to Ma. Just in case it doesn't go accordin' to plan.'

I cocked my ears up straight away and couldn't keep my mouth shut. 'Tha' means yeh won't be goin' back to Canada, Phil.' I was so happy to hear he might be staying.

'It all depends on this fella I'm goin' to meet in the next half an hour. If he can get me in on the site he's workin' on, I'll be away in a hack. He was tellin' me yeh get paid by the house. Oh, another thing, Alan, it's all rollers now. I'd be able to get through a couple of houses a week. I'm a flyer when I get goin'. Jaysus! When I think about it. I'd be on savage money, if this all goes well.' He stood up to go. 'Anyway, Kathleen, yeh'll be out in a day or two, so I'll see yeh when yeh come home. Let yeh know wha's happenin'.' He gave me a wink on his way out.

'Alan, I'm gettin' me stitches out in the mornin'. Nurse said if all is well the doctor could let me home by dinner-time.'

'Tha's great news, Kathleen.'

'Jaysus! I was nearly forgettin' to tell yeh, we were talkin' tha' much to Phil. The doctor wants to see yeh before I leave.'

'I wonder wha' tha's all about?'

We sat talking and laughing. But the laugh was soon to be put on the other side of Alan's face when the doctor walked in the following day. He had a very serious face on him as he stood at the end of the bed, and looked at the two of us for a few seconds.

'Kathleen, I will be letting you home today. Everything seems to be fine.' Both of us had a smile on our faces the length of the ward. Then he went on: 'I understand you're newly-weds?'

'Tha's righ', Doctor,' Alan answered, as proud as punch.

'Well . . .' he said, putting his hand to his mouth and giving a little cough. 'I'm afraid you will have to put your sex life on hold for at least three months.'

Alan looked straight at me; as soon as I heard the word 'sex' I held my head down and wouldn't look at either of them. The doctor went on to explain the 'dos' and the 'don'ts', the 'whys' and 'why-nots'. I was only half-listening. I was too busy thinking to myself: *Jaysus, this is great! I have a good excuse now – for a couple of months, anyway.*

Then I looked over at Alan. That soon stopped me in my stride. He was trying to take everything in. When the doctor left the room, all he said was: 'Tha' was a right mouthful, Kathleen.'

I didn't know what to say, so I said nothing. As Ma always said, 'Unless yeh know and understand wha's comin' out of yer mouth, keep it shut.'

* * *

We made our way up to Ma and Da as soon as I left the hospital. I was dying to see the little ones. They hadn't been allowed in to see me as they were too young.

When we walked in, Ma was sitting there feeding Mano, who was about five weeks old at that stage. Paul was asleep in the pram beside her. Da was in the kitchen, as usual cleaning up the mess after everyone. He was great when he wasn't on the drink, always helping Ma with one thing or another.

'Hi, Ma.'

'Ah! There yeh are, Kathleen. Come in. Sit down. Alan, pull over a chair. Phil, look who's here.'

'Yeh're lookin' grand, Kathleen.'

'Thanks, Da! Here, I have a few things – cakes, sweets and some biscuits. I wasn't goin' to leave them in the hospital, when I knew yiz could do with them.'

'Yeh never said a truer word. Phil, put the teapot on and hide them few bits – put them up on the top shelf, so's the kids won't see them. I'll share them out later tonight for a surprise.'

Alan sat in the kitchen with Da. They always had something to talk about. If it wasn't the boxing, it was football. They always got on very well together.

'Where's all the kids, Ma?'

'I got Clare and Marion to take them up to the park for a

while. Get them from under me feet, so's I might get a few things done around here. Kathleen, yer father took the pledge the other day. Let's hope it lasts a bit longer this time. He's a different man altogether when he's not in them pubs, as yeh well know more than anybody.'

'Tha's great news, Ma.' Just then little Paul woke up.

'He's been frettin' terrible after yeh. I've trouble every night tryin' to settle him.'

I went over and picked him up.

'How's my little fella?' He looked at me for a minute before he realised who I was. Then there was no end to the smiles I got.

'See wha' I mean, Kathleen? All I've got is cryin' since yeh left. I don't know wha' I'm goin' to do with him.'

'He'll be grand, Ma! I'll make sure I drop in every day. Won't I, little fella?' I gave him a big hug. He was as happy as anything.

It wasn't long before the rest of the gang started dribbling in. The house was full in no time. Phil made his way over to tell me that he'd got the job and wouldn't be going back to Canada. I was so happy with his news. I gave him a big hug.

'Does Ma and Da know?'

'I only got the word yesterday, so I told them straight away.'

I looked over at Ma. 'Isn't this great news about Phil stayin'?'

She held onto Mano with one hand and blessed herself with the other a half dozen times. 'Wha' have I always told yiz – Our Lady never forgets me; she always answers me prayers.'

I sat there for hours, Paul still in my arms, Jacinta and Patricia either side of my feet. Da made the dinner and Ma shared out the few goodies. Everybody got a taste.

'Ma, I'll bring Paul up to bed. Who's he sleepin' with now?'

'Stick him in between Marion and Clare. Not tha' it will make a difference. He's only down when the cryin' starts again. I had him in with Jacinta and Patricia the last few nights, but

Jacinta's pissin' rings around herself every night. I'll have to get tha' wan down to the clinic and get her checked. There's not enough hours in the day, I've tha' much to do. I don't know if I'm comin' or goin' half the time.'

'I told yeh, Ma, I'd be up real early in the mornin'. I'll bring Jacinta to the clinic while yeh're gettin' the little ones ready. Then we'll get stuck into the house.'

'Right yeh are, then.' And out came the diddy to give Mano a few sucks before putting him down for a couple of hours. 'Tha's it for me, Kathleen. Me diddies is all dryin' up now after all these years. I think it's time to retire them. It's a bottle for Mano from now on.'

'Tha' mightn't be any harm, Ma. Yeh've well done yer bit.'

I made my way upstairs to settle Paul. I was tiptoeing around in the dark so as not to wake any of them, but I should have known they wouldn't be asleep.

I slipped Paul in between the girls.

'Are yeh stayin' here tonight with us, Kathleen?' asked Marion.

'I'll stay for a little while. Then I have to go home with Alan.'

'But this is where yeh live,' went on poor Marion, being so innocent. 'Sure Alan can stay too. We'll move over and make room for him, won't we, Clare?'

'I can't, Marion, sure didn't I get married?'

None of them understood what I was trying to say.

'Don't be such a gobshite, Marion,' Noel butted in. 'Kathleen's left and she won't be stayin' here anymore, so yeh better get used to it.'

Marion started crying. Noel laughed at her. 'Na-na-nana-na! Look at the cry-baby.'

'Give it over, Noel, yeh don't have to tease her like tha'. It's as hard for me as it is for them.'

The kids settled after I told them I'd be up every day, and the only time I wouldn't be there was when they were asleep.

They seemed happy enough with that for the moment anyway and slowly, one by one, they dozed off.

When I got back downstairs, Alan had his jacket on.

'Are yeh right, Kathleen?' He handed me my coat.

'Yeh're off, then?' Da whispered. 'Don't take any notice of yer mother about helpin' out here. I'll look after all tha'. Just come up and see the kids and sit with yer mother for a while.'

'Okay, Da. It's gettin' late, so I best be goin'. I'll talk to yeh tomorrow.'

I could feel a lump in my throat. It was hitting me like a ton of bricks. I thought I felt bad the night before the wedding, but this was ten times worse. I really was never going to sleep there anymore. I wondered if everybody felt the same when leaving home for the first time, or was it me being childish?

Ma must have seen the panic in my face. She made her way over to me: 'I have to lock up now, so yeh better muffle yerself up there.' She wrapped an old scarf around my neck. 'I've to try and get meself a few hours' sleep before I start all over again tomorrow; now off with the two of yiz.'

That was it. I was outside the door before I knew it.

* * *

Alan's grandfather's house was just down the road so we were there in a couple of minutes. I felt strange walking in the door for the first time.

'Pop must be in bed,' said Alan. 'I asked him to make sure and keep the fire goin'. I wanted to have the place nice and cosy for when yeh came home.'

I was glad to hear this. It gave us a chance to be on our own, for a little while anyway. We stayed up talking for ages, Alan going on about one thing and another. 'Yeh'll end up back in the hospital if yeh don't listen to me.' But I was only half-listening, thinking to myself, *I don't want to be here. I want to go home.*

I'd have promised him the sun, moon and stars that night,

and said anything to make him happy for being so patient with me. We finally made our way upstairs. I could feel the cold hitting me in the face as soon as we opened the bedroom door. It was like walking into a fridge. There was a small fire in the corner, which must not have been lit in years. Alan was stripped and in the bed in seconds. I knelt down beside the bed as I always did. Alan peeped out over the eiderdown quilt.

'Wha' are yeh doin', Kathleen?'

'I'm sayin' me few prayers.'

He quickly pulled the quilt over his head.

'Are you laughin' at me, Alan McGrath?'

'I'm not, I swear, Kathleen.'

'I can hear yeh!'

He popped his head out with the pillow stuck in his mouth, laughing.

'Okay, I am – sorry, love.'

'Is it because I'm sayin' me prayers yeh're laughin'? Yeh must think I'm a right tick, Alan.'

'No, yeh're not – it's just, religion is very strong in yer family and tha's the way yeh are, but yeh don't have to kneel out there in the cold. Yeh can just as well say yer prayers beside me. Now get in before yeh freeze to death.'

I jumped into the bed, shaking with the cold, but I couldn't get the heat into me.

'Oh my God, Alan, this bed is so cold.'

'Tha's easily sorted out. I'll pick up a couple of water bottles on me way home from work tomorrow evenin', and an hour or two before we go to bed I'll light tha' small fire in the room. Tha'll take the nip outta the air. Then when yeh slip in beside me yeh'll be nice and cosy. Wha' de say? It'll be like yeh never left home, Kathleen.'

I don't know about tha', I thought to myself. *It's goin' to take a lot more than two hot water bottles to help me settle in this house.* 'Alan, it wasn't tha' Ma had blazin' fires lightin' in the bedrooms, or anythin' like tha'. It was just, by the time I used to get to bed the kids would have the sheets nice and warm and I would slip in between them, tha's all.'

'Yeh won't know yerself tomorrow night by the time I'm finished here. Now try and get a few hours' sleep. Yeh know yeh'll be up at the crack of dawn, wantin' to go up to yer Ma's.'

When we came down the next morning, Alan's granddad was already up and about. It felt strange sitting there, looking across the table at this little old man. He was blowing on a spoonful of porridge.

'Will yeh have some?' he asked. I looked at his hands; you could have made mud pies with the dirt under his nails; and looking at the rest of him, a good wash wouldn't have gone astray either. 'I said, *will yeh have some?*' He didn't even call me by my name.

'No, thanks very much . . . em . . . em . . .' I didn't know what to call him.

Alan was on the ball straight away. 'Kathleen, yeh can call him "Pop".'

'Is tha' ok?' I asked.

'Tha's the name I go by. Now are yeh havin' a drop of this or wha'?' He was getting crankier by the minute.

'I'll just do meself a bit of toast, if yeh don't mind. I'm not one for eatin' much in the mornin's.'

'Suit yerself, then. De yeh want some, Alan?'

'I'm okay, Pop. A cup of tea and a smoke does me until lunchtime. Just look after yerself.'

'I won't be goin' to this trouble again, yeh can be sure,' he mumbled.

I thought, *Thank God for tha'*.

While Alan cleaned out the fire, I gave the place a quick tidy around and then I was out of there. Alan dropped me off at Ma's on his way to work.

'I'll pick yeh up when I'm finished. And remember wha' I said about overdoin' it.'

'Will yeh stop worryin'?' I gave him a big kiss.

* * *

The weeks went by so fast, with me going up to Ma's every day, helping her with one thing or another. Before I knew it the three months were coming to an end and I was well over my operation. I would have been happy enough to leave things with a kiss and cuddle, but I could see Alan was raring to go. Every night I got into bed, I would say to myself: *This is it; I'm really goin' to do it tonight.* But it didn't happen. I'd freeze each time.

I started bringing little Paul home a couple of nights a week, pretending he was still fretting and to give Ma a break. I'd stick him in the bed between us. Alan knew full well what I was up to, but said nothing.

A few more months went by and I could see that his patience was starting to run out with me. He started getting very quiet and when he did have something to say he was snappy. I didn't blame him: any other fella would have lost it long before that.

I wasn't sleeping very well with the worry of all this. I was lying there one night, Alan asleep with his arms wrapped around me so tight. I looked at him and thought: *I love you so much, Alan, and I'm not goin' to lose you, but if I don't do somethin' about this problem, I will.*

That's when I made up my mind, there and then: I would go and see Dr Johnson the next day.

I was outside the doctor's surgery long before he arrived, making sure that no one got in front of me, so I'd be his first patient. I didn't want to have to sit in a waiting room, thinking, getting more nervous by the minute. At least when he arrived I could walk straight in and just say it. That was the plan, anyway.

He arrived after ten minutes. In that time I must have walked in and out of the garden fifty times: going, staying, going, staying, in and out; my head was all over the place.

I finally sat in the chair.

'Well now, Kathleen. How have you been since your stay in hospital? That was a right scare for you, but from the report they sent me all went well. What has you up here today?' He got his notepad ready.

I looked at him, trying to get the words in my head to come out of my mouth. I just couldn't.

'Kathleen, what is it?'

'I . . . em . . . em . . . I've, I'm . . . I can't sleep, I can't eat and me stomach is sick, Doctor.'

'Well then, we know what might be wrong here, don't we, Kathleen?'

'We do, Doctor?'

'You have all the signs. I'll just have to send off a sample to confirm it. Lie down there on the couch 'til I check and make sure everything is alright.'

'Confirm wha', Doctor?'

'You could be pregnant, Kathleen.'

When he said that, the tears started flowing out of me like a river. 'I'm not pregnant, Dr Johnson. I can't be. Yeh don't understand.' And then I said it at last: *'I've never had sex – never, ever, ever.'*

He sat looking at me for a few seconds with his mouth open. Then he moved his chair over beside me and held my hand.

'Calm down, Kathleen. Have you spoken to anybody else about this?'

'Only me brother Phil, but it didn't make any difference.'

'What about Alan? Has he?'

'I don't think so. We don't even talk to one another about this, never mind other people.'

'I have never had a patient myself with this problem, but I know a few doctors who have. You're not the only couple, Kathleen.'

That didn't make me feel any better.

He sat there with me for a long time. Usually I'd be in and out in five minutes, a piece of paper in my hand, trying to remember if I'd told him everything I went for in the first place; but not this time, even though I could hear the doorbell ringing every couple of minutes. The queue must have been out the door and halfway down the street. He still didn't rush. He went into everything with me, wanting to know every little detail. He examined me down below to make sure everything was where it was supposed to be, and that there were no lumps or bumps that shouldn't be there. When he was finished, he sat back down in his chair.

'Everything seems in order there. Now, the way I see it, Kathleen, there's nothing medically wrong with you. For whatever reason, you have put this blockage in your head; be it your mother, father, religion – they probably all did play a part in your mind, but I think fear of the unknown is what is wrong here. You have put it in your head that it's going to hurt you. That's why you won't let it happen. So what I want you to do for me is . . .' As he was talking to me, he was bending over to the press in front of him. He took out a jar and put it into my hand. I looked down at it and looked back up at him as quick.

'It's a jar of Vaseline, Doctor.'

'That's right, Kathleen. Plain old Vaseline, and this is what's going to sort a lot of this problem out for you. Before I go any further, would you like me to talk to Alan?'

I thought for a few seconds. 'No, I'll do it. If I'm goin' to try and get past this, we're going to have to talk to one another about it, together.'

'Good, Kathleen! That's the way to be thinking. Now, what I want you to do is not let tonight go by, no matter what. You are to make love tonight. It's the only way. Put plenty of Vaseline on where I just examined you and tell Alan he's to do the same. Oh, yes, another thing – he's to take it slow and easy, not to go charging in like a racehorse. He'll know what I mean.' I cringed when he said that. He stood up then and put his arm around me. 'In time, as you learn to relax, you will start to enjoy lovemaking. That's all I can say. It's up to you now, Kathleen. Drop up in a week or two and let me know how things are.'

'I will, Doctor, and thanks for listenin' to me.'

When I left his office I felt a lot better in myself and determined to do everything he'd said.

* * *

I thought the day would never end, waiting for Alan to pick me up from Ma's. Usually I would be stalling with the time, dragging my heels, dreading the thoughts of going down to Pop's. But not tonight; I just about gave Alan time to finish his cup of tea in Ma's when I started to put my coat on.

'Yeh're headin' off early,' said Ma. 'Are yeh goin' somewhere, Kathleen?'

I made up some lame excuse about my washing piling up and Alan having to sort the back garden out. Alan frowned over at me; he didn't say a word until we got into the car.

'Wha' was all tha' about, Kathleen?'

'Just let me wave to Ma and the kids. Paul was cryin' to come with me so I promised him I would blow lots of kisses to him and he was to catch each one and hold onto them until I come up tomorrow, and then he can blow them all back to me.' Paul was happy enough with that and was smiling as we pulled away.

'Well, wha's up, Kathleen?

'I'm sayin' nothin' not until I'm sittin' down and lookin' at yeh straight in the eye.'

'This sounds serious, Kathleen. Is somethin' bad after happenin'?'

'It's good, Alan. I mean, I think, I hope. Look, here we are; I'll tell yeh in two minutes.'

I never saw Alan get out of the car so quick. Usually, he'd

have a look in the mirror, take his comb out and fix his quiff and then light up a smoke, but not tonight. He was out of the car and in the door like a light.

Pop wasn't there, which was great.

'I'll make us a cup of tea.'

'Jaysus, Kathleen. Will yeh stop stallin'?'

'Right then. I've somethin' to tell yeh. I was up with Doctor Johnson today. I went to talk about us.' Alan was about to say something, but I held up my hand. 'No, Alan, I don't want yeh to say anythin' until I'm finished. I told him all about wha's happenin' between us. Yeh know, about . . .' I hesitated for a second. I was going to say 'the other', but I didn't. I just came right out and said '. . . our sex problem'.

I could see Alan's eyebrows rising and that little grin showing on the corner of his mouth when he heard me say the word 'sex'. That's when I took out the jar of Vaseline. 'Alan, this is wha's goin' to sort me out.' He looked at the jar and then at me, with a look of astonishment on his face. 'Before yeh open yer mouth, Alan, let me finish.'

'Right then. I'm listenin'.'

'We're doin' it tonight, no matter wha'. You've to put some Vaseline on you know where, and I've to do the same. Tha' way it'll make things a bit easier. Oh yeah, another thing – yeh're to take yer time and make sure yeh don't go chargin' in like a racehorse. The doctor said yeh'd know wha' he meant by tha'.' The grin on Alan's face was getting wider by the minute. 'Then maybe I won't be so tense and will learn how to relax. The rest will just come natural. Well, wha' de yeh think, Alan?'

I could see that he was stunned but very happy at the same time. He put his arms around me.

'Kathleen, I can't believe yeh went and did this on yer own.'

'Either can I, Alan.'

'Well, wha' I think is . . .' He gave me a big kiss. 'Pop's not here; Paul's not here; so there's no time like the present.'

He took me by the hand and we headed for the stairs. We

just about got to the bedroom door when I suddenly stopped in my tracks.

'Alan, stop, stop!' I ran back down the stairs.

'Ah Jaysus, Kathleen, not again, not again.'

I made my way back up. 'It's okay, Alan, I just forgot the Vaseline.' The relief on his face as we walked into the bedroom!

I can't say that I was floating on air or heard violins or anything like it that night. Between the slipping and the sliding, the hitting and the missing, there was a bit of laughing going on, which helped me relax and not be so tense or afraid. The main thing for me that night was that I faced up to the traumatic fears that I had built up inside my head, which could have destroyed us. We weren't long making up for lost time. There wasn't a night went by that one of us wasn't giving the nod and the eye over at the other to make our way upstairs.

And in time, I learned how to enjoy something that is so easy and natural.

From such an early age, I always had to be so grown-up for Ma's world, but now and only now was I ready to be grown up for me and ready to go out into the real world for Kathleen.

Epilogue

I kept my promise to Ma, dropping in every day, still cleaning, helping and slipping her a few shillings when I could. As soon as each of the kids hit fourteen years, they were out in the world, fending for themselves and earning their keep.

Slowly but surely, life started to get easier for Ma. There were still blips and rows along the way, but nothing that she couldn't master, building a lovely home around the family, which she well deserved. Each and every one of the kids did very well for themselves – how could they not with the full force of Ma behind them!

Da lived to be seventy years old, falling on and off the wagon over the years, but it never stopped any of us loving him. Ma lived to be eighty-four years old. She had twelve children, twenty-seven grandchildren, nineteen great-grandchildren and one great-great grandchild. She remained a strong influence in all her children's lives up until her death, surrounded by all those who loved her dearly.

Alan and I were delighted with the arrival of our first child, Martina, followed by Alan Junior and then Amanda to complete our family. I finally had a chance to follow a lifelong dream to train as a hairdresser, and went on to open three very successful salons of my own . . . but of course I couldn't have done it without the total support of Alan.

In 2008 we celebrated our fortieth wedding anniversary, surrounded by our three kids, three granddaughters and one-great-grandson.

* * *

I wasn't long coming back from the past with the roars of Ma in my face.

'Kathleen, will yeh answer me! I have been talkin' to meself here for I don't know how long. Every time I look at yeh, yeh're miles away in tha' head of yours. Even as a child yeh were always gettin' lost in yer thoughts. Wha'ever yeh do be thinkin', I'll never know.'

'Thoughts from a child, Ma, tha's all, just thoughts from a child. But I'll tell yeh one thing I was thinkin' about – and this has been goin' around in me head for ages. I think I'll write a book about yeh.'

'About me? Sure wha' have I done in me life tha's worth writin' about, only nothin'?'

'Ah now, Ma, yeh'd be surprised, yeh'd be very surprised.'

'Well then, get the kettle on and we'll have a nice cup of tea out of them fancy china cups of yers, and as soon as yeh have tha' done, sit yerself down there and I'll tell yeh a few yarns. But before I do start about the goings-on of me life, I'll tell yeh one more thing for nothin'.'

She sat there in the kitchen, looking around, giving it the once-over.

'Yeh've done well for yerself, Kathleen, so yeh have. It's a far cry from jam jars to china yeh've come.'

The End.

If you enjoyed *What Would Ma Say?*,
why not try her next book,
In Ma's Footsteps, also published by Poolbeg.

Here is a sneak preview of the prologue
followed by Chapter one . . .

In Ma's
Footsteps

KATHLEEN DOYLE

POOLBEG

Prologue

I've been enjoying every minute of my retirement. Our family
are all grown up, each of them doing well for themselves. Both
Alan and I have our health. What more could I ask for?

We were lucky enough to be able to buy a little apartment in
Portugal about five years ago and I have to say it was one of the
best things we ever did. We always loved Portugal and the people
there. Our apartment has become a home from home.

As I lay back in the heat of the Portuguese sun, I thought
about all the hard work that Alan and myself had done over
the years. Looking around me now at what we have today, it
was worth every hour we put in. We've been married now for
over forty years and love each other as much as we did when
we first met.

Not that things came easy for us – far from it. We had some
very tough times, but between us we always came through it in
the end. I've always been good at counting the pennies – I got
that from Ma – and would make sure that I would save every
which way I could. No matter how small it was, there was
always some money put by.

'All the same,' I said to Alan, who was lying beside me on
the beach, 'did yeh ever think tha' yeh'd see us havin' our own

little place in the sun, bein' able to come away on holidays like this? I mean, when yeh think back to when we lived with yer Grandad Pop, we didn't even have a bath to wash ourselves in. If we were lucky, we'd just about enough money to get by from week to week.'

'We've come a long way since then, Kathleen, but tha' was sheer determination and hard grafting from the pair of us. So tha's wha' has us sittin' here today – enjoyin' ourselves like this.'

'Yeh're so righ', Alan. I get tired just thinkin' about all the hours we put in between us. I must ask yeh, Alan, if yeh had yer time over again, would yeh have done anythin' different with yer life?'

'Yeh mean as regards you and me, is tha' wha' yeh're tryin' to say, Kathleen?'

'Well, actually, tha's not wha' I mean. I was thinkin' more about yeh givin' up yer job in Gallaghers and buyin' the ice-cream van. But seein' tha' yeh brought up you and me, wha' would yeh change?'

'Well now, let me see Kathleen . . . If I'd known yeh were goin' to be the biggest chatterbox tha' stood on this earth, I'd have traded yeh in years ago, and tha's for sure.'

I looked at him with half a smile. 'Jaysus, Alan, are yeh serious?'

He was laughing his head off as he spoke. 'Would yeh stop it, Kathleen! Yeh know I wouldn't change a hair on yer head for anythin' or anyone.'

'Tha's alrigh', Alan, 'cause I wouldn't change you either, so now.'

'As far as the ice-cream van is concerned, I think I would've thought it through a bit more, Kathleen, instead of jumpin' straight in the way I did. I mean, look at the way yeh had to start doin' the markets on Sundays after doin' a week's work because I wasn't bringin' in enough money in the winter. And when the van would break down and I'd be off work – it was times like tha' I was sorry.'

'Ah, would yeh get away with yerself, Alan. Yeh love bein' yer own boss and I never minded any of the extra work. Anyway, I used to enjoy headin' off for the day to spend a bit of time with me sisters. I had some craic with them over the years.'

'Wha' about yerself, Kathleen? Would you have done anythin' different?'

'There is one thing tha' I definitely wouldn't do again, and tha's live with Pop. Ma tried to warn me about livin' on somebody else's floor, as yer Da did with you, but I suppose yeh can't put an old head on young shoulders. We had to make our own mistakes. Now, havin' said tha', I was very happy livin' there and it did break me heart when we had to leave tha' little house. You know tha' more than anybody.'

'We never should've moved there in the first place, Kathleen. Tha' was all my fault.'

'It was meant to be, Alan, because so many doors opened up for us after we moved. I went out and started mixin' with people a lot more, somethin' I never did, which helped me become more outgoin', and tha's how I was able to go on and follow me dream to become a hairdresser. I really do believe everythin' happens for a reason.'

'Ah, maybe yeh're righ', Kathleen. Who knows? All I know is tha' we're at a very happy place at this time in our lives and tha's all tha' matters at the minute. Now, are yeh comin' down for a swim or are yeh goin' to keep rammagin' on all day?'

'You go ahead, Alan. I think I'll stay here for a while and get a bit of heat into me bones.'

As I lay back on the chair and closed my eyes, I listened to the sound of the waves on the beach – it was so relaxing. I thought of Ma and how tough her life had been. Between having us twelve kids, it took her all her time to keep her head above water. I'd love nothing better than to have her here with me now. I would spoil her so much. I know it's a bit of a cliché to say that we were poor but in our way we were happy, but that's the truth for my family. Anyway, I've told that story already.[1] This one's for us – for Alan and me.

[1] See *What Would Ma Say?*

1

The Geyser

I was ready to settle down to married life at last. I was so happy being married and living with Alan; he was everything I had ever wished for and more. We were still lodging with Alan's granddad, 'Pop', in Kimmage, but hopefully that wouldn't be for too long. Alan was working really hard to get enough money together for a deposit for our own house, just as he'd promised.

'Alan,' I said as we sat there drinking a cup of tea one morning, 'I'm goin' to see if I can get meself a job at the hairdressin'. It's wha' I always wanted to do and then I'll be able to help with the savin's. It's not fair on you havin' to look after everythin'.'

'Kathleen, didn't I tell yeh I'd take care of all tha'? Now, don't be worryin' yer pretty little head, will yeh? Anyway, I was just lookin' at yer Ma the other evenin' and by the looks of her she needs yeh more.'

'I have to agree with yeh, Alan, she looks so tired and worn out. Maybe I will leave it for another while. She's not able for the last two babies.' These were my little brothers, Paul, who was only two years old, and Mano, barely twelve months. Mano was the last of Ma's kids – number twelve. I was the second, after young Phil.

'Come on, Kathleen, get yerself ready and I'll drop yeh off before I head off to work,' he said, giving me a nice big kiss.

'De yeh know somethin', Alan? Yeh're so good. Tha's why I love yeh so much.'

* * *

And that was it. Every morning, as soon as I had the place tidied and my washing done, I'd make my way up to Ma's house in Crumlin every day, helping her clean up and look after the kids. Phil and Carmel were working away and Noel hadn't been too long out there in the workforce, starting to fend for himself. Da had got a couple of rises in his pay packet and Ma made sure each time that he handed them over to her. Life was starting to get a little bit easier at last.

We were heading down towards Old County Road one day, making our way to the clinic to get Mano one of his needles, when Ma turned around to me and said, 'Kathleen, I have a bit of news for yeh.'

I stopped dead in my tracks, stood and looked her straight in the face 'Jaysus, Ma, don't tell me yeh're havin' a baby – please don't say yeh're havin' another baby!'

'Ah, for fuck sake, Kathleen, will yeh give it over. Didn't I tell yeh tha' door was long closed after little Mano was born? Didn't I say tha' to yeh?'

'I know, Ma. I know yeh did, but –'

'There's no buts about it, Kathleen. Now yeh're after gettin' me all annoyed and ruinin' me bit of news.'

'Sorry, Ma. Go on, tell us wha' it is.'

'Well. Well . . .' She pushed the pram through the doors of the clinic, still holding on to the words, but you could see she was bursting to tell me. 'Kathleen, I have enough money to buy the geyser for the hot water. Everybody will be able to have a proper bath from now on.'

'Jaysus, Ma, tha's great news. How did yeh manage to put the few bob by?'

'Well, Kathleen, when Noel started work I said to meself, "I don't care, I'm puttin' some of his wages by. No matter wha', come rain or shine, I'm not touchin' it." And I didn't. So will yeh come in to the gas company with me and help me pick one out?'

That's exactly what we did the very next day.

* * *

So the day finally came when there was hot water in Crumlin. No more running up and down the stairs for any of the kids the way us older ones had to, with your pot of water, getting ready to wash all your bits.

There was great excitement among the younger kids the day the geyser was installed. Even Da made his way home early that day. Ma was as proud as Punch, standing there waiting on the men to finish. They were only out the door when she was over to the taps to test the water. When that hot water came pouring out of the tap, the look on her face was priceless. She had waited so long for that day to come.

All the kids were pushing, shoving, screaming and shouting to see who'd be the first to have a splash in the bath. Ma wasn't long quietening them all down with one of her famous looks. She then turned around to me.

'Kathleen,' she said, 'I know yeh don't live here anymore, but yeh waited so long to have tha' bubble bath of yers in this house, I think you should be the first.' She handed me a bottle of bubbles. I couldn't believe Ma had remembered the way I had always gone on about that.

I got such a lump in my throat it took me all my time to hold back the tears.

'Oh, and another thing, Kathleen – when yeh're finished don't let the water out. Tha'll do a few of the younger ones to have a good wash and keep the bill down at the one time. Just because I have a few of them older ones workin' now doesn't mean I still don't have to watch me few pennies around here.'

She was still rammaging on as she gathered all the kids and made her way downstairs.

'Yer mother is righ',' Da said. 'You should be the first to hansel the bath.' He gave me a little wink as he closed the door behind him.

I thought to myself as I slipped into the water, *Things are really startin' to look up around here and it feels good.*

* * *

The months seemed to go by very quickly. I was so happy and in love that I didn't realise at first how quiet Alan had become – probably because I never stopped talking and he didn't get much of a chance to get a word in anyway. But he was extra quiet and seemed to be a million miles away, thinking to himself all the time.

'Wha's wrong with yeh, Alan?' I asked as we drove away from Ma's one evening. 'Yeh're not yerself. Is it me? Are yeh fed up? Wha' is it? Tell me.'

'Jaysus, it's nothin' like tha', Kathleen. It's me job. Me Da has to let me go. He barely has enough work for himself.'

'Oh my God, Alan, why didn't yeh tell me?'

'I was tryin' to hang out as long as I could, hopin' things might pick up.'

'How did this happen? Yer Da is always busy.'

'Ah, there's this fella after settin' himself up in business. He's goin' around the doors collectin' and deliverin' the shoes for repair. Sure, we're only gettin' half the work now. I've been sittin' on me arse for the past couple of weeks, doin' nothin'. I can't expect me Da to keep payin' me wages, so I said I'd finish up this week. I'll go around the factories, see if I can get some work. But I'll tell yeh one thing for nothin', Kathleen, I won't be gettin' anythin' like the money me Da was payin' me.'

'Tha's it, Alan, I'm definitely gettin' meself some work, I don't care wha' yeh say.'

* * *

Sure enough, a few days later, Alan had a job working in a handbag factory called Freedex, and into the bargain he got me a job there as well. Although it was only part-time, it paid more than I would have got from hairdressing, which suited me down to the ground at the time. I was bringing in a few shillings to help out with the bills and I was still able to go up to Ma when I was finished. But the money we were making between us was nothing like what Alan used to make and we were finding it a bit hard to manage. That's when Alan hit me with the bombshell.

'Kathleen, I want to talk to yeh about maybe us stayin' on here – livin' with Pop. There's no way I'm able to save any more money and we're just about gettin' by at the moment. So wha' I was thinkin', yeh know, the money tha' we have saved, we could put it into this house, and by the time I'm finished doin' it up, I promise yeh, yeh'll be well pleased with the results. It's either tha' or we try and get a flat. And believe me, they're not cheap.'

'Does tha' mean we'll never ever get our own house, Alan?'

'Who knows wha' lies ahead, love? All I know is, I'm tryin' to do the best for us for now. And stayin' here to me would be the best option.'

'Okay, if yeh think it's the righ' thing to do. But wha' if he says no?'

'By the time I'm finished suckin' up to him, tha' won't be a problem.'

341

* * *

Now on top of all that I had just found out I was pregnant, which wasn't supposed to be in the plans. Not at that moment in time anyway. Everything went arse about face. To top it off, Ma went crazy mad when I told her my bit of news.

'In the name of Jaysus, Kathleen,' she roared – I think half the road must have heard her that day – 'Have yeh learnt nothin' over the years, lookin' at me and rearin' most of them kids for me. Was tha' not enough to put yeh off, at least for a few years anyway? And now yeh say yeh're not goin' to have yer own house. Yeh'll be stuck down there with tha' oul' fella.'

'Ah, he's not tha' bad, Ma. Sure yeh wouldn't even know he was there half the time. Anyway I'm hardly ever there meself. If I'm not in work I do be up here with you.'

'Tha'll all change when yeh have yer own child. Mark my words, Kathleen.' Her voice was getting louder and louder.

Jaysus, I thought, *she's sayin' 'child' not 'baby'. She's really pissed off with me. I'd better try and change the subject before she has a fit altogether'.*

'Ma, Phil tells me he's goin' steady; did yeh ask him when we're goin' to meet her?'

She looked over at me, giving me one of her dagger looks, knowing full well what I was up to. 'Hmm! So I believe. He calls her Joan. She's a nurse.'

'Tha's right, Ma, he said she's real nice.'

That was it; I knew once I got her talking about Phil she'd be on a roll and that would take the suss off me, for a little while anyway.

* * *

Alan spoke to Pop about us staying on and everything was okay there.

'Yiz can stay for as long as yiz want,' he said. 'Sure I'm only too glad of the bit of company.'

'Tha's great, Pop. So is it okay if I paint and wallpaper the house? Maybe stick a bit of new furniture in. Would yeh mind us doin' tha'?'

'The place hasn't been touched in years, Alan, and I know it could do with a good overhaul, so yeh have me permission to do wha'ever yeh want. Just don't ask me to help!' I was so happy when I heard him say that.

'Yeh're all righ' there, Pop. Once I get meself goin' I'll have the place done up in no time at all.'

So we went and put every penny that we had saved into doing the house up. We already had our furniture for the bedroom, so we started there first, working our way down, painting all the woodwork white, with matching blinds for all the windows and fresh new wallpaper throughout the house. The carpet in both rooms and on the stairs was to match, a lovely chocolate brown and cream, with a wood-type lino, which was only coming into fashion at the time, in the sitting room and running on into the kitchen.

The kitchen was so small it was more like a little scullery and – can you believe this? – the bath was actually behind the kitchen door along with the sink! Not that Pop used it for washing himself in, no way; he had it filled up with turf. So that was the first thing to go, making room for a small table and chairs.

The toilet was outside the house, just off the kitchen, and it needed a right going-over, which I left for Alan to do. By the time he was finished it was spick and span. The last thing to buy was our black leather suite. (It was plastic really, but I didn't care.) I thought it was massive; with a few orange cushions here and there it really looked the part.

It took us a good few months to do but it was worth the wait and looked very well by the time we were finished. With everything so bright and fresh-looking, and with the new furniture and our bits and bobs, I was happy enough to stay living there. It felt like a proper little home now, ready to welcome our baby – which, by the way, was due any day now.

• ◦ •

If you enjoyed this chapter from

In Ma's Footsteps by Kathleen Doyle

why not order the full book online
@ www.poolbeg.com
and enjoy a 10% discount on all
Poolbeg books

See last page for details.

• ◦ •

PUBLISHED BY POOLBEG

IN MA'S FOOTSTEPS

KATHLEEN DOYLE

In the phenomenal and hilarious bestseller, *What Would Ma Say?*, Kathleen Doyle introduced us to her remarkable family and their exploits growing up in working-class Dublin in the 1950s and 1960s. Now she is walking *In Ma's Footsteps*, picking up where the first book left off.

Kathleen describes marital bliss with Alan and how they raised their own (smaller) family of three in difficult times. From a shed in her back garden, Kathleen started cutting hair for her neighbours, eventually owning three hairdressing salons.

Along the way, Kathleen's sharp tongue brightens up her stories, such as how the family rooster, "Dick the Cock", sent her into premature labour; Alan getting "the snip"; the mysterious vandalising of Kathleen's knickers; and how her daughter Martina ran away from home at the age of 11 – but only for the one night, mind. Kathleen herself became a grandmother at the age of 38, and is now a great-grandmother.

There were also tragedies, most of them, incredibly, happening in just one year: Da's agonising death from cancer; Ma's operation to remove a brain tumour; Kathleen's own brush with cancer, which resulted in her having her "bits" taken out; and, most heartbreaking of all, Kathleen's brother Phil dying, also from a brain tumour.

Throughout it all, Kathleen remains philosophical, never losing her sense of humour. She's a true survivor.

ISBN 978-1-84223-427-3

POOLBEG WISHES TO
THANK YOU
for buying a Poolbeg book.
As a loyal customer we will give you
10% OFF (and free postage*)
on any book bought on our website
www.poolbeg.com

Select the book(s) you wish to buy
and click to checkout.

Then click on the 'Add a Coupon' button
(located under 'Checkout') and enter
this coupon code

POOLBEG

USMWR15173

POOLBEG

(Not valid with any other offer!)

WHY NOT JOIN OUR MAILING LIST
@ www.poolbeg.com and get some
fantastic offers on Poolbeg books

*See website for details